DUESENBERG
OWNER'S COMPANION

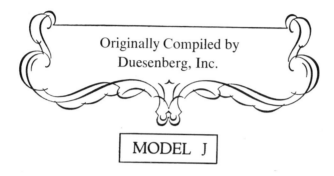

Originally Compiled by
Duesenberg, Inc.

MODEL J

A FOUNTAINHEAD GUIDE FOR
THE DUESENBERG ENTHUSIAST—
REPRODUCING IN A MASTER VOLUME
THOSE FACTORY-ISSUED PRIMARY REFERENCES
SO FLEETING IN THEIR ORIGINAL ISSUE

POST-ERA BOOKS
Arcadia CA 91006

©

Copyright

1974

Dan R. Post

ISBN-0-911160-53-1

CONTENTS

Master page numbering as indicated here does not appear on individual folios; it is blind. Delineation above shows chronology . . . Numbers in evidence on most pages of the Companion are reproduced from the original matter and relate directly within individual sections.

†This collation of 30 layouts is believed to represent the company's national class magazine program practically in its entirety, from pre-introduction to closing days.

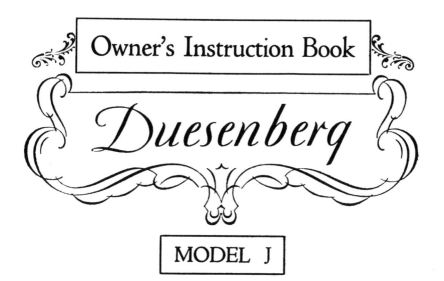

Owner's Instruction Book

Duesenberg

MODEL J

Price $5.00

Compiled by the

General Service Department

DUESENBERG, INC.
Indianapolis, Ind., U. S. A.

Printed in U. S. A.

Foreword

The motoring public, in its thirst for the "unusual" in motor car performance, has accepted, without question, the present series of cars representing our ideal in automotive engineering.

Not one iota of expense has been spared, thru the efforts of Mr. E. L. Cord, to produce a car giving the utmost in Beauty, Power, Speed, Comfort and Safety. This achievement has been made possible by the dynamic genius of Mr. F. S. Duesenberg, world famous engineer, in supplying fundamentals in design and construction, which have advanced the entire automotive industry.

Quality, superior to any previous conception, will be maintained at all times, thus, eliminating irregularities in manufacture, occurring with many present day quantity production practices.

It is understood that further interest and attention to the product is necessary to give the owner unfaltering performance. Therefore, in keeping with our appreciation of the innate value to each owner, we submit the following information for your guidance.

Printed in U. S. A.

W arranty

Should the parts of any new automobile manufactured by us prove defective in workmanship or material, under normal use, within 1 year after shipment thereof from our factory, and such defective part be returned to us at our factory in Indianapolis, Indiana, within said time, transportation charges paid, we will deliver to the purchaser, f. o. b. Indianapolis, Indiana, a new part in lieu of such returned part, providing the returned part be determined by us to have been defective in material and workmanship.

We make no warranty with respect to tires, rims, ignition apparatus, horns or other signaling devices, starting devices, generators, batteries, speedometers or other accessories, or with respect to used or second hand cars, nor are we responsible for any warranties or agreements made by our dealers. In no case will we pay any bills for repairs made outside our factory, nor shall the above agreements apply to any automobile which may be in any way altered or repaired outside our factory nor to any defects developed by misuse, negligence, or accident.

Except as above expressly provided, no warranty or guarantee of the quality of any automobile manufactured by us, or the parts thereof, or any parts, accessories, or repairs, or of the other materials or workmanship therein, or of the suitableness thereof for the purpose intended, or the freedom thereof from defects, latent or patent, is made or given, nor shall any such warranty or guarantee ever arise by implication of law or otherwise.

DUESENBERG, INC.
Indianapolis, Ind.

Duesenberg, Inc., reserves the right to make improvements at any time without incurring any obligations to install same on cars previously sold or to install the old part, which has been changed, improved or omitted, on cars subsequently sold.

Dealer's Service Policy

The following outline is given to acquaint the owner with our service policies. It is our sincere desire to assist you in every way to secure the utmost in pleasant transportation through the ownership of your Duesenberg automobile and our entire organization is always at your disposal toward that realization.

1. We will make all necessary adjustments to a new car for a period of 90 days after delivery, provided it is returned to our service station and has not been tampered with or injured through accident or neglect.

2. Within one year after delivery to the original purchaser we will dismantle, repair or replace and reassemble to perfect working condition without expense to the owner either for parts, labor, or transportation, any part or parts determined by the factory to be defective; the owner to assume responsibility of all charges pending factory decision.

3. When it is necessary for the convenience of the owner to render service at a distance from our service station, whether regular maintenance or warranty work, the expenses of the workman for transportation, meals, lodging, etc., will be charged to the owner.

4. All inspections and maintenance instructions given by our service personnel concerning the operation of Duesenberg motor cars are made on behalf and in the interest of the owner. The owner therefore, assumes the responsibility for any oversight or fault in connection therewith.

5. All repairs and regular maintenance service corrections to include, cleaning carbon, grinding valves, etc., for which the owner is directly responsible will be charged for at the regular rates. An estimate of charges will be given when it is possible to determine amount of work necessary.

Instructions for Ordering Parts

It has been found impractical and impossible to provide owners with parts price lists that will be complete and up-to-date at all times.

Information on parts not contained in this book may be obtained at our service station.

Parts in most frequent demand are shown in this book. The numbers appearing on the illustrations are part numbers and all parts must be ordered by this number and description given therewith.

IN ALL CASES POSSIBLE, PARTS SHOULD BE ORDERED OR RETURNED FOR CREDIT THROUGH OUR DEALER OR DISTRIBUTOR.

WHEN THIS IS NOT POSSIBLE THE OWNER MAY OBTAIN SERVICE ON PARTS DIRECT FROM THE FACTORY. PARTS ORDERED AND CORRECTLY SHIPPED MAY NOT BE RETURNED FOR CREDIT OR EXCHANGE UNLESS PERMISSION IS OBTAINED FROM THE FACTORY; WHEREUPON A HANDLING CHARGE OF 10 PER CENT WILL BE DEDUCTED FROM CREDIT DUE.

WHEN ORDERING PARTS be sure to give the following information:

1. Name and description of part
2. Part number
3. Serial number of car
4. Serial number of unit assembly for which part is desired.
5. If part is desired for body, give body make, number, type, style and sample of part or small sketch of same.

WHEN RETURNING PARTS for credit be sure to give the same information requested above as when ordering parts and in addition the following:

6. Reason for returning part, giving in detail difficulty experienced with same.
7. Date car was delivered to owner.
8. Order number on which new part was supplied.
9. Mileage of car at time part was changed.
10. Owner's name and address.

License and Insurance Data

Number of cylinders.. 8
Cylinder bore...3¾ in.
Stroke...4¾ in.
Piston displacement...420 cu. in.
Horse Power (SAE rating)...45

The car serial number will be found on front of dash upper left-hand side.

The motor number is stamped on the left rear motor support leg.

The front axle number is stamped on top flange center section of I beam.

The rear axle number is stamped on top of center section of steel housing.

Approximate Shipping Weights for Standard Types

2-4 Pass. Roadster Convertible Coupe............142½ W. B. 5250 lbs.
4 Pass. Convertible Sedan......................142½ W. B. 5550 lbs.
5 Pass. Standard Sedan.........................142½ W. B. 5450 lbs.
4 Pass. Sport Phaeton..........................142½ W. B. 5250 lbs.
7 Pass. Standard Sedan.........................153½ W. B. 5850 lbs.
      Chassis (Only)...........................142½ W. B. 4450 lbs.
      Chassis (Only)...........................153½ W. B. 4550 lbs.

Illustrations

1. Instruments
2. Lubricating system of motor
3. Cross-sectional view-left side of motor
4. Photograph and cross-sectional view-front of motor
5. Valve and ignition timing diagram
6. Photograph of carburetor and cross-sectional view of fuel pump.
7. Cross-sectional view of clutch, and transmission.
8. Cross-sectional view of rear axle and torque tube.
9. Cross-sectional view of front axle and external view of brake assembly
10. Master cylinder assembly
11. Plan view of chassis
12. Shackle assembly
13. Wiring diagram

INSTRUMENTS AND CONTROLS

(1) Ignition Switch

The ignition switch located on the instrument board when turned
to the right snaps out to the "on" position and closes the circuit
between the storage battery and the ignition system. Thus, current
is supplied for igniting the gasoline in the cylinders, which is the
first step in starting the motor. Always stop the motor by turning
off the ignition switch and be very careful to see that switch is
never turned on when the motor is not running as the battery may
be completely discharged.

(2) Throttle Control Lever

The hand throttle is closed when the lever is in its upper-most
position and should be opened by moving the lever downward approximately ½" on quadrant for the second step in starting the
motor. The speed of the motor may thus be regulated by the hand
lever or foot pedal.

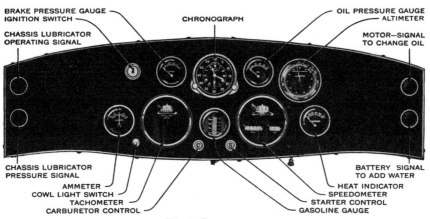

Fig. 1. Instruments

(3) Spark Control Lever

The ignition timing is retarded when the lever is in its uppermost
position and should be moved to approximately mid position of
the quadrant for the third step in starting the motor. As soon as
the motor has started the ignition should be advanced by moving
lever downward to position where maximum performance of the
motor is obtained. Learn to regulate position of spark lever for
different motor speeds, keeping it in the advanced positions for
higher motor speeds and retarding it as required for maximum
power at lower speeds.

(4) ACCELERATOR PEDAL

The accelerator pedal performs the same function as the hand throttle lever and ordinarily is used in preference to the hand lever.

(5) CARBURETOR CONTROL

The carburetor control is to be used for enriching the carburetor mixture as required when the motor is cold. The fourth step in starting the motor is to pull the carburetor control out as far as possible until the motor starts to fire, and immediately return it gradually to its normal position as the motor warms up. Under extremely cold weather conditions it may be necessary to leave the control pulled out approximately ½″ for a few minutes to give the correct carbureton until the water temperature is normal. The control should be pushed all the way in to the instrument board as the warming up process is completed to prevent excessive oil dilution and resultant cylinder wear.

(6) STARTER CONTROL

The engaging of the starting motor is accomplished by pulling the control button located on instrument board out as far as possible and is the fifth and last step in starting the motor. The starter should be engaged at intervals of 10-15 seconds and should not remain engaged for longer periods as this will discharge the battery rapidly. If the motor does not start after two or three attempts, an immediate investigation should be made to determine the trouble by checking the following items.

1. Gasoline supply may be exhausted.

2. Gasoline mixture may be too rich or lean. Carburetor may be choked excessively by leaving dash control out too long.

3. Open throttle approximately half way to start when motor has been choked excessively.

4. Check gasoline supply at carburetor by removing hexagon drain plug in bowl near the front on the outside. It may be necessary to remove and clean strainer bowl assembly Part No. J-1232 Fig. 3 and prime the system by operating gasoline pump by hand.

5. Be sure switch is on and check to see if electrical terminals are tight at the distributor and ignition coils back of the instrument board.

6. In cold weather depress the clutch pedal so as to eliminate the load on the starting motor of turning the transmission.

7. Check starter ground strap from starter to frame and battery terminals to see that they are absolutely tight.

8. Check battery charge.

(7) CLUTCH PEDAL

The clutch pedal controls the operation of the clutch and releases or disengages the motor to permit shifting and engaging the transmission gears. A clearance of 1″ to 1½″ should be maintained between the return position of the pedal and the floor board at all times to insure proper clutch action. (See clutch). The foot should not be permitted to rest on the clutch pedal while driving as this subjects the clutch parts to unnecessary wear.

(8) BRAKE PEDAL)

The foot brake pedal operates the 4 wheel hydraulic brakes commonly known as service brakes. Application and control of brakes is accomplished by depressing the pedal in the conventional manner, the braking effect being directly proportional to amount of pressure exerted on the pedal.

(9) GEAR SHIFT AND LEVER

The transmission is of the conventional three speeds forward with the standard universal gear shift. Due to the special design of the transmission a lightning shift of gears may be made even at high motor speeds.

(10) LIGHT CONTROL LEVER

The lighting switch is located at the base of the steering column and is operated by the third control lever on top of steering column. Extreme position to the left is for cowl and tail lamps, next position to right all lights off and the two positions to the extreme right for headlights and tail light with the headlight beams deflected for one of the positions.

(11) HAND BRAKE LEVER

The hand brake lever operating the emergency brake is to be used for locking car in position when parked. Form the habit of locking the brake when the car is parked.

(12) WINDSHIELD WIPER

The windshield wiper is operated from the vacuum in the manifold and is controlled at the assembly by a thumb screw.

(13) TACHOMETER

The tachometer is a revolution counter attached to the rear of one camshaft giving direct revolutions per minute of motor speed.

(14) SPEEDOMETER

The speedometer instrument gives the direct reading in miles per hour up to 150, together with total and trip mileage.

(15) CHRONOGRAPH (Clock and Split Second Stop Watch)

The clock is an eight day instrument incorporating in its movements a split second watch by the use of which actual developed speed can be figured from the specific time and distance covered.

(16) ALTIMETER

The altimeter records barometric pressure in inches of mercury together with altitude measured in feet. The graduated scale for altitude may be shifted, thus allowing the scale to be set at zero with dial indicator whereby variations in altitude are indicated directly for different localities. By setting the altitude dial to the exact altitude of a given locality according to the corresponding barometer reading, weather conditions or changes may be approximated.

(17) OIL PRESSURE GAUGE

The oil pressure gauge indicates the condition of the oil pressure system for the motor and gives the pressure reading in pounds per square inch. Form the habit of observing the oil gauge to see that it shows correct pressure at all times. If pressure should drop below normal, lack of oil or very thin oil may be the reason.

(18) GASOLINE GAUGE

The gasoline gauge indicates in gallons the amount of gasoline in the tank. This gauge is calibrated or set at the factory and should require no attention thru the lifetime of the car.

(19) BRAKE PRESSURE GAUGE

The brake pressure gauge indicates the hydraulic pressure developed upon application of the brakes or in other words the working condition of the system. The brakes ordinarily require approximately 200 pounds pressure for operation but the system is capable of developing 500 pounds pressure in emergencies; thus a high factor of safety is maintained for breaking effect in controlling the car.

(20) AMMETER

The ammeter indicates the working condition of the electrical system or in other words the rate of charge or discharge of the battery. The ammeter should indicate a charging rate of 10-12 amperes with all lights turned off at a road speed of 20-30 M. P. H.

(21) HEAT INDICATOR

The heat indicator gives the temperature of the water cooling system in degrees of Fahrenheit. The most efficient operating temperature is from 160-200 degrees although in extremely warm or cold climates the temperature may run slightly higher or lower.

(22) INSTRUMENT BOARD SIGNAL LIGHTS

The green signal light at the right side marked "Bat" when burning approximately every 1500 miles reminds you that the battery should be inspected and pure distilled water added to bring the solution to within 3/8" of top.

The red signal light at the right side marked "Oil" when burning approximately 750 miles indicates that the motor oil should be changed.

The red signal light at the left side when burning approximately every 60-80 miles indicates that the chassis lubricating mechanism is operating and immediately afterward the green signal light should flash showing that oil is being delivered to the various shackle bearings. Should the second light fail to operate check the oil supply in chassis lubricator supply tank at the right front side of the dash.

(23) HOOD LOCK

To lock the hood properly it is necessary to place the lock control handle upright when dropping hood in position, then turn handle down in right hand direction, pushing cylinder of key lock "in" to lock control lever in down position.

Tool box and battery compartment locks operate in the same manner.

(24) RADIATOR CAP

When removing radiator cap care should be taken to unscrew cap as far as possible before lifting from shell, otherwise cap will not return to its proper locking position when again installed.

Paragraphs 25-29 inclusive discontinued.

OPERATION

In the designing and building of this car every effort has been made, to make it as complete as possible and to eliminate the many annoyances of periodic inspection and lubrication so essential to prolonging the life of the average motor car.

In furthering this motive the manufacturing division has taken all possible precautions in building and testing this car to eliminate various items of checking and preparation usually necessary upon receipt of the car at its destination.

When cars are shipped it will be necessary to check the following items.

(30) PREPARING CAR FOR SERVICE

1. Remove spark plugs and insert approximately ½ oz. of cylinder oil into each cylinder.
2. Fill radiator with clean water (capacity 7 gal.) In cold weather an anti-freeze solution should be used. See paragraph 73.
3. Fill gasoline tank (capacity 26 gal.)
4. Be sure oil in crankcase is up to proper level which is indicated by oil level gauge on left side of motor. (capacity 3 gal.)
5. Check air pressure of tires, which should be 40 lbs. for front, 38 lbs. for rear.
6. Test battery with hydrometer and see that all plates are covered with water.
7. Check all lights to see that they burn properly.

(31) RUNNING A NEW MOTOR

The most critical period in the life of the motor is the first 1000 miles of operation. Permanent injury or damage may result through the failure to observe the simple but fundamental laws of "working in" the new motor.

During this initial period of operation, additional cylinder lubrication should be supplied by adding one quart of light crystal engine oil to each ten gallons of gasoline used.

Sustained or continued high motor speeds are extremely detrimental until the motor has passed the initial 1000 miles of operation. Even after this mileage the motor should never be raced, especially when cold.

(32) OPERATING THE CAR

Operating the car, that is, starting the motor, shifting gears, controlling and stopping the car is all accomplished in the conventional manner with which all operators are familiar. It is therefore needless to narrate this simple procedure, but we will give a list of driving suggestions which we trust will assist in operating the car and adding comfort for its passengers.

1. Use the power of the motor and brakes moderately in controlling the car.

2. Drive with the carburetor control all the way in against the dash at all times except when starting with the motor cold. Rich mixtures cause rapid oil dilution and excessive cylinder wear.

3. Form the habit of glancing at the instrument panel. The instruments indicate the operating condition of the lubricating, electrical and cooling systems. Watch the oil gauge to see that it shows normal pressure at all times.

4. Do not ride with foot on the clutch pedal or disengage clutch when coasting down steep grades as these practices cause early service replacements and expense.

5. Leave ignition "On" when coasting. Failure to do this allows gasoline to wash the cylinder walls and thin lubricating oil, while unburnt gasses passed into the muffler may produce great damage when ignited later as the switch is turned "On".

6. Learn to regulate the spark control in relation to motor speed, driving with it in the advance position for high motor speeds and retarding it for ascending steep grades at low speeds.

(33) INSPECTION AND LUBRICATION

In listing the items which must necessarily be checked at different intervals we have assumed that the owner is thoroughly familiar with the attention necessary to water in the cooling system, water in the battery, gasoline, oil supply in the crankcase, lights, tire pressure and the daily routine essential to successful motor car operation. However, descriptive details for the above mentioned items will be found under their respective explanations in other parts of this book.

It is imperative that the following items be checked very thoroughly at intervals of 2500 and 5000 miles.

INSPECTION AND LUBRICATION SCHEDULE

2500 MILES

CHASSIS LUBRICATION—Replenish oil supply in chassis lubricator supply tank on right front of dash with Bijur special oil which may be obtained at our service stations or at Bijur Lubricating Co., 250 W. 54th St., New York City.

5000 MILES

COMPRESSION—Check cylinder compression by turning motor with hand crank if compression is not uniform check valve clearance.

DISTRIBUTOR—Wipe distributor head clean, inspect and adjust contact points.

TIMING—Check ignition timing.

FAN—Check fan belt adjustment.

SPARK PLUGS—Clean and adjust.

GENERATOR—Inspect coupling, commutator, and brushes, and clean them if necessary. Add 10-15 drops of oil to each bearing.

GASOLINE STRAINER—Remove and clean screens, etc.

WATER PUMP—Inspect water pump packing for leaks. Tighten packing nut if necessary.

WHEELS—Align front wheels and pack front wheel bearings with a good grade of light cup grease similar to alemite.

STEERING GEAR—Inspect for lost motion, pack gear with Whitmores' "65" lubricant, pack pivot pin bearings and tie rod joints with cup grease.

BRAKES—Adjust if necessary. Fill supply tank to within ½" of top with genuine Lockheed brake fluid.

CLUTCH—Inspect for 1" to 1½" free travel of clutch pedal and adjust if necessary.

AXLE-REAR—Inspect grease supply and bring to height of level plug with Whitmore's "0" lubricant.

TRANSMISSION—Inspect grease supply and bring to height of level plug with Whitmore's "0" lubricant.

BATTERY—Remove terminals, clean, grease, and tighten.

BODY BOLTS—Tighten.

AXLE SPRING CLIPS—Tighten.

SHOCK ABSORBERS—Inspect and replenish oil supply if necessary.

CHASSIS LUBRICATOR—Remove signal box pump housing cap (J-1159) Fig. 3 to clean felt and screen. Do not remove plugs in lower part of cap housing as a supply of glycerine is retained in well at this point to protect pressure switch.

Whitmore's lubricant for transmission, rear axle and steering gear may be obtained at our service station or Whitmore Manufacturing Co., Cleveland, Ohio.

ENGINE

(34) LUBRICATION SYSTEM

Efficient and adequate lubrication is supplied with positive pressure to all bearings and wearing surfaces of the motor. The diagram explaining the oil circulation system will be given by illustration No. 2. You will note the location of the oil pump at the lowest point in the oil sump where the oil is picked up after being filtered and screened and then discharged to the main pressure line feeding the entire system. From the main pressure line oil is first distributed to the main bearings, connecting rod bearings and piston pins, which in turn lubricate cylinder walls and piston rings. From this point in the main line a supply is also sent directly to all camshaft bearings, accessory drive shafts and idler sprockets for timing chain mechanism. The excess of oil supplied to camshaft bearings is maintained at the specific level in the camshaft housings to provide a bath of oil for all parts of the valve mechanism. Overflow or drain holes in the camshaft housing allow surplus oil to drain back into crank case and is thus kept in circulation. The oil filter located on the right side of the cylinder block is constantly filtering and removing all foreign matter in the oil supply taken from the pressure line after pressure is supplied to all units.

(35) OIL PUMP

The oil pump is of the conventional gear type, having a capacity much greater than is actually necessary to supply an abundance of pressure at all times. The pump is driven by a vertical shaft through the side gears mounted on generator drive shaft. It is mounted to the first cross web of the cylinder block and crank case by two cap screws and is coupled to its vertical drive shaft by means of a square sleeve coupling. The main pressure line from pump to cylinder block may be disassembled after loosening tube packing lock nut. In order to remove oil pump it is first necessary to remove the oil pan and sump and then detach from its mounting.

(36) OIL PRESSURE

The oil pressure adjustment is located on the lower left hand side of the cylinder block just in front of the oil float gauge indicator. By changing this adjustment screw and turning in a clockwise direction the pressure will be increased as indicated on the gauge on the instrument board. Turning in an anti-clockwise direction reduces the pressure accordingly. This adjusting screw is connected by a flexible cable to the relief valve sleeve in the oil pump; consequently when the adjusting screw in the block is changed you are merely increasing or decreasing spring tension on relief valve at the oil pump. The surplus oil by-passed by the relief valve is discharged directly back in the oil supply.

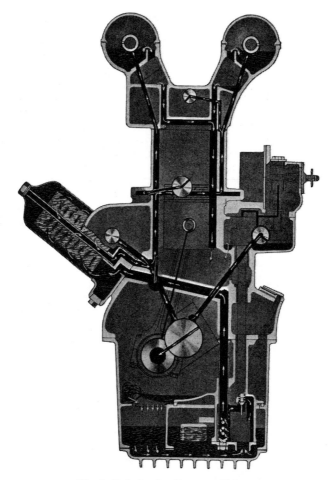

Fig. 2. Lubricating System of Motor

The correct oil pressure to be maintained at all times is approximately 2 to 10 pounds for low idling speeds and approximately one pound for every mile per hour with a maximum of 80 to 100 pounds for high speed operation. It is very essential that this correct pressure is maintained at all times.

(37) Oil Supply and Float Gauge

The capacity of the crankcase is 12 quarts and this supply is indicated by a float indicator gauge located at the lower front left hand side of the cylinder block.

Publisher's Note: This illustration did not appear in the original manual but has been added in order to rectify pagination.

Fig. 3. PARTS DESCRIPTION

J- 101	Front main bearing cap	J- 467	Cam cover rear cap gasket
J- 103	Center main bearing cap	J- 468	Cam cover front and center packing
J- 104	Rear main bearing cap	J- 469	Cam cover rear packing
J- 105	Front main bearing bushing	J- 472	Cam cover large hand nut assembly
J- 107	Center main bearing bushing	J- 474	Cam cover large hand nut stud
J- 108	Rear main bearing bushing	J- 475	Cam cover small hand nut retainer
J- 109	Main Bearing Stud		Wire
J- 110	Main bearing stud nut	J- 476	Cam cover small hand nut retainer
J- 112	Rear main bearing oil retainer	J- 477	Cam cover small hand nut assembly
J- 121	Rear main bearing oil retainer	J- 484	Camshaft bearing cap dowel
	Gasket	J- 485	Crankshaft plug
J- 124	Cylinder water plate screw	J- 489	Tachometer drive plug
J- 130	Main bearing bushing retainer screw	J- 490	Tachometer drive cover
J- 138	Chain case cap short screw	J- 551	Crankshaft sprocket
J- 140	Oil filler body	J- 552	Lower adjusting sprocket assembly
J- 146	Rear main bearing oil retainer screw	J- 553	Accessory shaft Sprocket
J- 150	Breather body	J- 555	Transfer sprocket assembly
J- 151	Breather body Gasket	J- 556	Upper adjusting sprocket assembly
J- 153	Breather body cap	J- 558	Lower chain
J- 154	Breather body cap screw	J- 559	Upper chain
J- 160	Oil gauge float bracket screw	J- 560	Crankshaft sprocket lock washer
J- 162	Oil gauge flexible shaft	J- 562	Gen. shaft sprocket oil slinger
J- 165	Oil gauge flexible shaft lower end	J- 567	Camshaft sprocket cap screw
J- 166	Oil gauge float bracket bushing	J- 585	Transfer sprocket assembly stud
J- 167	Oil gauge indicator	J- 586	Adjusting sprocket assembly stud
J- 171	Oil gauge face plate	J- 654	Gen. coupling disc screw
J- 172	Oil gauge indicator nut	J- 659	Distributor base
J- 176	Oil drain valve	J- 660	Generator drive shaft front bearing
J- 178	Oil drain valve body	J- 661	Generator drive shaft rear bearing
J- 179	Oil drain valve spring		bushing
J- 181	Oil drain valve stem collar	J- 665	Distributor control shaft
J- 182	Oil drain valve lift pin	J- 680	Gen. shaft rear housing cap screw
J- 184	Oil drain valve flex shaft upper end	J- 681	Gen. drive shaft
J- 185	Oil drain valve flex shaft lower end	J- 682	Gen. drive shaft thrust washer
J- 187	Oil drain valve flex shaft packing	J- 683	Gen. drive shaft rear oil slinger
	nut	J- 684	Gen. drive shaft rear housing cap
J- 189	Oil drain valve lever	J- 687	Gen. drive coupling shaft
J- 191	Oil drain valve lever screw	J- 688	Gen. drive coupling shaft end
J- 203	Oil pan front packing	J- 689	Gen. drive coupling shaft pilot
J- 204	Oil pan rear packing	J- 691	Generator coupling
J- 300	Crankshaft	J- 695	Generator strap
J- 301	Crankshaft thrust washer	J- 698	Generator strap stud
J- 302	Crankshaft oil hole plug	J- 699	Generator strap nut
J- 303	Crankshaft oil hole plug gasket	J- 785	Fan assembly
J- 306	Connecting rod bushing	J- 790	Fan drive pulley lock washer
J- 309	Connecting rod	J- 859	Oil pump body to cylinder screw
J- 310	Connecting rod cap	J- 880	Relief valve
J- 311	Connecting rod bolt	J- 882	Relief valve spring
J- 312	Connecting rod bolt nut	J- 883	Relief valve flexible shaft assembly
J- 313	Piston	J- 886	Relief valve flexible shaft lower end
J- 314	Piston pin	J- 983	Intake manifold core hole plug
J- 315	Piston pin lock ring	J- 989	Intake manifold core hole plug
J- 316	Piston compression ring		gasket
J- 317	Piston oil ring	J-1012	Crankcase ventilator flange
J- 318	Fly-wheel	J-1100	Fuel pump assembly
J- 319	Fly-wheel ring gear	J-1232	Gasoline filter bowl
J- 320	Fly-wheel bolt	J-1111	Fuel pump drive housing cover
J- 321	Fly-wheel housing	J-1118	Fuel pump shaft handle
J- 323	Fly-wheel cover plate	J-1124	Fuel pump housing cover screw
J- 324	Starting jaw	J-1127	Signal box cover gasket
J- 325	Starting jaw cap	J-1130	Signal box stud nut
J- 326	Starting jaw packing	J-1156	Signal box pump housing
J- 327	Starting jaw cap gasket	J-1159	Signal box pump housing cap
J- 328	Starting jaw spring	J-1170	Signal box cap
J- 329	Starting jaw spring retainer	J-1180	Signal box pump reg. guide screw
J- 330	Starting jaw pin	J-1188	Signal box car gasket
J- 331	Fly-wheel housing cap screw	J-1193	Signal box pump reg. spring
J- 401	Cylinder head gasket		assembly
J- 450	Camshaft front bearing cap	J-1507	Clutch pilot bearing
J- 451	Camshaft inter bearing cap	J-1508	Clutch pilot bearing retainer
J- 453	Exhaust camshaft center bearing cap	0113	Hex. head cap screw
J- 454	Camshaft front bearing bushing	0115	Flat head machine screw
J- 455	Camshaft inter bearing bushing	0119	Plain cut washer
J- 458	Camshaft rear bearing bushing	0125	Tapper pin
J- 460	Intake cam front cover	0130	Woodruff key
J- 461	Intake cam rear cover	0131	Woodruff key
J- 465	Intake cam rear cover gasket	0113	Hex head cap screw

(38) CHANGING OIL

This quantity of oil should be maintained in the crankcase at all times and drained, to be replaced, after 750 miles as indicated by operation of the signal light on the instrument board marked "Oil". Never flush motor with kerosene or flushing oil as it is impossible to remove a portion of this fluid which will remain in the different reservoirs. Ten drops of light engine oil should be added to generator shaft bearings at the same time motor oil is changed. The oil filter on the right hand side of the cylinder block contains a mesh covered cartridge, which removes and retains all sludge and foreign material found in the oil. This filter should be disassembled and cleaned thoroughly with gasoline at 10,000 miles and after 20,000 miles it is advisable to replace this cartridge. The filter may be completely disassembled after removing large hex nut on top.

(39) OIL SPECIFICATIONS

It is not possible to use the same grade of engine oil for all seasons of the year except in extremely mild climates.
An "extra heavy" grade of oil should be used for the warm seasons with specifications as follows:

Viscosity at 100° F	1421 Saybolt
Viscosity at 210° F	105 Saybolt
Flash	455° F
Cold Test	16° F

This grade of oil may be obtained in many nationally advertised brands and is classified in most cases as "extra heavy" or S. A. E. specification No. 60. Use only the very best oil obtainable.
For the winter months the next lightest grade should be used which is S. A. E. No. 50 or where the cold weather is extremely severe S. A. E. No. 40 oil may be desirable.

(40) CRANKSHAFT

The crankshaft is one of the vital factors contributing to the smooth and uniform flow of power at all speeds. The shaft, machined on all surfaces, is balanced statically to within one-onehundredth of an ounce and then given a dynamic balance with the same limits for all motor speeds. Further than this, cartridges or tubes partially filled with mercury are attached to the cheek of the shaft; the shifting of the mercury in the tubes thus eliminating even the slightest variation in power impulses.
The shaft of chrome-nickel-manganese steel has eight connecting rod throws and five main journals of ample size with extremely large connecting cheeks giving a positive alignment and rigidity under all loads. The center four connecting rod bearings are in one plan, at right angles "90 degrees" to the two end pairs. Oil supplied at the main bearing journals is transmitted to the connecting rod bearings through holes drilled in the cheeks of the shaft, where an enlarged chamber pockets any sludge that may be present in the oil and thus gives absolutely clean oil to the bearings.

(41) MAIN BEARINGS

Five main bearings with a large diameter of 2¾" lined with "Mogul Genuine" bearing metal support the crankshaft. Main bearings are fitted with .0015" clearance to allow a full cushion of oil for supporting the shaft. End thrust is taken at the front main bearing and held to .0015" limit. No shims are provided for tightening bearings as this operation should not be necessary in the life of the motor. However bearings may be tightened by removing each lower half using very fine emery cloth on a surface plate to remove desired amount of metal from the top faces of cap. Be sure to tighten bearing cap nuts securely.

(42) CONNECTING RODS

The connecting rods made of duralumin using a steel cap, provide a very light and strong unit, adding greatly to the efficiency of the engine. Rod bearings with a large diameter of 2-7/16" are lined with "Mogul Genuine" bearing metal and fitted with .0015"—.002" clearance. One webb of the I-beam section of the rod is gun-drilled to provide oil pressure to piston pin bushings. No shims are provided for tightening bearings as the shims will not allow correct alignment of lower half with upper half of rod. Also it ordinarily is unnecessary to tighten bearings in the life of the motor but may be accomplished in the same manner as explained in the previous paragraph for the main bearing. Be sure cap nuts are anchored securely.

(43) PISTON, PINS, RINGS

The pistons used are made of extremely light aluminum alloy, the design of which allows and maintains uniform expansion of the skirt with the cylinder walls for all motor temperatures. The skirt of the piston is separated from the head on the circumference, thus causing heat to be dissipated from the head of the piston into the pin bosses and connecting rods before the skirt has received only ⅓ the amount of heat normally transmitted by other conventional designs. Pistons are fitted with .0025"—.003" clearance and maintain this clearance through many thousand miles of operation. Four piston rings are used; three compression ⅛" wide, one double duty oil regulating ring 3/16" wide. Rings are fitted with .014" to .016" end clearance.

A hollow piston pin 1-1/16" in diameter floats in the piston pin or connecting rod bushing and is locked in the piston by means of two steel snap rings at each end. The pin is given a just free fit in the bushing and a slight driving fit in the piston.

(44) CYLINDER BLOCK—CRANKCASE

The eight cylinders are cast en bloc with the upper half of the crankcase using a detachable cylinder head. The material of block is chrome-nickel casting, giving long wearing life to cylinder bores. All cylinder barrels are water-jacketed for the full circumference and the entire length. Aluminum cover plates enclose the water jackets on both sides of the block to provide a protection to casting in case of freezing.

Connecting rod and piston assemblies may be removed from the bottom of the block by rotating crankshaft during the operation

(45) OIL BASE—LOWER HALF OF CRANKCASE

The oil base is an aluminum casting with long deep cooling fins on the underneath side. Two breathers mounted on the left side of the cylinder block provide additional ventilation for cooling the oil supply in the crankcase. A baffle pan and fine mesh screen at a height of 2½" covers the entire inside area of the oil base giving a large surface for removing foreign material in oil supply before entering the pump. It is not necessary to remove screen for cleaning when changing oil, but should be done if oil base is removed at any time. To remove crankcase it is necessary to remove, screws anchoring mud pans on top flange, 31-⅜" cap screws underneath anchoring top flange to cylinder block, 5-⅜" cap screws underneath bolting rear flange to flywheel housing.

A large circular plate is located in the bottom which may be removed for inspection of the oil pump, oil drain valve and oil float gauge.

(46) FLYWHEEL

The flywheel is a steel forging 14-15/16" in diameter completely machined on all surfaces. A hardened steel ring gear with 119 teeth is shrunk on the flywheel to engage with the starting motor. Twelve 7/16" bolts and nuts unevenly spaced anchor flywheel to crankshaft flange so that it is impossible to assemble the flywheel to the shaft in the wrong position. Markings on the flywheel indicate top centers for both No. 1 and No. 8 in this manner: 1 and 8, TOP. Marks appear before and after center to give reference for ignition and valve timing which is given in inches and degrees before or after center.

(47) CYLINDER HEAD

The cylinder head is a chrome nickel casting carrying the valve mechanism and overhead camshafts directly above the valves. The head is removable and may be detached from the cylinder block by removing upper chain cover, chain driving camshafts, cylinder head stud nuts accessories etc., as explained under "Carbon and Valves". Water passages encircle valves and spark plug chambers on all sides, giving positive and abundant cooling for all parts even for the most severe conditions. Two intake and two exhaust valves are used to give increased power by permitting a full charge of fresh gas to enter the combustion chamber and then expelling it through the large area thus eliminating the necessity of excessive heat being passed over single valves, as takes place in conventional cylinder combustion design.

(48) Valve Mechanism

The valves are mounted at 35 degree angles to vertical center line of cylinder head with camshaft mounted directly above and operating valves through sleeve tappet between shaft and valve. Excess oil supplied to camshaft bearings under pressure is trapped in the camshaft housing and maintained at a level above tappets to provide an oil bath for valve tappets, guides and contact of tappet against cam. An oil vapor thus passes through tappet assembly to lubricate valve stem and guide beneath. Consequently a very quiet and trouble-free valve operation is maintained at all times.

(49) Valves

Intake valves are made of chrome-nickel steel, with 1½" diameter head, 11/32" diameter stem and 30 degree seat.
Exhaust valves are made of silichrome steel with 1-7/16" diameter head, 11/32" diameter stem and 30 degree seat.

(50) Valve Tappets and Tappet Guides

Valve tappet guides are a just free fit into cylinder head and anchored in pairs by means of two clamps each. A clearance fit of .0015 inches between tappet and guide is maintained at all times using a special steel for both units.

(51) Valve Adjustment

Adjustment of valves is provided by adjusting nut (J-420, Fig. 3 and adjusting sleeve J-421, Fig. 3). This adjusting nut assembly makes contact between end of valve stem and underneath surface of tappet. Shims of the desired thickness are assembled between adjusting nut and sleeve to give the required clearance of .022" between the tappet and camshaft. An ordinary thickness or feeler gauge may be used for checking clearance between tappet and heel of cam, while 1-inch micrometers will be needed for checking thickness of adjusting nut to give correct clearance by addition or removal of shims in nut. In order to perform the operation of adjusting valves, it is first necessary to remove camshaft covers, upper chain cover, upper chain, distributor, camshafts, tappets, etc., to give access to adjusting nuts directly on top of valves. Be sure to check tappet clearance with feeler gauge for each valve before removing camshaft and make pencil notes of all settings in order to be able to change adjusting nut thickness to the desired dimension and thus obtain correct clearance.

Printed in U. S. A.

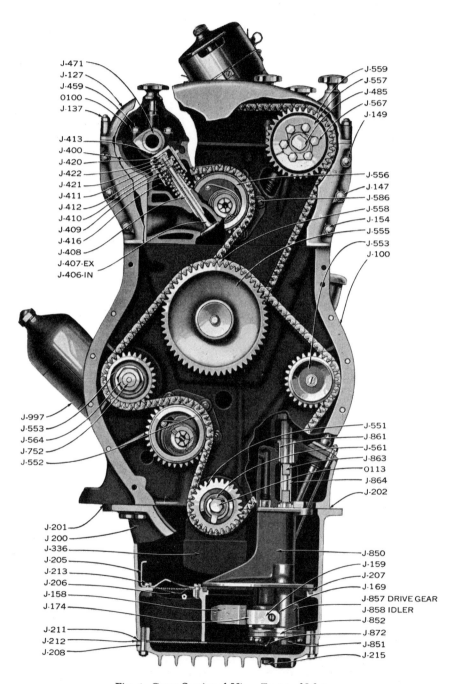

J-471
J-127
J-459
0100
J-137

J-413
J-400
J-420
J-422
J-421
J-411
J-412
J-410
J-409
J-416
J-408
J-407-EX
J-406-IN

J-559
J-557
J-485
J-567
J-149

J-556
J-147
J-586
J-558
J-154
J-555
J-553
J-100

J-997
J-553
J-564
J-752
J-552

J-551
J-861
J-561
J-863
0113
J-864
J-202

J-201
J 200
J-336
J-205
J-213
J-206
J-158
J-174

J-211
J-212
J-208

J-850
J-159
J-207
J-169
J-857 DRIVE GEAR
J-858 IDLER
J-852
J-872
J-851
J-215

Fig. 4. Cross Sectional View Front of Motor

Fig. 4. PARTS DESCRIPTION

J- 100	Cylinder block	J- 420	Valve tappet adjusting nut
J- 127	Chain case cap	J- 421	Valve tappet adjusting sleeve
J- 137	Chain case cap long screw	J- 422	Valve tappet adjusting shim
J- 147	Chain case upper cover dowel screw	J- 459	Camshaft bearing stud
		J- 471	Exhaust camshaft
J- 149	Chain case upper cover long screw	J- 485	Camshaft plug
		J- 551	Crankshaft sprocket
J- 154	Breather body cap screw	J- 552	Lower adjusting sprocket assembly
J- 158	Oil gauge float	J- 553	Accessory shaft sprocket
J- 159	Oil gauge float bracket	J- 555	Transfer sprocket assembly
J- 169	Oil gauge bevel gear	J- 556	Upper adjusting sprocket assembly
J- 174	Oil gauge float assembly	J- 557	Camshaft sprocket
J- 200	Oil pan	J- 558	Lower chain
J- 201	Oil pan R. H. gasket	J- 559	Upper chain
J- 202	Oil pan L. H. gasket	J- 561	Crankshaft sprocket lock washer
J- 205	Oil pan baffle plate	J- 564	Water pump shaft sprocket lock nut
J- 206	Oil pan screen	J- 567	Camshaft sprocket cap screw
J- 207	Oil pan to oil pump packing	J- 586	Adjusting sprocket assembly stud
J- 208	Oil pan strainer body	J- 752	Water pump drive shaft
J- 211	Oil pan strainer body gasket	J- 850	Oil pump body
J- 212	Oil pan strainer screen assembly	J- 851	Oil pump cover
J- 213	Oil pan baffle plate screw	J- 852	Oil pump cover gasket
J- 215	Oil pan strainer body long stud	J- 857	Oil pump gear
J- 336	Crankshaft small counterweight	J- 858	Oil pump idler gear
J- 400	Cylinder head	J- 861	Oil pump drive shaft lower bushing
J- 406	Intake valve	J- 863	Oil pump drive shaft
J- 407	Exhaust valve	J- 864	Oil pump drive shaft coupling
J- 408	Valve guide	J- 865	Oil pump shaft
J- 409	Inner Valve spring	J- 867	Oil pump shaft lower bushing
J- 410	Outer valve spring	J- 872	Oil pump pressure tube nut
J- 411	Valve spring retainer	J- 873	Oil pump pressure tube lower gasket
J- 412	Valve spring retainer wedge	J- 874	Oil pump pressure tube lower washer
J- 413	Valve tappet	J- 997	Oil filter assembly
J- 416	Valve tappet guide	0100	Plain hex nut 5/16" - 24
J- 418	Valve tappet guide clamp stud	0113	Hex head cap screw 1/2" - 20 - 1 1/4"

(52) VALVE GUIDES

The valve guides are special steel with press fit in cylinder head and a ream clearance fit of .001" for valve stem.

(53) VALVE SPRINGS AND RETAINERS

The valve springs are made of the best grade electric furnace steel available; two springs being used for each valve and assembled in the conventional manner using aeroplane type retaining washer locks to anchor retaining washer to valve stem. The retaining washer lock is in two halves with outside tapered diameter resting in retainer washer and clamping valve stem at the three ring groove.

(54) CAMSHAFT AND BEARINGS

The camshafts are made of special steel and supported by five bearings each 1¼" in diameter. The bearings are lined with "Mogul Genuine" bearing metal and given a clearance fit of .0015" for camshaft journals. End thrust is taken at front bearing maintained at .002" to .003". Valve lift for intake shaft is .350" and .360" for exhaust.

(55) TIMING CHAIN

Two endless silent timing chains with automatic adjustment are used to drive camshafts and accessory shafts. The lower chain part number J-558, Fig. 3, 2 inches wide and approximately 47 inches in length with ⅜″ pitch drives the generator shaft, water pump shaft, and transfer sprocket for upper chain. The automatic idler sprocket part number J-552, Fig. 3, retains the correct amount of tension on the chain at all times by means of its spring loaded hub and automatically adjusts the chain for wear. The chain may be removed after first removing chain cover and then disassembling automatic idler as explained under "Valve Timing" for the upper chain. The lower chain may be assembled in mesh for any position on all sprockets.

The upper chain, J-559, Fig. 3, 1-11/16 inches wide and approximately 52 inches in length with a ⅜″ pitch drives the two camshafts from driven transfer sprocket of lower chain. An automatic idler J-556, Fig. 3, maintains the correct tension which automatically compensates for wear. Oil pressure supplied to idler sprockets provide an oil bath for the complete chain mechanism. To remove upper chain first disassemble adjusting idler sprocket. Remove cotter pin and plain washer then with screw driver or thin tool pry forward the sprocket bushing and spring assembly J-574 until spring is almost ready to slip out of the notch in mounting shaft. With special tool part No. J-7016, release tension of spring from notch and pull forward, then allowing the spring to unwind. The idler sprocket may then be removed and the chain lifted off camshaft sprockets. The lower chain may be removed in the same manner after removing covers, etc. In assembling upper chain to sprockets as when setting the valve timing be sure to keep chain taut in the pull direction at all times. Assemble idler sprocket and bushing using special tool to center spring and bushing assembly setting spring with twelve notches or two complete turns. Turn motor with starter to allow chain to assume normal position and reset the tension on spring to 9 notches or 1½ turns.

(56) VALVE TIMING

The valve timing may be checked or reset as outlined in Fig. 5. In order to check timing first remove inspection plate on top of flywheel, exhaust cam cover and front intake cam cover. Rotate crankshaft with pry-bar through inspection plate hole against teeth of flywheel ring gear until crankshaft is on top center for Number 1 and 8 cylinders determined by markings on flywheel as follows No. 1 and 8 Top. Remove distributor head and with spark control advanced note if the main rotor arm is in correct position to fire No. 8 cylinder as explained in Fig. 5. If its position is incorrect rotate crankshaft one complete revolution to bring distributor in firing position for number 8 cylinder when No. 1 intake and exhaust cams are downward as illustrated.

With pry-bar through inspection hole in flywheel housing rotate crankshaft backwards approximately 6 inches on the flywheel and rotate forward until intake valve No. 1 is starting to open. The No. 1 and 8 center line on the flywheel should be just ⅜″ ahead of center line on flywheel housing.

A straddle clamp should be used to clamp and twist tappet J-413 as the crankshaft is rotated to determine the exact time when the camshaft contacts to open valve. Turn flywheel ahead and with clamp on exhaust valve tappet J-413 the valve should close, or the tappet release, when No. 1 and 8 center line is $1\frac{1}{4}''$ past center line of flywheel housing. The valve clearance should be .023" to .025" to give this timing.

To change or set timing it is necessary to remove upper timing chain cover, radiator, fan, and disassemble chain mechanism as explained under "Timing Chain".

In reassembling chain and sprockets to give the correct timing it will be necessary to remove the six 5/16" capscrews and shift timing chain sprockets on each camshaft in order to obtain the correct timing with respect to crankshaft. A block of wood should be wedged between chain on transfer sprocket and case to prevent chain dropping down at this lowest point. The flywheel should be set within $\frac{1}{4}''$ of the respective points for setting camshaft to allow for the slack in the chain. The chain should be kept taut at all times in assembling.

When valve timing is changed it is obvious that the ignition timing should be checked and set as explained under "Ignition Timing".

(57) VALVE GRINDING

Procedure for grinding valves.

1. Remove hood.

2. Remove radiator. (Remove brace rods, radiator hose connections, hold down nuts, and lift radiator directly upwards).

3. Remove fan. (Remove eccentric locking bolt in cover and pull fan forward from its mounting.)

4. Remove camshaft covers upper chain cover, distributor and control, spark plugs and wires, tachometer cable at rear of intake camshaft, heat indicator line and bulb in water manifold, water manifold, exhaust manifold, intake manifold, carburetor, exhaust heat connection across cylinder block, etc.

5. Disassemble upper chain as explained under "Timing Chain".

6. Remove cylinder head stud "acorn" nuts.

7. Assemble special eye bolts and hooks to spark plug holes to provide anchors for hoist in lifting cylinder head.

8. After head is removed and placed on bench, camshaft, valve tappets, springs and valves may be removed. A special tool part No. J-7017 should be used in depressing valve springs for removing valves.

9. An improvised rack should be made for carrying tappets, adjusting nuts, and valves and so marked in order to reassemble these parts in their original location. Failure to

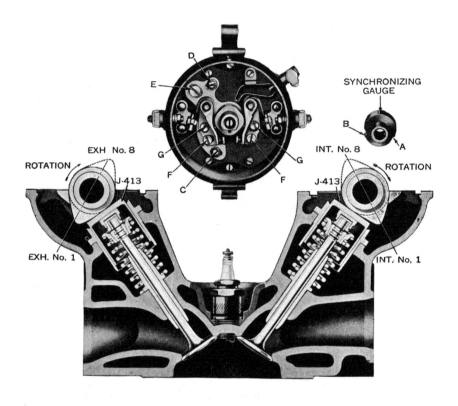

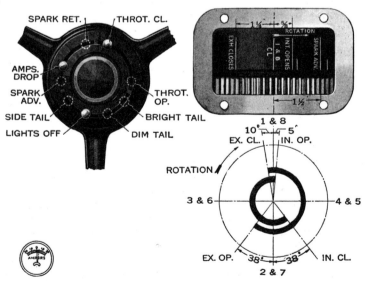

Fig. 5. Valve and Ignition Timing Diagram

do this will cause a great amount of additional work in setting valve clearances.

10. In grinding valves, seats should not be given a greater width than 3/32″. In case it is necessary to grind seats, to a greater width in order to obtain a full bearing for the complete circumference a valve seat sweeping tool should be used to narrow the seats.

11. Reassemble valves, springs, keepers, tappet valves, adjusting nuts and camshafts. Be sure tappet guide clamps and all camshaft bearing caps are tight. Rotate camshafts and with feeler gauge blades obtain actual clearance between cams and tappets. Remove camshafts, tappets and tappet adjusting nuts and with shims of varying thickness change length of adjusting nut to the required dimension to give .023″ to .025″ clearance. One inch micrometers must necessarily be used to check length of adjusting nut before and after removing shims.

12. Assemble cylinder head and units to motor being sure to set valve and ignition timing as illustrated in Fig. 5 and described under their respective headings.

(58) CARBON DEPOSIT

Ordinarily it is not necessary to clean out carbon and grind valves under 15,000 to 25,000 miles, provided a clean burning high compression gas is used at all times. Oil changes must be made as recommended to eliminate crankcase dilution and carbon deposits.

Carbon can only be removed by scraping after cylinder head is removed as described under "Grinding Valves".

FUEL SYSTEM

Gasoline is supplied to the carburetor from the 26 gallon tank at the rear by means of a mechanically operated bellows pump in conjunction with an electric booster pump. A gasoline chamois strainer bowl is placed just ahead of the pump to trap dirt and sediment which has accumulated in the gas tank. A positive supply of clean gas is thus maintained at the carburetor under all operating conditions.

(59) CARBURETOR

The special Schebler carburetor is a duplex air metering type supplying the two separate manifold chambers from one fuel chamber and bowl. The carburetor has two 1¼″ throat openings with adjustments for each one similar to two carburetors and thus metering the gas mixture separately to Nos. 3, 4, 5, 6 and 1, 2, 7, 8 cylinders as is readily determined by observing the intake manifold.

CONTROL HOOK-UP

The control tubing is fastened securely in the clamp and screw

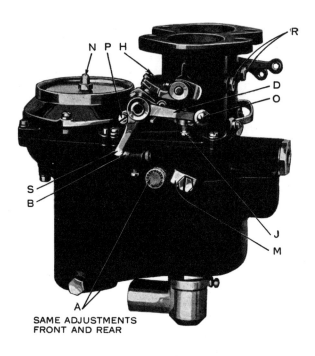

SAME ADJUSTMENTS
FRONT AND REAR

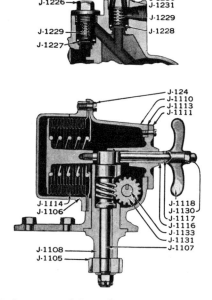

Fig. 6. Carburetor and Cross Sectional View of Fuel Pump

Printed in U. S. A.

Fig. 6. PARTS DESCRIPTION

J- 124 Fuel pump drive housing screw	J-1117 Fuel pump shaft rod
J-1105 Fuel pump driven gear	J-1118 Fuel pump shaft handle
J-1106 Fuel pump bellows housing	J-1130 Fuel pump shaft bottom nut
J-1107 Fuel pump drive shaft	J-1131 Signal box driven gear
J-1108 Fuel pump drive shaft bearing	J-1133 Signal box drive shaft
J-1110 Fuel pump drive housing	J-1226 Fuel pump intake plug
J-1111 Fuel pump drive housing cover	J-1227 Fuel pump intake valve
J-1113 Fuel pump drive housing cover gasket	J-1228 Fuel pump outlet valve
	J-1229 Fuel pump valve spring
J-1114 Fuel pump bellows assembly	J-1230 Fuel pump pressure dome
J-1116 Fuel pump operating shaft	J-1231 Fuel pump valve plug gasket

assembly "M" with tubing projecting about 1/16" beyond the clamp and the control wire in binding post "O" so there is about 1/16" play between the loose lever "D" and screw "P." When the throttle is closed after tightening binding post "O" straighten out the control wire so that the loose lever "D" does not bind the dash control lever "S" and cause it to stick open when moved. Use this control only in starting and warming up motor as explained in Part I of this book under "Instruments and Controls". If trouble is had in starting a warm motor open the throttle half way.

IDLING ADJUSTMENT—There are two idle adjustments as marked "A" one on the front side and one at the rear. The motor should be thoroughly warmed up before making the idle adjustments. Both spark and throttle should be fully retarded.
Before making idle adjustments "A" in front disconnect spark plug wires to Nos. 3, 4, 5, and 6 cylinders and allow the engine to run as a four cylinder motor.
Turning "A" in front, to the right (clockwise) makes the mixture leaner for cylinders 1, 2, 7, and 8; to the left makes the mixture richer.
Disconnect spark plug wires to 1, 2, 7 and 8 cylinders before changing idle adjustment "A" in rear.
Turning "A" in rear as if it were connecting to the same shaft as "A" in front, leans or richens the mixture for cylinders No. 3. 4, 5 and 6, The motor should idle down to approximately 200 r p m on the tachometer when running as a four cylinder motor or approximately 350 r p m when running as an eight cylinder motor.
To change the idle speed, adjust the idle screw "H". After making above adjustments and engine is running as an eight cylinder motor it may be necessary to change both adjustments the same number of clicks to make the total mixture lean or rich.

RANGE ADJUSTMENT—This adjustment is only effective in the driving range at speeds from 20 to 70 miles per hour and does not effect acceleration or hill climbing with wide open throttle. The adjustment is made by turning the range adjusting screw "B" to the left for a lean mixture and to the right for a rich mixture. This adjustment as shipped from the factory is usually found to be best.
To obtain the original factory setting, screw the range adjusting screw "B" in or out so the head is flush with the edge bushing enclosing it. Whenever the range adjustment is changed it is necessary to readjust the idle mixture.

Printed in U. S. A.

SECOND METHOD OF ADJUSTMENT—In case the carburetor cannot be adjusted in the above manner to give the desired results the following procedure may be used.

Set range screw "B" to original factory setting as explained in the previous paragraph.

With spark and throttle fully retarded idle the motor on each set of four cylinders and lean the respective idle adjustment on each set until motor stops, then back up or enrichen 8-14 notches until motor runs smoothly. This adjustment must be made separately for each set of four cylinders. Any variation in r p m for the two sets may be altered by turning screw "R" in to speed up, or out to slow down its group of cylinders. The total idling speed of the motor operating on eight cylinders may be set by turning screw "H".

WIDE OPEN THROTTLE ADJUSTMENT—The extreme high speed adjustment may necessarily need to be changed in some localities but this should only be done by an authorized Schebler service station. This adjustment is made at the contact cam screw "J" operating against throttle cam.

(60) CARBURETOR HEAT CONTROL

Exhaust heat is passed from the exhaust manifold across the cylinder block to the chamber around the intake manifold and then discharged through auxiliary pipe and muffler mounted along the left side of the frame. The amount of heat by-passed is regulated by means of a thermostatically controlled valve at the exhaust manifold. This valve automatically opens when motor temperatures are low and closes as the motor maintains the correct running temperature. The temperature at the top of the intake manifold is maintained at 125°F and 150°F to give uniform carburetion. Should the manifold receive too much heat the connecting link between the thermostat and valve at the exhaust manifold should be lengthened. A butterfly valve operated by the throttle rod further controls this heat as it leaves the intake manifold into the pipe and auxiliary muffler. This valve operates to compensate for variation of pressure in the exhaust system by closing when the pressure in the exhaust manifold is greatest and opening when pressure is low.

(61) FUEL PUMP

A spring loaded diaphram or bellows, operated by means of a cam, driven from a side gear on the generator shaft constitutes the fuel pump. As the cam compresses the bellows, the inlet check valve under the large hexagon nut just at the rear of the gas filter opens and allows gas to pass into pump. Immediately as the cam action releases and allows the bellows to expand with the spring tension, the outlet valve opens under the dome expansion chamber and gas passes to the carburetor. The dome expansion chamber filled with air equalizes the pressure of the pump for the carburetor.

Should the pump fail to deliver gas to the carburetor, remove and clean, check valves under the hexagon nut at the rear of the filter and under dome expansion chamber.

The entire mechanism runs in a bath of oil eliminating any necessity for attention and adjustment. A handle at the side of the pump is attached to the diaphram shaft and when operated by hand for a few strokes will prime the entire system. The strainer bowl should be removed and cleaned or slushed every 5,000 miles.

(62) ELECTRIC BOOSTER PUMP

An electric booster fuel pump is mounted in the left frame side member underneath the front seat. This pump further insures a uniform pressure in the gasoline line at all speeds and requires no attention. The ignition switch controls the operation of this unit.

(63) GASOLINE GAUGE

The gasoline gauge on the instrument board indicates at all times the amount of fuel in the rear tank. It is operated by the weight of gasoline pressing on a column of air which in turn causes the red liquid in the gauge head to rise or fall. Should the car be left standing for a week or longer the gauge may show less than the tank contains but driving the car for several blocks will cause the reading to be corrected.

If any difficulty is encountered with the gauge proceed as follows. Disconnect the air line at the gauge head. The liquid must come to rest exactly at zero. If necessary adjust the height of the column or add to or remove a few driops of liquid at the top of the brass tube. To remove liquid absord some on a toothpick or match.

Caution. Use only the special telegage liquid obtainable from the factory or the King-Seeley Corporation, Ann Arbor, Mich. Remove gas tank filler cap and blow air line dry with 50 full vigorous strokes of a hand tire pump. Do not use compressed air. Connect air line at gauge head and see that line is air tight at tank unit. The gauge will read zero until the car is driven a few blocks, whereupon the correct reading will be maintained.

Printed in U. S. A.

IGNITION SYSTEM

The ignition system may be classified as two distinct units with one set of breaker points and coil firing the center four cylinders (3, 4, 5, 6) and the other set of points and coil firing the two end pairs (1, 2, 7, 8). This type ignition permits low speed breaker point contacting thus giving positive firing of spark plugs under all speeds. The spark plugs are located directly over each piston and at the center of gas turbulence in the combustion chamber.

(64) DISTRIBUTOR

The distributor is mounted in casting above center of intake camshaft and locked in position by retaining plate and four "acorn" headed studs. By removing studs and plate with spark control lever the distributor may be removed. The head and rotor are of the single jump spark type using side outlet cap. A four lobe cam and double breaker arms in parallel circuit with the coils fire the cylinders in the following order. 1-6-2-5-8-3-7-4.

(65) SPARK ADVANCE

The distributor is a semi-automatic advance with the rotation in a clockwise direction viewing from the top. A manual advance of 20 degrees is obtained by shifting the distributor in its mounting. An automatic advance of 40 degrees is obtained through spring controlled governor weights of the marine type located beneath the breaker plate in the distributor cup and require no attention. As the speed of the motor and distributor shaft increases, when accelerating, the weights are gradually thrown outward and advance the cam in the direction of rotation.

(66) CONTACT POINTS

The contact points should be inspected every 5,000 to 10,000 miles and set at .018"—.024" clearance when fully opened by cam. To adjust points for this dimension loosen screws "F" and turn screws "G". Fig. 5. Points should present a "frosted" appearance and if black should be cleaned with fine emery cloth on a flat tool surface. Do not attempt to synchronize points by setting with different clearances but shift points on anchor plate as described under "Ignition Timing".

(67) IGNITION TIMING

Turn motor until intake and exhaust cams are in the same position as shown in Fig. 5, which is the firing center for No. 8 cylinder and four lobe cam should be in position as shown.

In timing the ignition it is quite necessary to set both sets of points so that they are absolutely synchronized and fire all cylinders at same time with relation to their respective center lines on the flywheel. The points may be synchronized in the following manner by use of special synchronizing tool J-6965 as illustrated in Fig. 5. Considerable time can be saved in retiming the engine by marking position of rotor and four lobe cam before removing so that it may be put back in the same position.

Loosen the screw in center of cam mounting the second time and remove cam, but do not tighten screw as synchronizing gauge should be free to turn when placed on this shaft. Rotate the gauge until the breaker arm rubbing blocks drop into the notches on its surface. Then holding the shoulder of the one notch firmly against the side of the block at "A" loosen the screws "C" and "D" and turn eccentric "E" until the side of the other block is in contact with the shoulder of the notch at "B". With the arms in this position tighten screws "C" and "D". The adjustment can be checked by holding the gauge solidly against the rubbing blocks and lifting each breaker arm in turn. If they are properly set a slight friction will be felt as the arms are raised from the gauge. Remove synchronizing tool and place four lobe cam on mounting post and lock in position so that No. 8 cylinder will fire at $1\frac{1}{2}''$ before top center with spark control fully advanced. No. 3 cylinder should fire just 90 degrees later on the flywheel at $1\frac{1}{2}''$ before its top center. These firing points may be determined by turning flywheel, using prybar with ignition switch "On" and noting when ammeter drops to zero.

(68) DISTRIBUTOR HEAD

The distributor has one high tension lead for each coil and eight spark plug leads with terminals marked in the same manner as the wires are attached to the plugs. The firing order 1-6-2-5-8-3-7-4 is thus obtained by each end of the dual arm rotor firing the respective cylinders in this order.

(69) CARE OF DISTRIBUTOR

Eight to ten drops of light engine oil should be placed in side oiler every 5,000 to 10,000 miles. Also when points are adjusted a very thin film of vaseline should be placed on cam to lubricate fibre rubbing block contact. The center plunger and the brass track inside the head should always make contact with rotor at center and carbon rubbing brush. The carbon brush may be broken quite easily in case head is not removed properly.

(70) CONDENSERS

Two condensers are mounted inside the distributor housing beneath breaker plate assembly and connected in parallel with the respective set of points.

(71) SPARK PLUGS

The spark plugs used are built specially for this motor using a standard 18 mm. thread. Points should be set at .022—.028 inches.

In no case should different plugs be used and when replacement is necessary be sure to obtain plugs with the exact specifications on the porcelain as given on the original ones.

(72) COILS

Two coils mounted on rear of instrument board are connected in parallel circuits to the respective set of coil points. A single ignition switch controls the complete circuit.

COOLING SYSTEM

(73) COOLING SYSTEM

Ample cooling is supplied by means of a large capacity radiator with positive circulation direct from centrifugal water pump located pump located at right front side of motor.

The capacity of the entire system is 7 gallon with a drain valve located at the bottom of the radiator on the left hand side to be used for flushing. A drain cock is also provided at the right rear side of the cylinder block to drain portion of water remaining around cylinder chambers.

A non-freezing solution of water and alcohol (only) is recommended for use during the winter months. Many other non-freeze solutions are recommended individually by their respective manufacturers as nothing has been found more satisfactory in every manner than alcohol.

A table is given below for your convenience in preparing the correct mixture proportions for desired temperatures.

Atmospheric Tem.	Alcohol	Water
10° F. above Zero	6 qts.	22 qts.
0° F. Zero	8 qts.	20 qts.
10° F. below Zero	9½ qts.	18½ qts.
20° F. below Zero	11½ qts.	16½ qts.
30° F. below Zero	13½ qts.	14½ qts.

Should alcohol be spilled on the lacquer wash immediately with water to avoid dissolution.

(74) HOSE CONNECTIONS

The two radiator hose connections should be inspected every few months and clamps tightened to prevent any leaks occurring at these points. Hose connections should be replaced at the end of the winter months as the anti-freeze solution may deteriorate the inside and thus restrict water passages and circulation.

(75) WATER PUMP AND FAN

The water pump located on the right front side of the cylinder block is driven by means of a safety coupling from accessory shaft and lower chain. A stainless steel shaft with brass rotor impellor and aluminum housing forms a non-corrosive unit to provide efficient operation throughout the life of the car. A long non-gran bronze bushing and steel thrust button eliminate the necessity of adjustments or replacements and the only attention necessary is the occasional tightening of the packing nut. New packing may be installed without removing water pump.

The fan is supported on plain annular ball bearings and should be packed with alemite grease every 10,000 miles. To adjust fan belt, loosen eccentric locking bolt at top of mounting and turn top of eccentric with spanner wrench to left side of car to remove slack in belt. It is not necessary to have belt absolutely taut.

CLUTCH

The clutch is a dual-plate, dry disc type, designed especially for ruggedness, ease and smoothness of operation.

It is composed of two major units; the cover and pressure plate assemblies, the driven member using a special dampening element for absorbing and storing the power impulses of the motor into an uninterrupted torque at all speeds.

(76) CONSTRUCTION

The driven member or dual plate assembly consists of a hardened splined hub, two driven discs to which the friction facings are attached and the center driving plate.

Twelve coil springs are located between the splined hub flange recesses and the driving blocks that are riveted to the discs. This feature allows a determined amount of lateral movement between the discs and the hub to compensate for lapse of power between power impulses of the motor.

The cover plate assembly consists of the outer driving plate and the stamped cover plate in which are mounted the twelve pressure springs and six release levers. These springs produce a pressure against the outer and inner pressure plates and flywheel face to engage the friction faces of the lining for the drive discs. The pressure exerted by these springs is far in excess for the actual requirement to compensate for wear on the facings and thus eliminate any necessity for future adjustments to units within the assembly. The only adjustment necessary is at the clutch pedal and this should be maintained so as to produce 1″ to 1½″ free movement of the pedal from the floor board. The clutch release bearing being completely enclosed and lubricated automatically by the chassis lubricating system relieves any necessary attention for lubrication.

(77) DISASSEMBLING AND ASSEMBLING

To disassemble the clutch it is first necessary to remove the transmission. In moving the transmission from its mounting be sure nto not allow the weight of the unit to rest on the clutch shaft when partially removed from clutch assembly. Remove the six ⅜″ cap screws at the outer edge in the cover plate assembly. The complete unit may then be removed from the flywheel.

Mounted in the cover plate there are three center plate adjustment screws. When installing the assembly on the flywheel the three center driving plate and adjustment screws should be backed out until their ends are flush with the face of the pressure plate.

In placing the complete clutch on the flywheel a splined dummy shaft should be used to align the splined hub with the forward pilot bearing while the six cap screws in the cover plate are being tightened down. After the above operation the three center plate adjusting screws should be screwed forward as far as possible and then backed off four notches.

It is then only necessary to adjust the pedal position as described in previous paragraph. Should a splined dummy shaft not be available for aligning splined hub in the assembly the transmission may be placed in position and then the six cap screws tightened thru

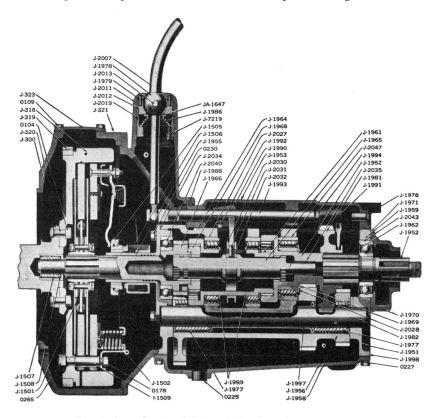

Fig. 7. Cross Sectional View of Clutch and Transmission

Printed in U. S. A.

Fig. 7. PARTS DESCRIPTION

J- 300	Crankshaft	J-1986	Gear shift lever support
J- 318	Flywheel	J-1988	Gear shift bracket dust felt
J- 319	Flywheel ring gear	J-1990	Shifter high & intermediate fork
J- 320	Flywheel bolt	J-1991	Shifter low and reverse fork
J- 321	Flywheel housing	J-1992	Shifter fork screw
J- 323	Flywheel housing cover plate	J-1993	Shifter high and second rail
J-1501	Clutch driven member assembly	J-1994	Shifter low and reverse rail
J-1502	Clutch cover plate assembly	J-1997	Countershaft gear bearing spacer
J-1505	Clutch release bearing	J-1998	Transmission case pan.
J-1506	Clutch release sleeve	J-1999	Eccentric gear snap ring
J-1507	Clutch pilot bearing	J-2007	Transmission case pan gasket
J-1508	Clutch pilot bearing retainer	J-2011	Gear shift bracket
J-1509	Clutch driving stud	J-2012	Gear shift lever socket
JA-1647	Gear shift lever spring washer	J-2013	Gear shift lever fulcrum pin
J-1951	Transmission case	J-2019	Gear shift lever socket nut
J-1952	Main shaft	J-2027	Eccentric gear (NC-212) bearing
J-1953	Shaft frame	J-2028	Main shaft bearing washer
J-1955	Main drive gear bearing retainer	J-2030	Clutch gear shift collar
J-1956	Transmission case pan	J-2031	Clutch gear shift collar pin
J-1958	Countershaft gears	J-2032	Clutch gear shift collar ring
J-1959	Main shaft rear bearing adapter	J-2034	Main drive gear bearing retainer gasket
J-1961	Eccentric gear		
J-1962	Main shaft oil retainer rear washer	J-2035	Main shaft pilot bushing
J-1964	Shift frame gasket	J-2040	Main drive gear bearing (No. 1211)
J-1965	Direct and second speed clutch gear	J-2043	Main shaft rear bearing (No. 1308)
J-1966	Main drive gear	J-2047	Main shaft front bearing (No. 211)
J-1938	Second speed drive gear	J-7219	Gear shift lever socket nut screw
J-1969	Main shaft snap ring	0104	7/16 - 20 plain hex nut
J-1970	Main shaft rear bearing retainer	0109	5/16 - 24 - 5/8" hex head cap screw
J-1971	Main shaft rear bearing retainer gasket	0178	3/8" - 25 - 7/8" hex head cap screw
J-1976	Back up switch plunger		
J-1977	Countershaft gear bearing	0225	3/4" Briggs std. allen pipe plug
J-1978	Gear shift lever (lower end of lever) ball	0227	5/16" - 18 - 3/4" hex head cap screw
J-1979	Gear shift lever socket pin	0230	3/8" - 16 - 7/8" hex head cap screw
J-1981	Main shaft low and reverse gear		
J-1982	Countershaft	0265	9/16" - 18 plain hex nut

opening in the transmission housing with gear shift assembly and plate removed. The three screws may then be adjusted.

(78) CLUTCH SERVICE POLICY

To save the individual dealer the expense of procuring assembly fixtures and tools for the replacement of clutch parts the following service method has been adopted:

For a nominal charge the cover plate assembly and the driven member assembly may be returned to the factory to be reconditioned. This work will be done with all worn parts replaced and the units will be the same as when new.

TRANSMISSION

(79) TRANSMISSION

The transmission is supplied with three speeds forward and one reverse but is a "four speed forward type" of design. An internal over-running gear gives a direct drive in both second speed and high gear allowing an absolutely quiet second gear. This design also permits an exceedingly quick shift between high and second speeds.

A conventional countershaft with quill gear drives the low and reverse sliding gear, on the main shaft at the rear of the transmission giving the low and reverse gear.

Roller bearings are used throughout the entire unit except for the main shaft bearings at the front and rear to give a positive alignment and add further to quietness.

The standard universal gear shift positions are used.

The transmission should be drained every 10,000 miles and a fresh supply of Whitmore's "0" lubricant added. Approximately 5 pints is required to bring oil to level of filler plug.

In order to disassemble transmission from car it is first necessary to remove universal joints and shaft as explained under "Universal Joints".

Remove clutch and brake pedals, shift lever and pedestal hand brake lever and controls backing light connection front muffler cover and nuts bolting transmission to flywheel housing, etc. The transmission may then be removed by pulling to the rear and lifting left side slightly to allow clutch release shaft to pass master cylinder. *Do not allow* the weight of the transmission to hang on clutch shaft as the alignment of the complete assembly will be disturbed. If the clutch is removed be sure to use centering tool for locating driven disc in correct position as explained under "Clutch".

(80) SPEEDOMETER GEARS

Gears at the rear of the transmission drive the speedometer. The Speedometer drive and driven gear are enclosed in the small housing at the rear of the transmission and can only be removed after universals and shaft is removed. Any change in rear axle ratio will necessitate a change in speedometer gears.

(81) HAND BRAKE

The hand brake mounted at the rear of the transmission proves a very simple and efficient mechanism. To adjust brake shoes loosen screw in equalizer sleeve at the center of the shaft, Fig. 11, which expands and contracts the shoes. Tighten adjusting nut on end of shaft to the position where hand brake lever will lock brake when in the fifth notch on its ratchet. When lever has locked brake in this position tighten screw in equalizer sleeve.

(82) UNIVERSAL JOINTS

Two universal joints are used, one cushion ball joint and one mechanical joint. The cushion ball joint contains eight rubber balls to cushion and insulate drive line from power plant. The mechanical joint is lubricated automatically from the propeller shaft bearing at the torque yoke. To disassemble universal joints remove the eight bolts thru flange for rear universal and the four large bolts thru front universal. Disassemble hand brake shoes from mounting and the complete shaft unit may be removed. If rubber joint is completely disassembled a clamping ring will be necessary to hold balls with drive cross and blocks to proper position for engaging in steel casing. The mechanical joint may be completely disassembled and parts replaced without special tools.

REAR AXLE

The rear axle exemplifies simplicity and rigidity in its general construction and employs the very latest in hypoid gearing for the final drive. The gears or bearings should not require any attention or adjustment throughout the life of the car provided the unit receives adequate lubrication.

(83) LUBRICATION

It is very essential that Whitmore's gear lubricant No. "0" be used in the rear axle as this is the only grease that is particularly suited for the hypoid gearing. This grease may be purchased at Duesenberg service stations or may be obtained direct from the Whitmore Manufacturing Co., of Cleveland, Ohio, and their representatives. The rear wheel bearings are lubricated from the supply in center of the axle and a composition washer located inside the brake drum assembly against the bearing retainer seals the lubricant at this point, thus preventing it from passing into the brake assembly. However do not fail to drain lubricant and flush ever 10,000 miles and refill with a fresh supply. The reason for this is that metal dust and sludge forming with the old oil will be extremely detrimental to all parts if allowed to remain in use.

(84) PINION AND RING GEAR

The hypoid gear construction provides for the pinion being off center (2 inches) which permits torque drive to be exceptionally low, allowing the chassis gravity center to be low and adding to the safety in operating the car. The assembly is mounted on ball bearings throughout with a sleeve adjustment for maintaining the correct position of the ring gear.

The correct position of the pinion is maintained by shims (J-3040)
the removal of which brings the pinion in deeper mesh with the
ring gear. In cases where the unit is disassembled for any reason,
the dimension marked on the face of the pinion, is the distance from
the face of the pinion to the center of ring gear assembly and should
be set for this exact dimension for trial setting of gears. This position should never be altered only in cases where it is necessary.
The ring gear and differential unit may be disassembled from the
axle housing by first removing the axle shafts as described in the
succeeding paragraph, second, removing, differential cover and the
two halves of carrier bosses secured in position by the four hex

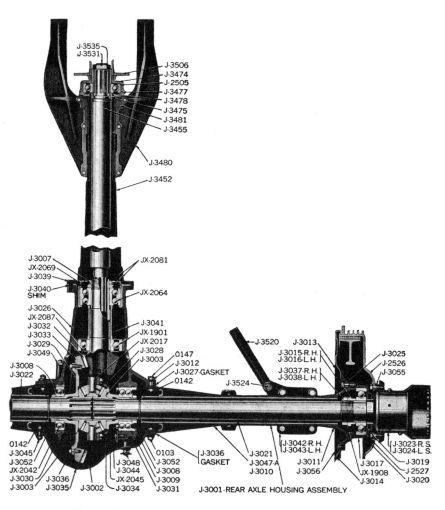

Fig. 8. Cross Sectional View Rear Axle and Torque Tube

Fig. 8. PARTS DESCRIPTION

JX-1901	Rear axle wheel pinion bearing	J-3031	Differential carrier right side cap
JX-1908	Rear axle wheel bearing nut lock	J-3032	Rear axle hypoid 14-53 pinion
	washer	J-3033	Rear axle hypoid 14-53 gear
JX-2017	Differential spider arm	J-3034	Differential right side ball
JX-2042	Differential L. H. bearing		bearing
JX-2045	Differential bearing lock screw	J-3035	Differential gear cover
JX-2064	Drive pinion front bearing	J-3036	Differential ring gear bolt
	(double row)	J-3037	Rear axle wheel bearing R. H.
JX-2069	Pinion bearing retainer nut		lock nut
JX-2081	Bevel pinion nut	J-3038	Rear axle wheel bearing L. H.
JX-2087	Bevel drive pinion washer		lock nut
J-2526	Brake drum	J-3039	Drive pinion bearing retainer
J-2527	Brake drum screw	J-3040	Drive pinion bearing retainer
J-3001	Rear axle housing assembly		shim
J-3002	Differential bevel pinion	J-3041	Bevel drive pinion bearing spacer
J-3003	Differential side gear	J-3042	Rear spring R. H. seat
J-3007	Bevel pinion nut lock washer	J-3043	Rear spring L. H. seat
J-3008	Differential bearing nut lock	J-3044	Differential bearing retainer lock
	washer	J-3045	Differential gear cover stud
J-3009	Differential carrier R. H. stud	J-3047-A	Shock absorber saddle
	nut	J-3048	Differential carrier right side
J-3010	Rear axle housing		stud
J-3011	Rear axle housing end	J-3049	Differential carrier left side stud
J-3012	Differential carrier stud	J-3052	Differential bearing nut
J-3013	Rear brake upper-half cover	J-3055	Rear brake drum pilot
J-3014	Rear brake lower-half cover	J-3056	Rear brake cover bolt
J-3015	Rear axle wheel bearing R. H.	J-3452	Torque tube assembly
	nut	J-3455	Propeller shaft assembly
J-3016	Rear axle wheel bearing L. H.	J-3474	Torque yoke bearing cap
	nut	J-3475	Torque yoke bearing spacer ring
J-3017	Rear axle wheel bearing retainer	J-3477	Torque yoke bearing retainer
J-3019	Rear axle packing	J-3478	Torque yoke bearing retainer
J-3020	Rear axle packing retainer		shim
J-3021	Rear axle R. H. shaft	J-3480	Torque tube yoke
J-3022	Rear axle L. H. shaft	J-3481	Torque tube yoke cap
J-3023	Wire wheel R. H. rear hub	J-3506	Universal joint rear flange
J-3024	Wire wheel L. H. rear hub	J-3520	Radius rod assembly
J-3025	Wheel bearing retainer bolt	J-3524	Radius rod eye bolt
J-3026	Differential carrier	J-3531	Universal joint cotter
J-3027	Differential carrier gasket	J-3535	Universal joint shaft nut
J-3028	Differential right case	0103	3/8" - 24 plain hex nut
J-3029	Differential left case	0142	3/8" - 24 jam nut
J-3030	Differential carrier left side cap	0147	3/8" - 24 Castle nut

nuts. The unit may then be removed. This practice of disassembling is to be discouraged however, because in reassembling it is impossible to observe the tooth contact or bearings in setting the gears. Therefore in all cases it is the best policy to completely remove the rear axle assembly from under the car when major repairs or disassembling is necessary to obtain proper tooth contact.

(85) AXLE SHAFTS AND BEARINGS

The axle shafts are hollow and extremely large to provide a great factor of safety in carrying the load and at the same time eliminating excess weight. The shafts are supported at the outer end on large annular ball bearings which require no attention or adjustment throughout the lifetime of the car. The axle shaft, brake drum and bearing assemblies may be disassembled from the axle as a complete unit by first removing the 8-3/8" cap screws J-3025 and then tapping lightly outward against the inner edge of the drum.

(86) Torque Tube—Propellor Shaft

The torque tube encloses the propellor shaft and maintains a positive alignment for complete line of drive. The tube is anchored to the frame crossmember thru a yoke and rubber insulators allowing a cushioned drive direct to rear axle independent of springs and shackles. The propellor shaft is supported at the front by means of an annular ball bearing automatically lubricated and is connected to the pinion shaft at the rear thru a splined slip joint.

The torque tube may be disassembled after removing complete unit with rear axle or after removing universal joints. To dismantle complete unit remove spring clips lower half torque yoke insulator brackets, rear universal flange bolts, brake line flexible connection, chassis lubricator connection to propellor shaft bearing, etc. The propellor shaft can then be pulled forward out of tube after removing the front bearing retainer screws.

FRONT AXLE

(87) Front Axle

The front axle is a chrome molybdenum forging of I beam section with reinforced flanges of ample strength to carry all radial and vertical stresses. The pivot pins are anchored in the axle forging with the steering knuckle and brake mechanism revolving about a double row radial bearing at the top and at ball thrust bearing at the bottom. An adjustment for end thrust is provided at the lower bearing by means of shims, J-2532 and adjusting nut, J-2531, Fig. 9. To make this adjustment remove locking bar J-2548 and back off adjusting nut J-2531. Remove one thin shim J-2532 and tighten nut securely. Remove sufficient shims until there is no perceptible up and down movement of steering knuckle or until a slight drag is noticed on revolving knuckle about pivot pin.

Pivot pin bearings should be packed with alemite cup grease every 10,000 miles using Zerk Gun and fitting in axle forging.

(88) Tie Rod

The tie rod or steering cross rod has an automatic adjusting ball joint at each end. These joints should be packed with alemite cup grease every 10,000 miles and otherwise no attention or adjustment is necessary. A right hand and a left hand thread is provided at the respective ends of the rod to screw into ball joints.

The ball joints at each end of the drag link or rod from the steering drop arm to the left steering arm should be adjusted so that the rod may be twisted when gripped firmly by the hand. To obtain this adjustment, tighten ball ends as far as possible and then back off until cotter pin can be inserted.

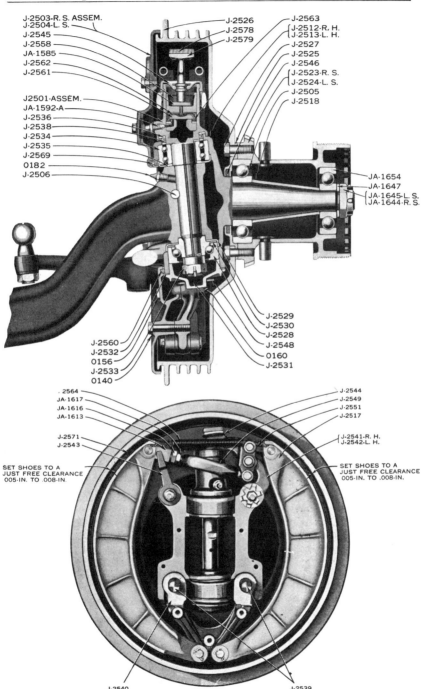

J-2503-R. S. ASSEM.
J-2504-L. S.
J-2545
J-2558
JA-1585
J-2562
J-2561

J2501-ASSEM.
JA-1592-A
J-2536
J-2538
J-2534
J-2535
J-2569
0182
J-2506

J-2526
J-2578
J-2579

J-2563
J-2512-R. H.
J-2513-L. H.
J-2527
J-2525
J-2546
J-2523-R. S.
J-2524-L. S.
J-2505
J-2518

JA-1654
JA-1647
JA-1645-L. S.
JA-1644-R. S.

J-2560
J-2532
0156
J-2533
0140

J-2529
J-2530
J-2528
J-2548
0160
J-2531

. 2564
JA-1617
JA-1616
JA-1613

J-2571
J-2543

SET SHOES TO A
JUST FREE CLEARANCE
005-IN. TO .008-IN.

J-2544
J-2549
J-2551
J-2517

J-2541-R. H.
J-2542-L. H.

SET SHOES TO A
JUST FREE CLEARANCE
005-IN. TO .008-IN.

J-2540   J-2539

Fig. 9. Cross Sectional View of Front Axle and Wheel Brake Assembly

Fig. 9. PARTS DESCRIPTION

JA-1585	Front brake piston disc	J-2533	Steering pivot pin nut
JA-1592A	Front brake hydraulic air bleeder screw	J-2534	Steering knuckle radial ball bearing
JA-1644	Front wheel R. H. nut	J-2535	Steering knuckle radial bearing cover
JA-1645	Front wheel L. H. nut	J-2536	Steering knuckle radial bearing felt
JA-1647	Front wheel nut washer		
JA-1654	Front wheel outer bearing	J-2538	Steering knuckle radial bearing felt retainer
J-2501	Steering knuckles pivot pin assembly		
J-2503	Front brake cover R. H. assembly	J-2545	Front brake cylinder block
J-2504	Front brake cover L. H. assembly	J-2546	Front hub bearing retainer felt
J-2505	Front wheel inner bearing	J-2548	Thurst bearing retainer nut lock
J-2506	Steering knuckle pivot pin lock	J-2558	Front brake hydraulic piston
J-2512	Steering R. H. knuckle	J-2560	Front brake lower cover felt
J-2513	Steering L. H. knuckle	J-2561	Brake piston cup washer insert
J-2518	Front wheel hub bearing spacer	J-2562	Brake cylinder piston seal cup
J-2523	Front wire wheel R. H. hub	J-2563	Brake cylinder piston seal cup spreader spring
J-2524	Front wire wheel L. H. hub		
J-2525	Front hub bearing retainer	J-2569	Front brake cover upper felt
J-2526	Front brake drum	J-2578	Front brake toggle arm pad
J-2527	Front brake drum screw	J-2579	Front brake toggle arm pad rivet
J-2528	Steering pivot pin thrust ball bearing	0140	Hex head cap screw 5/16" - 24 - 1-1/2"
J-2529	Steering pivot pin thrust ball bearing cover	0156	Hex head cap screw 5/16" - 24 - 1-1/4"
J-2530	Steering pivot pin thrust bearing cover felt	0160	Hex head cap screw 5/16" - 24 - 1/2"
J-2531	Steering pivot pin thrust bearing retainer nut	0182	Zerk lubricator fitting (straight) 1/8" pipe thread
J-2532	Steering pivot pin thrust bearing retainer shim		
JA-1613	Brake toggle adjusting block	J-2542	Front brake toggle L. H. support
JA-1616	Brake toggle adjusting nut	J-2543	Front brake adjusting link guide
JA-1617	Brake toggle adjusting lock nut	J-2544	Front brake toggle arm
J-2517	Brake shoe	J-2549	Front brake toggle adjusting link
J-2539	Steering arm rod	J-2551	Front brake toggle link
J-2540	Front brake shoe (lower support	J-2564	Brake shoe spring
J-2541	Front brake toggle R. H. suppirt	J-2571	Brake lining

(89) ALIGNING FRONT WHEELS

It is very necessary that the front wheels be properly aligned to give satisfactory steering and long wearing life to tires. The wheels should stand 1/8" to 1/4" closer together in front than in the rear. This dimension should be taken at one to two inches below the center of the wheel.

To check "Toe in" do not jack up front of car. First make a thin mark or line at the center of each tire in front and set device or gauge to this dimension. Roll the car backwards until the marks are at the correct height in the rear and with gauge note the difference from the original dimension in front. This dimension may be changed by loosening the two clamp bolts at each ball joint and twisting the tie rod in the proper direction. It is not necessary to disassemble tie rod for changing "toe in" as the right and left hand thread at each end changes the length of the assembly when rod is turned.

(90) FRONT WHEEL BEARINGS

The front wheels are carried on two annular ball bearings, which are given a tapping fit into the hub and onto the spindle. These bearings require no adjustment but should be packed with alemite grease every 5,000 miles.

To remove hub assembly it is necessary to obtain a puller which can be supplied on special order.

BRAKES

The hydraulic breaking system embodies all the latest development in hydraulics, giving the utmost in efficiency and simplicity of construction. The system consists of four completely sealed, internal expanding brakes operated directly from hydraulic pressure developed at the master cylinder assembly upon depressing foot pedal. The brake pedal, when depressed, moves the piston within the master cylinder, thus displacing the brake fluid out thru the lead lines to the four wheel cylinders. The brake fluid enters into each of the wheel cylinders causing the piston to move upward, thus operating a reducing lever to expand the shoes against the brake drums. As pressure on the pedal is increased greater pressure is developed in the system and consequently greater braking effect is obtained. Equal and undiminished hydraulic pressure is transmitted to each brake assembly and therefore inherent equalization of braking is obtained at all times.

(91) MASTER CYLINDER

The master cylinder is contained within the supply tank, being operated thru a connecting linkage attached to the brake pedal. The supply tank carries the reserve supply of fluid and protects the master cylinder submerged in the fluid from taking in air, dirt or water. In the head of the master cylinder, held in place by a return spring, is a combination inlet and outlet check valve. When the foot pedal is depressed and the master cylinder is pushed outward, the fluid opens the outlet check valve as it is being forced into the system. When the foot pedal is released, the master piston return spring forces the piston to its "off" position against its stop. At the same time the wheel cylinder pistons are being returned by the brake shoe return springs forcing the fluid back thru the inlet check valve until the fluid pressure balances the weight of the master piston return spring at which point the inlet valve closes. As the master cylinder returns to the "off" position, liquid is allowed to enter or be expelled, thus maintaining a constant volume of fluid in the system at all times, compensating for expansion or contraction and replenishing any loss resulting from leaks. It is imperative that the master piston be in its "off" position or fully returned when the brake pedal is resting against the toe board, else this compensating feature will be lost and the proper pressure and braking will not be maintained. To check for this setting remove the clevis pins at pedal linkage and note that the piston is fully returned. Th change the position of the piston with relation to the foot pedal it will be necessary to shift bell crank J-4803 on its shaft in the desired direction of rotation.

(92) BRAKE SUPPLY TANK

The supply tank described under the heading of "Master cylinder" is a simple reservoir and carries the surplus supply of brake fluid.

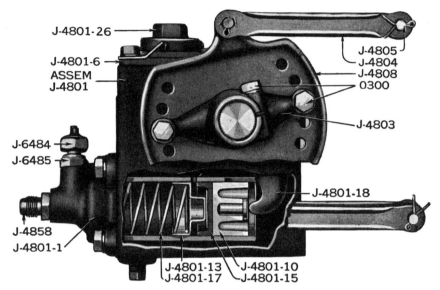

Fig. 10. Master Cylinder Assembly

0300	Master cylinder lever cap screw	J-4801-26	Master cylinder filler plug assembly
J-4801	Master cylinder assembly		
J-4801-1	Master cylinder supply tank	J-4803	Master cylinder lever
J-4801-6	Master cylinder supply tank cover	J-4804	Master cylinder lever link
J-4801-10	Master cylinder piston assembly	J-4805	Master cylinder lever link pin
J-4801-13	Master cylinder piston return spring retainer	J-4808	Master cylinder lever adjusting Plate
J-4801-15	Master cylinder piston cup	J-4858	Master cylinder to brake line union connection
J-4801-17	Master cylinder piston return spring	J-6484	Master cylinder light switch
J-4801-18	Master cylinder brake shaft lever	J-6485	Master cylinder light switch adapter

The filler plug (J-4801-26) in the tank is fitted with a breather valve sealing the tank and thus preventing evaporation of fluid and dirt entering. The supply of fluid should be maintained to within ½″ of the rop of the tank. Use only "Lockheed" brake fluid.

(93) WHEEL BRAKE ASSEMBLIES

The four wheel brake assemblies are identical in construction. Adjustment is only necessary to compensate for wear of the lining and the frequency of this operation depends entirely upon the service they are subjected to. Any unequal braking that may occur will undoubtedly be due to some foreign substance such as paint, grease, oil coming in contact with the lining. This condition may be remedied by thoroughly cleaning the lining with gasoline and roughening the surface with a file. In event the lining becomes thoroughly saturated with oil or grease it will be necessary to reline the shoes.

(94) ADJUSTMENTS

Adjustments of the brakes will not be necessary until such time when the foot pedal goes to the floor board and satisfactory application of the brakes is not obtained. The necessary adjustments can readily be made by moving or expanding the shoes as outlined below.

1. Jack up each individual wheel preferably all at the same time.

2. Remove plates at front assemblies on inside dust cover marked "adjust brake here." Disassemble upper section of rear inside dust cover by removing two (5/16″) caps screw and two (5/16″) nuts for each section.

3. The adjusting nut (JA-1616) and locking nut (JA-1617) Fig. 9 are identical for all assemblies and provide the only and complete adjustment for the correct position of the shoes. The lock nut contains a left hand thread while the adjusting nut contains both a right and left hand thread for elongating and shortening the link connecting the shoes.

4. Loosen lock nut and turn adjusting nut in the opposite direction, expanding the shoe until the brake drags slightly against the drum (noted by rotating the wheel by hand.) Let the adjustment remain at this point for the time being. Perform this same operation for the 4 assemblies and when a slight drag has been produced on all of them, depress the foot pedal to the floor board. Depressing the pedal and applying pressure to the system allows the two shoes of each assembly to centralize or equalize their position as a unit. Upon rotation of the wheels it will be found that the brakes are again free.

5. Repeat the above operation of adjusting the shoes out against the drum and depressing the foot pedal until the brakes do not free up after depressing foot pedal. When the above adjustment is performed the last time and there remains a slight drag on each wheel, it will be necessary to back off or reverse the adjusting nut (JA-1616) 3 hexagons or one half turn and again depress the foot pedal. The brakes will then be free and all shoes will have the same correct clearance at the drums. The brakes will then be restored to their original setting and effectiveness.

(95) RELINING SHOES

To remove shoes and reline it is necessary to first remove all brake drums. The rear ones are removed as a unit with the axle shaft as described under "Rear Axle Shafts and Bearings". To remove front drums, first remove, spindle lock nut and then tap lightly against inner edge of drum with lead or brass hammer until assembly may be dismounted from spindle. Remove inside dust covers. Remove toggle pins anchoring each shoe at the upper and lower ends. The shoes may then be removed.

(96) WHEEL CYLINDER AND PISTON

To remove pistons at wheel cylinder it is first necessary to remove brake drums as described above. Then by lifting toggle arm (J-2544) up and to the rear, using a lever of sufficient strength the brake assembly will be shifted slightly to the rear and the piston may then be lifted out of the cylinder.

The piston may be removed more easily if the bleeder screw is opened. Use only alcohol to clean piston and cup washer.

(97) BLEEDING SYSTEM

When any of the pressure units or connections are disassembled or disconnected for any reason it will be necessary to "bleed" the system in order to expel the air. Before attempting to "bleed" the system fill the supply tank with genuine Lockheed Brake Fluid and keep the tank at least half full all the time. Unscrew bleeder screw (JA-1592A) ½ turn at one wheel; on front assemblies it will be necessary to remove plate marked "bleed here" and attach rubber hose to protruding shank of screw allowing tube to hang into container such as bottle. Depress foot pedal slowly by hand and return to normal position. Approximately ten complete strokes of pedal will be necessary to bleed each cylinder. Depressing the pedal forces fluid through lines and out at wheel cylinders expelling any air which may be in the system. When no air bubbles are heard or appear at the end of the hose tighten bleeder screw. A bleeder screw in brake line connection at front of dash and should be bled last to expel air trapped at this point. Fluid withdrawn in bleeding operation may be used again in the supply tank provided no dirt is allowed to enter the liquid.

STEERING GEAR

(98) STEERING GEAR

The steering gear is of a special design cam-lever type with constant pitch cam. This design gives what is known as an irreversible steering, preventing road shock being transmitted to the hand wheel and at the same time permitting very easy steering due to the small number of friction surfaces.

Lubrication is the most important factor in maintaining a steering gear at its highest efficiency. It prevents wear and rattle. Remove pipe plug and fill housing completely with *Whitmore's "65" Gear Lubricant* every 5,000 miles.

Only two adjustments are necessary to eliminate all lash in the system. All adjustments should be made with the front wheels jacked up and with the steering drop arm removed. With the front wheels set straight ahead, turn the steering wheel hand to midposition. This is the position at which the steering drop arm should be assembled and locked securely on the trunion shaft after proper adjustments have been made.

To eliminate up and down movement of the steering wheel or end play in the column, remove locking stud with washer and back off large hexagon nut at the top of the steering gear housing. Remove one of thin shims between large nut and housing and tighten nut securely. Shims of the desired thickness should be removed until a slight drag is produced on moving the steering wheel.

To eliminate lash of lever arm in cam, adjust trunion shaft stop screw located in side gear cover plate at back of housing. Loosen hexagon lock nut and turn screw to right or clockwise until a slight drag is produced on moving the steering wheel. Tighten locking nut securely. Be sure to anchor steering drop arm with trunion arm in midposition of cam as explained above.

The steering column or wheel position may be shifted up or down after loosening the four bolts anchoring steering gear housing to frame and toe board bracket screws. Loosen screws on gate clamp at instrument board bracket and raise or lower wheel to the desired position.

CHASSIS

The chassis unit being built exceptionally low and sturdy permits a driving ease and feeling of safety even at excessive high speeds. The absolute insulation of the power plant and torque drive from the frame by means of rubberized supports eliminates any foreign noises from these units being transmitted to the frame and allows the units to maintain a true alignment with relation to one another. The line or drive is virtually in the same plane as the power plant unit, the angle of deflection being so slight as to eliminate angular stress on the universal joints. The unique design and uniform distribution of weight, produce an equilibrium throughout the chassis giving approximately the same load at each wheel.

(99) FRAME

The frame being of 7/32″ stock, 8½″ depth, crossed braced by four tubular, and two square shelled cross members gives a rigidity which absolutely prevents even the slightest frame flexure. The cross member at the front of the motor is braced longitudinally from each side of the motor to frame just above the front spring rear shackle. This one feature alone increases the rigidity to an equivalent of a frame twice the thickness as used. The four shell cross members riveted and gusseted at the center section of the frame insures rigidity in a like manner.

(100) CHASSIS LUBRICATING SYSTEM

All points of the chassis requiring regular and systematic lubrication, are automatically lubricated by a special pressure pump at the motor, supplying pressure through the oil supply tank at the dash to shackles, universal joints, propellor shaft bearing, steering drag link, shock absorber arms, etc. The pressure pump at the motor is a unit of the signal box assembly mounted just ahead of the fuel pump.

The pressure pump normally operates once every 60 to 80 miles, to supply oil under pressure to the chassis bearings. The correct supply of oil to each bearing or unit is controlled thru metering valves located at these points. It is quite necessary that the oil supply be maintained in the reservoir located on the front of the dash, else air and water, causing corrosion at the various units may impair the entire system, or lack of oil may damage pump. The two signal lights at the extreme left of the instrument board indicate the operating of the system explained under "Instrument Controls".

Should the lights burn continuously or not at all the electrical contacts may be at fault.

Other units of the chassis to be lubricated less frequently and not lubricated automatically are listed under "Operation of Cars".

Printed in U. S. A.

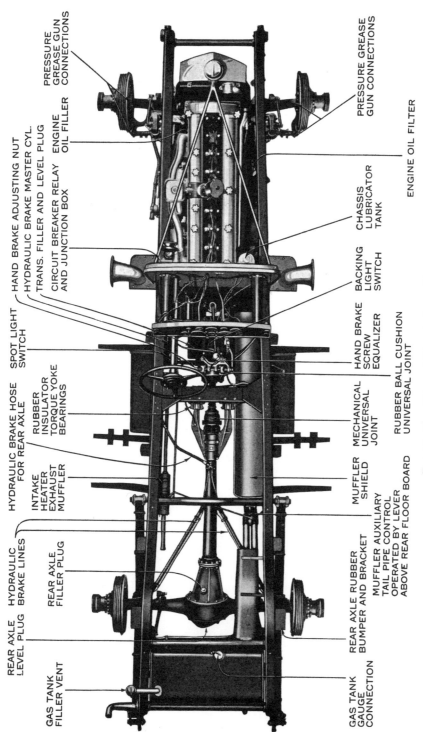

PRESSURE GREASE GUN CONNECTIONS

PRESSURE GREASE GUN CONNECTIONS

ENGINE OIL FILTER

ENGINE OIL FILTER

HAND BRAKE ADJUSTING NUT

HYDRAULIC BRAKE MASTER CYL.

TRANS. FILLER AND LEVEL PLUG

ENGINE OIL FILLER

CIRCUIT BREAKER RELAY AND JUNCTION BOX

CHASSIS LUBRICATOR TANK

SPOT LIGHT SWITCH

BACKING LIGHT SWITCH

HYDRAULIC BRAKE HOSE FOR REAR AXLE

RUBBER INSULATOR TORQUE YOKE BEARINGS

HAND BRAKE SCREW EQUALIZER

RUBBER BALL CUSHION UNIVERSAL JOINT

INTAKE HEATER EXHAUST MUFFLER

MECHANICAL UNIVERSAL JOINT

HYDRAULIC BRAKE LINES

MUFFLER SHIELD

REAR AXLE FILLER PLUG

MUFFLER AUXILIARY TAIL PIPE CONTROL OPERATED BY LEVER ABOVE REAR FLOOR BOARD

REAR AXLE LEVEL PLUG

REAR AXLE RUBBER BUMPER AND BRACKET

GAS TANK FILLER VENT

GAS TANK GAUGE CONNECTION

Fig. 11. Plan View of Chassis Assembly

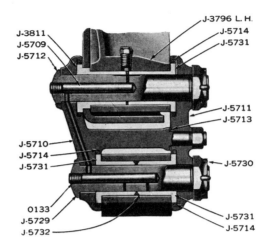

Fig. 12. Front Spring Rear Shackle Assembly

J-3796	Front engine & spring rear L. H. support	J-5712	Offset shackle pivot pin
		J-5713	Offset shackle adjusting shim
J-3811	Offset shackle front pin outer Bushing	J-5714	Offset shackle packing
		J-5729	Spring shackle bolt
J-5709	Offset shackle pivot pin filler plug	J-5730	Spring shackle bolt nut
J-5710	Offset spring shackle	J-5731	Spring eye bushing
J-5711	Offset shackle side arm	J-5732	Spring eye bushing packing
		0133	Pipe plug allen 1/8″ briggs std.

(101) SHACKLES

The shackles are of conventional design, using the very best grade of non-gran bronze obtainable as a bearing for the hardened steel shackle bolts. The bushings and bolts are extremely large, thereby eliminating excessive bearing pressure and resultant wear.

Incorporated in the design of the shackle is a special feature, whereby a supply of oil is maintained even against the end thrust faces of the bolts and bushing, eliminating wear at this point and the frequency of tightening and adjusting shackles. The correct end clearance is maintained by tightening the bolts and nuts to a just free clearance, and for the rear shackles of both front and rear springs, shims of a corresponding thickness should be removed on the bolt connecting each leg of the shackle to allow end thrust faces to remain parallel to each other. This operation of tightening or adjusting shackles will only be necessary every 10,000 to 20,000 miles.

(102) SPRINGS

The springs are semi-elliptic in design and are made unusually long and wide with thin leaves to give the greatest strength and desired resilence for the weight of the car.

(103) SHOCK ABSORBERS

The shock absorbers, control or check the spring action for extreme movement both in the upward and downward directions.
Thus it will be found that under all road conditions exceptionally good riding qualities will be maintained.
The shock absorbers require no adjustment throughout the life time of the car. It will of course be necessary to maintain the proper supply of liquid in each unit, using only Delco-Remy shock absorber liquid obtainable at any of their branches.

ELECTRICAL SYSTEM

The ignition system is described under paragraph 64.

(104) GENERATOR

The generator is driven at crankshaft speed from accessory shaft on the left side of motor, thru short shaft using two flexible disc couplings. The armature rotates clockwise on two annular ball bearings which should receive 10 drops of light engine oil every 750 miles at the same time oil is changed in the motor. The generator is a two pole shunt unit using third brush regulation with cut out relay mounted directly on housing.

(105) CHARGING RATE

The charging rate is determined by means of the position of the third brush. To change the position of the brush loosen the round head locking screw located at one side of the bearing cover on the commutator end frame. Remove the cover band and shift the third brush in the direction of armature rotation to increase the output and in the opposite direction to decrease the output. When the adjustment is completed tighten the round head screw securely to prevent brush changing position. The charging rate should not be higher than 12 amperes when generator is hot and lesser charging rates are recommended when lights and starting motor are not used excessively.
The third brush control is supplemented by a thermostat which is an automatic switch operated by the heat inside the generator. When the battery is fully charged or the internal temperature of the generator reaches 165 degrees F. the contact points open and a resistance is placed in series with the generator field with the result that the generator output is reduced approximately 40 per cent. This type of control permits a higher charging rate on short drives longer period in the winter time which helps to restore the battery charge.
The brushes should be examined occasionally to see that they are not worn excessively and if necessary clean armature with No. 00 sandpaper.

Printed in U. S. A.

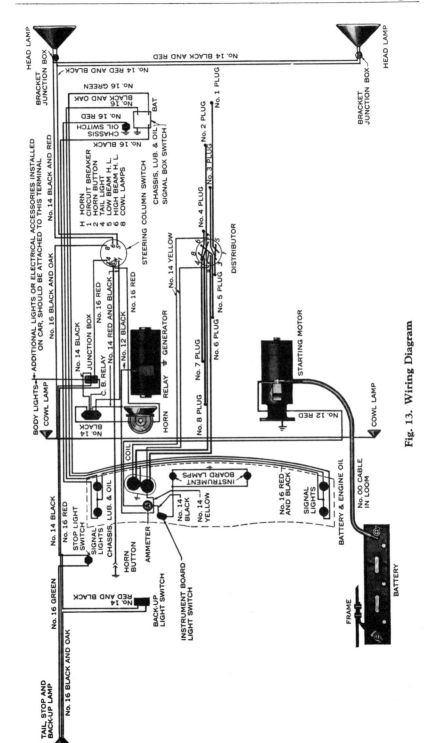

Fig. 13. Wiring Diagram

(106) CUT-OUT RELAY

The cut-out relay mounted on the generator frame serves to automatically connect the generator to the battery circuit when the voltage of the generator is equal to the voltage of the battery and to disconnect the circuit when the generator stops or the voltage drops.

(107) STARTING MOTOR

The starting motor is a six volt, six brush, six pole series wound unit equipped with a bendix drive to engage ring gear on flywheel. The bendix drive automatically engages when starter control is pulled out at dash. The armature is carried in graphite bronze bushings which do not require lubrication. Do not lubricate spiral shaft of bendix drive as it is only necessary that it be thoroughly clean. The cover band should be removed occasionally to inspect brushes to see that they are not worn and commutator cleaned with No. 00 sandpaper.

(108) CIRCUIT BREAKER

The circuit breaker mounted in front of dash on left hand side is a protective device to disconnect any circuit where there is an abnormal discharge or a short circuit. This unit serves the purpose of fuses and gives a buzzing signal to warn operator of the condition of system.

(109) LIGHTING SWITCH

The lighting switch is located at the bottom of the steering column and is controlled by the third lever at the steering quadrant. No attention should be necessary other than to keep the connections tight.

(110) AMMETER

The ammeter on the instrument panel indicates charging and discharging rates of the battery or the correct operating condition of the entire system.

(111) HORN

The horn is a six volt motor driven type and should receive a few drops of light engine oil periodically.

(112) STORAGE BATTERY

The 6 volt 160 ampere hour storage battery is carried in the compartment of the splash shield on the right side of the frame. The negative terminal is grounded as the entire system is of the single wire grounded type. The battery terminals should be cleaned periodically and given a thin coat of vaseline. Water should be added to the battery to keep liquid ½" above top of plates. The right hand upper signal light on the instrument board reminds you to inspect battery liquid every 1,500 miles.

(113) Lights

Standard light equipment is:
Headlight—High Beam 32CP, 6-8 Volts, S. C. base
Headlight—Low Beam 21CP, 6-8 Volts, S. C. base
Cowl Lights   3CP, 6-8 Volts, S. C. base
Instrument Light   3CP, 6-8 Volts, S. C. base
Tail Light   3CP, 6-8 Volts, S. C. base
Backing and Stop Light 21CP, 6-8 Volts, S. C. base
All connections should be inspected periodically to prevent open circuits and burning out bulbs.

BODY

(114) Body

Since practically all bodies supplied on the present chassis are custom built, it is impossible to include maintenance instructions and replacement details for all makes and types. However information may be obtained upon application from this factory or the respective body builders supplying the equipment. In all correspondence be sure to state, body manufacturer, body style and type seating capacity serial numbers and as many details as are available. In all cases give car number with above information.

Index

PARTS LIST

Duesenberg

MODEL J

PRICE $1.50

Compiled by the

General Service Department

DUESENBERG, INC.
Indianapolis, Ind., U. S. A.

CODE ADDRESS:
"Dusenautos"

Foreword

All prices quoted in this price list are net to Duesenberg owners, at Duesenberg, Inc., Indianapolis, Indiana, or at any Duesenberg Distributor or Dealer in the United States. Prices are effective on the date appearing at the lower right corner of each page, and Duesenberg, Inc., reserves the right to change prices without notice and is not responsible for the failure of the distributor or dealer to receive or note corrections thereto.

Warranty

Should the parts of any new automobile manufactured by us prove defective in workmanship or material, under normal use, within 1 year after shipment thereof from our factory, and such defective part be returned to us at our factory in Indianapolis, Indiana, within said time, transportation charges paid, we will deliver to the purchaser, f. o. b. Indianapolis, Indiana, a new part in lieu of such returned part, providing the returned part be determined by us to have been defective in material and workmanship.

We make no warranty with respect to tires, rims, ignition apparatus, horns or other signaling devices, starting devices, generators, batteries, speedometers or other accessories, or with respect to used or second hand cars, nor are we responsible for any warranties or agreements made by our dealers. In no case will we pay any bills for repairs made outside our factory, nor shall the above agreements apply to any automobile which may be in any way altered or repaired outside our factory nor to any defects developed by misuse, negligence or accident.

Except as above expressly provided, no warranty or guarantee of the quality of any automobile manufactured by us, or the parts thereof, or any parts, accessories or repairs, or of the other materials or workmanship therein, or of the suitableness thereof for the purpose intended, or the freedom thereof from defects, latent or patent, is made or given, nor shall any such warranty or guarantee ever arise by implication of law or otherwise.

DUESENBERG, INC.
Indianapolis, Indiana

Instructions for Ordering Parts

It has been found impractical and impossible to provide owners with parts price list that will be complete and up-to-date at all times.

Information on parts not contained in this book may be obtained at our service stations.

Parts in most frequent demand are shown in this book. The numbers appearing on the illustrations are part numbers and all parts must be ordered by this number and description given therewith.

IN ALL CASES POSSIBLE, PARTS SHOULD BE ORDERED OR RETURNED FOR CREDIT THROUGH OUR DEALER OR DISTRIBUTOR.

WHEN THIS IS NOT POSSIBLE THE OWNER MAY OBTAIN SERVICE ON PARTS DIRECT FROM THE FACTORY. PARTS ORDERED AND CORRECTLY SHIPPED MAY NOT BE RETURNED FOR CREDIT OR EXCHANGE UNLESS PERMISSION IS OBTAINED FROM THE FACTORY: WHEREUPON A HANDLING CHARGE OF 10 PER CENT WILL BE DEDUCTED FROM CREDIT DUE.

WHEN ORDERING PARTS be sure to use Duesenberg parts order form and give the following information:

1. Name and description of part.

2. Part number.

3. Serial number of car.

4. Serial number of unit assembly for which part is desired.

5. If part is desired for body, give body make, number, type, style and sample of part or small sketch of same.

WHEN RETURNING PARTS for credit be sure to use Duesenberg "Advice of parts returned" form and give the same information requested above as when ordering parts and in addition the following:

6. Reason for returning part, giving in detail difficulty experienced with same.

7. Date car was delivered to owner.

8. Order number on which new part was supplied.

9. Mileage of car at time part was changed.

10. Owner's name and address.

When Ordering by Code

The code system used in connection with our Parts List is the Acme Phase & Commodity Code System. The code words listed represent one each, part number, description and price; it therefore, becomes necessary only to show the code word when one part each is desired; for example:—

ACKON represents 1 J-413-AB Valve Tappet $4.35 each

In ordering greater quantities by code word it will be necessary to prefix the code word with a quantity word or quantity code word selected from the Acme Supplement.

NOTE—To gain the greatest benefit from the use of this code system, it will be necessary for you to secure from the Duesenberg Company a copy of the supplement to the Acme Phase & Commodity Code Book. Prices of these books will be given upon application at the main office, Indianapolis, Indiana, U. S. A.

Illustrations

CODE WORD	NO. USED PER CAR	PART NO.	DESCRIPTION	PRICE EACH
			CYLINDER BLOCK-CRANKCASE-MAIN BEARINGS AND OIL FITTINGS	
ABAAI	1	J-23	Engine (complete less clutch and transmission)....................Assembly	6,220 00
ABABJ	1	LYC J-6100	Cylinder block and crank case..Assembly	1,040 00
			(Always furnished with main bearing caps, bearings, studs, cylinder head studs, chain adjuster, stud and oil pump bushings as follows: less cylinder side plates including following parts to J-867 inclusive)	
			1 J-101 Front main bearing cap	
			10 J-122 Main bearing cap dowel	
			2 J-102 Intermediate main bearing cap	
			1 J-103 Center main bearing cap (with J-1067)	
			1 J-105 Front main bearing bushing	
			2 J-106 Intermediate main bearing bushing	
			1 J-107 Center main bearing bushing	
			1 J-108 Rear main bearing bushing	
			5 J-130 Main bearing bushing retaining screw	
			16 J-109 Main bearing stud	
			16 J-110 Main bearing stud nut	
			1 J-113 Crankcase main oil line tube	
			14 J-402 Cylinder head stud	
			4 J-402 Cylinder head stud (long)	
			6 J-586 Lower adjusting sprocket stud	
			7 J-585 Transfer shaft (to cylinder stud)	
			1 J-660 Generator drive saft front bearing (with 3 cap screws)	
			1 J-661 Generator drive shaft rear bearing bushing	
			1 J-750 Water pump drive shaft bearing (with 3 cap screws)	
			1 J-866 Oil pump shaft bushing (upper)	
			1 J-867 Oil pump shaft bushing (lower)	
ABACK	1	LYC J-7100	Cylinder block..Assembly	1,138 00
			(fitted same as above (J-6100) except includes pistons J-313, rings J-316, J-317, and pins J-314, J-315)	
ABADL	27	J-138	Fuel pump cap ....Screw	75
ABAEM	1	J-101	Front main bearing..Cap	17 50
ABAFN	12	J-122	Main Bearing ....Dowel	03
ABAGP	2	J-102	Intermediate main bearing..Cap	6 10
ABAHQ	1	J-103	Center main bearing...Cap	16 60
ABAIR	1	J-104	Rear main bearing..Cap	20 30
ABAJS	1	J-105	Front main bearing ....Bushing	6 25
ABAKT	2	J-106	Intermediate bearing...Bushing	2 40
ABALU	1	J-107	Center main bearing ....Bushing	2 80
ABAMV	1	J-108	Rear main bearing ....Bushing	3 10
ABANW	5	J-130	Main bearing bushing retaining...Screw	02
ABAOX	16	J-109	Main bearing...Stud	30
ABAPY	16	J-110	Main bearing stud...Nut	24
ABAQZ	1	J-111	Cylinder water thermostat...Plate	18 60
ABASA	22	J-124	Cylinder water plate...Screw	15
ABATB	1	J-112	Rear main bearing oil (upper)..Retainer	4 60
ABAUC	1	J-1069	Rear main bearing oil (lower)...Retainer	6 00
ABAVD	4	J-484	Rear main bearing oil dowel...Retainer	05
ABAWE	2	J-139	Rear main bearing screw..Lock Wire	10
ABAXF	8	J-146	Rear main bearing oil retainer...Screw	06
ABAYG	2	J-121	Rear main bearing oil retainer..Gasket	05
ABAZH	1	J-1067	Rear main bearing oil drain..Fitting	6 00
ABBAH	1	J-1071	Rear main bearing oil drain..Packing	10
ABBBI	1	OJ-1066	Rear main bearing oil drain...Block	6 30
			(fitted with 1—J-1068)	
ABBEL	2	J-146	Rear main bearing oil drain block..Screw	06
ABBGO	1	J-1068	Rear main bearing oil drain...Tube	
			(See OJ-1066)	
ABBIQ	1	J-113	Crankcase main oil line...Tube	2 95

CODE WORD	NO. USED PER CAR	PART NO.	DESCRIPTION	PRICE EACH
			CYLINDER WATER PLATE-CONTROL BELLOWS-CHAINCASE COVERS	
ABEZD	2	J-114	Cylinder water..Plate	6 10
ABFAD	44	J-124	Cylinder water plate ....Screw	15
ABFBE	3	J-115	Cylinder water plate...Gasket	05
ABFEH	1	J-116	Cylinder water inlet...Plate	9 15
ABFFI	20	J-124	Cylinder water plate...Screw	15
ABFIM	1	J-117	Cylinder water inlet plate...Gasket	05
ABFKO	1	J-118	Cylinder water inlet plate...Deflector	1 10
ABFOS	1	J-1045	Control bellows...Housing	3 60
ABFQU	1	J-1046	Control bellows..Cap	2 60
ABFUY	8	J-124	Water thermostat plate cover......................................Screw	15
ABFXA	1	J-1049	Control bellows cap...Gasket	05
ABFYB	1	J-125	Chaincase lower..Cover	40 75
ABGAB	14	J-154	Chaincase lower cover cap..Screw	55
ABGDE	2	J-122	Chaincase lower cover...Dowel	02
ABGEF	1	J-126	Chaincase upper..Cover	17 75
ABGGI	2	J-154	Chaincase upper cover cap..Screw	55
ABGIK	4	J-138	Chaincase upper cover cap (short)................................Screw	70
ABGMO	1	J-127	Chaincase...Cap	15 20
ABGOQ	6	J-138	Chaincase (short)...Capscrew	75
ABGSU	4	J-137	Chaincase (long)...Capscrew	90
ABGUW	4	J-135	Chaincase cap..Stud	06
ABGWY	4	J-136	Chaincase cap stud..Nut	09
ABGZA	1	J-128	Chaincase lower cover (R. H.)......................................Gasket	10
ABHAA	1	J-129	Chaincase lower cover (L. H.).......................................Gasket	10
ABHHI	1	J-131	Chaincase upper cover (R. H.)......................................Gasket	05
ABHIJ	1	J-132	Chaincase upper cover (L. H.).......................................Gasket	05
ABHNO	2	J-149	Chaincase upper cover (long)..Screw	1 40
ABHOP	2	J-147	Chaincase upper cover drive..Screw	1 00
ABHTU	2	J-148	Chaincase upper cover drive screw...................................Nut	70
ABHUV	1	J-133	Chaincase cap...Gasket	15
ABIBA	1	J-134	Chaincase cap (center)..Gasket	05
			OIL FILLER-OIL BREATHER-OIL GAUGE-OIL DRAIN-OIL PANS	
ABLOL	1	J-140	Oil filler..Body	3 90
ABLRO	1	J-6140	Oil filler body..Assembly	7 70
			(Includes J-142, J-143, J-144)	
ABLUR	3	J-138	Oil filler body cap..Screw	70
ABLXU	1	J-141	Oil filler body..Gasket	05
ABLYV	1	J-142	Oil filler body...Cap	1 95
ABMAW	1	J-143	Oil filler body cap..Spring	15
ABMCY	1	J-144	Oil filler body cap...Pin	15
ABMFA	1	J-145	Oil filler body...Screen	90
ABMIE	1	J-150	Breather..Body	3 10
ABMMI	1	J-6150	Breather body (includes J-153, J-154)......................Assembly	4 75
ABMOK	2	J-138	Breather body..Capscrew	70
ABMSO	1	J-151	Breather body..Gasket	05
ABMUQ	1	J-153	Breather body...Cap	1 15
ABMYU	1	J-154	Breather body (long)..Capscrew	55
ABNAV	1	OJ-174	Oil gauge float (includes J-158, J-159, J-169, J-170)........Assembly	17 10
ABNEZ	1	J-158	Oil gauge...Float	1 45

CODE WORD	NO. USED PER CAR	PART NO.	DESCRIPTION	PRICE EACH
ABNID	1	J-159	Oil gauge float...Bracket	1 20
ABNJE	1	J-169	Oil gauge bevel...Gear	1 35
ABNNI	3	J-170	Oil gauge bevel gear...Rivet	02
ABNOJ	2	J-160	Oil gauge float bracket..Screw	30
ABNTO	1	J-161	Oil gauge float bracket screw...Lock Wire	12
ABNUP	1	J-166	Oil gauge float bracket...Bushing	15
ABNYT	1	OJ-173	Oil gauge flexible shaft..Assembly	4 95
			(Includes OJ-162, J-163)	
ABNZU	1	OJ-162	Oil gauge flexible shaft..Assembly	5 25
			(Includes J-162, J-165, J-168)	
ABOAU	1	J-163	Oil gauge bevel...Pinion	1 10
ABOBV	1	J-165	Oil gauge flexible shaft (lower)...End	75
ABOCW	1	J-168	Oil gauge flexible shaft (upper)..End	75
ABODX	1	J-172	Oil gauge flexible shaft (upper) end.......................................Nut	10
ABOEY	1	J-167	Oil gauge..Indicator	1 75
ABOFZ	1	J-171	Oil gauge face..Plate	1 95
ABOGA	1	OJ-176	Oil drain valve...Assembly	5 20
			(Includes J-176, J-178, J-179AA, J-181, J-182)	
ABOHB	1	J-176	Oil drain..Valve	1 80
ABOIC	1	J-178	Oil drain valve..Body	2 35
ABOJD	1	J-179AA	Oil drain valve...Spring	10
ABOKE	1	J-181	Oil drain valve stem..Collar	15
ABOLF	1	J-182	Oil drain valve lift..Pin	06
ABOMG	2	J-213	Oil drain valve body..Screw	05
ABONH	1	OJ-186	Oil drain valve flexible shaft..Assembly	6 00
ABOOI	2	J-187	Oil drain valve flexible shaft packing....................................Nut	90
ABOPJ	2	J-188	Oil drain valve flexible shaft..Packing	05
ABOQK	1	J-189	Oil drain valve..Lever	1 50
ABORL	1	J-191	Oil drain valve lever..Screw	60
ABOSM	1	J-200AA	Oil (pan only)...Pan	123 30
ABOTN	1	LYC J-6200DA	Oil pan...Assembly	156 80
			(Includes following parts to J-145 inc.)	
			9 J-418 Oil pan strainer body stud	
			3 J-215 Oil pan strainer body (long) stud	
			1 OJ-1066 Oil drain (with J-1068) block	
			2 J-145 Oil filler body screen	
			NOTE—When using J-200AB new style pan omit J-1068, J-1066 and J-145.	
ABOUO	1	LYC J-7200AA	Oil Pan..Assembly	203 40
			(Includes following to OJ-176 inc.)	
			1 J-205AA Oil pan baffle plate	
			28 J-213 Oil pan baffle plate screw	
			1 J-206AA Oil pan screen	
			1 J-207 Oil pan pump bushing	
			1 J-208 Oil pan strainer body	
			1 OJ-212AA Oil pan strainer screen assembly	
			2 J-211 Oil pan strainer body gasket	
			1 OJ-176 Oil drain valve	
ABOVP	1	J-201	Oil pan (R. H.)...Gasket	25
ABOWQ	1	J-202	Oil pan (L. H.)..Gasket	30
ABOXR	1	J-203	Oil pan front...Packing	05
ABOYS	1	J-204	Oil pan rear..Packing	05
ABOZT	1	J-205AA	Oil pan baffle...Plate	6 40
ABPAT	28	J-213	Oil pan baffle plate...Screw	06
ABPBU	1	J-206AA	Oil pan...Screen	5 90
ABPFY	1	J-207	Oil pan pump..Packing	08
ABPHA	1	J-208	Oil pan strainer...Body	11 80
ABPIB	9	J-418	Oil pan strainer body..Stud	05
ABPLE	1	J-215	Oil pan strainer body (long)..Stud	15
ABPOH	1	OJ-212AA	Oil pan strainer screen...Assembly	2 25
ABPPI	1	J-211	Oil pan strainer body..Gasket	50

CODE WORD	NO. USED PER CAR	PART NO.	DESCRIPTION	PRICE EACH
			CRANKSHAFT	
ABUGV	1	OJ-300	Crankshaft..............Assembly	495 90
			(Includes J-336, J-337, J-338, J-339, J-340, OJ-300)	
ABUHW	1	OJ-6300	Crankshaft..............Assembly	605 50
			(Includes J-342, J-343)	
ABUIX	4	J-336	Crankshaft (small)..............Counterweight	2 80
ABUJY	3	J-337	Crankshaft (large)..............Counterweight	4 00
ABUKZ	1	J-338	Crankshaft rear check..............Counterweight	8 70
ABUMA	16	J-339	Crankshaft counterweight..............Bolt	70
ABUNB	8	J-340	Crankshaft counterweight..............Dowel	10
ABUOC	1	J-301	Crankshaft thrust..............Washer	2 45
ABUPD	8	J-302	Crankshaft oil hole..............Plug	75
ABUQE	8	J-303	Crankshaft oil hole plug..............Gasket	05
ABURF	1	J-551	Crankshaft..............Sprocket	8 25
ABUSG	1	J-561	Crankshaft sprocket lock..............Washer	06
			CONNECTING RODS-PISTONS	
ACAAJ	8	J-306	Connecting Rod..............Bushing	75
ACABK	4	LYC J-6309AA	Connecting rod..............Assembly	28 20
			(Includes J-311, J-312)	
			(The above is used in cylinders 1-3-5-7)	
			Note: Rebabbitting charge $5.00 net per rod	
ACACL	4	LYC J-6309AB	Connecting rod..............Assembly	28 20
			(Includes J-311, J-312)	
			(The above used in cylinders 2-4-6-8)	
			Note: Rebabbitting charge $5.00 net per rod	
ACADM	16	J-311	Connecting rod..............Bolt	70
ACAEN	16	J-312	Connecting rod bolt..............Nut	15
ACAFO	8	J-313	..............Piston	10 75
ACAGQ	8	LYC J-6313	Piston..............Assembly	11 35
			(Includes J-314 and J-315)	
ACAHR	8	LYC J-7313	Piston..............Assembly	13 90
			(Includes J-314, J-315, J-316, J-317)	
ACAIS	8	J-314	Piston..............Pin	1 20
ACAJT	16	J-315	Piston pin lock..............Ring	06
ACAKU	24	J-316	Piston (compression)..............Ring	50
ACALV	8	J-317	Piston (oil regulator)..............Ring	90

      August 15, 1929

CODE WORD	NO. USED PER CAR	PART NO.	DESCRIPTION	EACH
			FLYWHEEL-STARTING JAW-STARTING MOTOR	
ACEFK	1	J-318	(with ring gear J-319)..Flywheel	104 25
ACEGM	1	LYC	(with ring gear and	
		J-6318	J-1509AA)..Flywheel	110 10
ACEHN	6	J-1509AA	Clutch..Stud	70
ACEIO	1	J-319	Flywheel ring..Gear	3 00
ACEJP	12	J-320	Flywheel..Bolt	25
ACEKQ	1	J-321	Flywheel..Housing	80 50
ACELR	2	S-303	Flywheel housing..Dowel	10
ACEMS	3	J-778	Starting motor flange..Screw	85
ACENT	12	J-322	Flywheel housing transmission..Stud	20
ACEOU	11	J-331	Flywheel housing cap..Screw	10
ACEPV	2	J-332	Flywheel housing cap screw lock..Wire	15
ACEQW	1	J-323	Flywheel housing cover..Plate	2 55
ACERX	1	OJ-324	Starting jaw (Includes J-324, J-330)..Assembly	12 25
ACESY	1	J-324	Starting..Jaw	2 80
ACETZ	1	J-325	Starting jaw..Cap	5 50
ACEVA	1	J-326	Starting jaw..Packing	06
ACEWB	1	J-328	Starting jaw..Spring	15
ACEXC	1	J-329	Starting jaw spring..Retainer	60
ACEYD	1	J-330	Starting jaw..Pin	20
ACEZE	1	J-327	Starting jaw cap..Gasket	05
ACFAE	1	J-653	Starting motor..Assembly	72 50
			CYLINDER HEAD-CAMSHAFTS-BEARINGS-VALVES-TAPPETS- GUIDES-TIMING CHAINS-SPROCKETS AND CAMSHAFT COVERS	
ACIUV	1	J-400	Cylinder..Head	1,760 00
ACIVW	1	LYC J-9400	Cylinder head..Assembly	2,190 25
			(less camshafts, valve tappets, guides and clamps but as follows to J-148 inc.)	
			8 J-970 Exhaust manifold stud	
			4 J-972 Exhaust manifold clamp stud	
			8 J-970 Intake manifold stud	
			8 J-996 Water outlet manifold stud	
			4 J-996 Cam cover rear cap stud	
			4 J-148 Cam cover rear cap stud nut	
			16 J-406AA Intake valve	
			16 J-407AA Exhaust valve	
			32 J-408 Valve guide	
			32 J-409 Inner valve spring	
			32 J-410 Outer valve spring	
			32 J-418 Tappet guide clamp stud	
			32 J-411 Valve spring retainer	
			64 J-412 Valve spring retainer wedge	
			32 J-420AA Valve adjusting nut	
			32 J-421AA Valve adjusting sleeve	
			96 J-422 Valve adjusting (.002) shim	
			96 J-423 Valve adjusting (.005) shim	
			64 J-424 Valve adjusting (.010) shim	
			3 J-485 Camshaft plug	
			1 J-489 Tachometer drive plug	
			1 J-491 Tachometer drive sleeve	
			2 J-450 Front cam bearing cap	
			2 J-454 Front cam bearing cap	
			4 J-451 Intermediate cam bearing cap	
			4 J-455 Intermediate cam bearing bushing	
			1 J-452 Center cam bearing cap	

CODE WORD	NO. USED PER CAR	PART NO.	DESCRIPTION	PRICE EACH
		1 J-457	Center cam bearing (exhaust) bushing	
		1 J-456	Center cam bearing (intake) bushing	
		1 J-473	Center cam bearing (upper half) bushing	
		1 J-659	Distributor base	
		2 J-453	Rear cam bearing cap	
		2 J-458	Rear cam bearing bushing	
		1 J-463	Rear cam bearing cover	
		1 J-490	Tachometer drive cover	
		24 J-459	Camshaft bearing stud	
		16 J-484	Camshaft bearing cap dowel	
		2 J-658	Distributor base (short) stud	
		2 J-668	Distributor base (long) stud	
		2 J-148	Distributor base nuts	
ACIWX	1	LYC J-10400	Cylinder Head...Assembly (with all parts listed under J-9400 including J-413AB, J-416, J-417, J-470AA, J-471AA, J-467)	2,508 50
ACIXY	1	J-401	Cylinder head...Gasket	3 20
ACIYZ	14	J-402	Cylinder head...Stud	45
ACJBA	4	J-402X	Cylinder head (long)...Stud	60
ACJED	11	J-404	Cylinder head stud...Nut	1 25
ACJFE	2	J-405	Cylinder head stud (tall)...Nut	2 00
ACJII	5	J-707	Ignition wire cylinder spacer...Nut	1 90
ACJOO	5	J-708	Ignition wire cylinder..Screw	1 40
ACJUU	16	J-406AA	Intake...Valve	1 05
ACJYY	16	J-407AA	Exhaust...Valve	1 55
ACKAZ	32	J-408	Valve..Guide	75
ACKCA	32	J-409	Valve (inner)...Spring	25
ACKEC	32	J-410	Valve (outer)...Spring	40
ACKIH	32	J-411	Valve (retainer)..Spring	15
ACKJI	64	J-412	Valve spring retainer (halves)..Wedge	20
ACKON	32	J-413AB	Valve...Tappet	4 35
ACKPO	32	J-416	Valve tappet..Guide	1 30
ACKUT	32	J-417	Valve tappet guide...Clamp	50
ACKVU	32	J-418	Valve tapper guide clamp...Stud	05
ACKYX	32	J-420AA	Valve tappet adjusting...Nut	90
ACKZY	32	LYC J-6420AA	Valve tappet adjusting nut...Assembly (Includes J-421AA, J-422, J-423, J-424)	2 25
ACLAY	32	J-421AA	Valve tappet adjusting..Sleeve	1 35
ACLDA	96	J-422	Valve tappet adjusting (.002)...Shim	02
ACLEB	96	J-423	Valve tappet adjusting (.005)...Shim	02
ACLGE	64	J-424	Valve tappet adjusting (.010)...Shim	02
ACLIG	2	J-450	Camshaft front bearing...Cap	6 15
ACLKI	4	J-451	Camshaft intermediate bearing..Cap	5 90
ACLOM	1	J-452	Camshaft center bearing...Cap	6 75
ACLQO	14	J-484	Camshaft bearing cap...Dowel	03
ACLUS	4	J-453	Camshaft rear bearing cap cover..Retainer	8 10
ACLWU	4	J-418	Camshaft rear bearing cap retainer..Stud	05
ACLYW	2	J-454	Camshaft front bearing...Bushing	5 10
ACMAX	4	J-455	Camshaft inter bearing...Bushing	1 45
ACMBY	1	J-456	Intake camshaft center bearing...Bushing	6 60
ACMEA	1	J-457	Exhaust camshaft center bearing..Bushing	1 60
ACMHE	1	J-473	Intake camshaft center bearing upper...Bushing	6 60
ACMIF	2	J-458	Camshaft rear bearing...Bushing	3 30
ACMLI	24	J-459	Camshaft bearing...Stud	10
ACMOL	1	J-460	Intake cam cover...Front	23 35
ACMRO	4	J-468	Cam cover front and center..Packing	02
ACMUR	1	J-461	Intake cam (rear)...Cover	19 75
ACMXU	1	J-469AA	Cam cover rear...Packing	02
ACMYV	1	J-426	Exhaust cam...Cover	29 25
ACNAW	2	J-464	Intake cam cover (front)...Gasket	05
ACNCY	2	J-465	Intake cam cover (rear)..Gasket	05
ACNFA	2	J-466	Exhaust cam cover..Gasket	05
ACNIE	1	J-463	Cam cover rear..Cap	2 25
ACNMI	1	J-490	Tachometer drive..Cover	1 75
ACNOK	4	J-996	Cam cover rear cap..Stud	06
ACNSO	4	J-148	Cam cover rear cap stud..Nut	55
ACNUQ	2	J-467	Cam cover rear cap...Gasket	05
ACNYU	1	J-470AA	Intake..Camshaft	63 75

CODE WORD	NO. USED PER CAR	PART NO.	DESCRIPTION	PRICE EACH
ACOAV	1	J-471AA	Exhaust..Camshaft	60 00
ACOBW	2	J-557	Camshaft..Sprocket	9 75
ACOCX	12	J-567	Camshaft sprocket..Capscrew	05
ACODY	1	J-558	Timing (lower)..Chain	27 45
ACOEZ	2	J-568	Camshaft sprocket capscrew.................................Lockwire	10
ACOGB	1	J-559	Timing (upper)..Chain	24 90
ACOHC	3	J-485	Camshaft..Plug	25
ACOID	1	J-489	Tachometer drive..Plug	90
ACOJE	1	J-491	Tachometer drive...Sleeve	35
ACOKF	1	OJ-472	Cam cover large hand..Nut	1 35
ACOLG	4	J-475	Cam cover small hand nut retainer............................Wire	05
ACOMH	4	J-476	Cam cover small hand nut.......................................Retainer	15
ACONI	4	OJ-477	Cam cover small hand..Nut	1 30
			(Includes J-477, J-479)	
ACOOJ	9	J-480	Cam cover large hand nut retainer.............................Wire	10
ACOPK	9	J-482	Cam cover large hand nut.......................................Retainer	15
ACOQL	1	OJ-552	Lower adjusting sprocket......................................Assembly	23 85
ACORM	6	J-586	Lower adjusting sprocket...Stud	05
ACOSN	1	OJ-555	Transfer sprocket..Assembly	39 90
ACOTO	1	OJ-556	Upper adjusting sprocket......................................Assembly	23 85
ACOUP	6	J-586	Upper adjusting sprocket...Stud	05
ACOVQ	1	J-562	Generator shaft sprocket oil...................................Slinger	25
ACOWR	1	J-565	Transfer shaft..Stud	10
			(Included in OJ-555)	
ACOXS	1	J-566	Transfer shaft stud...Nut	05
			(Included in OJ-555)	

DISTRIBUTOR-GENERATOR-IGNITION COILS

CODE WORD	NO. USED PER CAR	PART NO.	DESCRIPTION	PRICE EACH
ACTYO	1	J-652	Ignition coil and lock..Assembly	27 50
ACUAP	1	J-651	Distributor...Assembly	45 00
ACUBQ	1	J-659	Distributor..Base	93 25
ACUCR	2	J-484	Distributor base..Dowel	05
ACUDS	2	J-658	Distributor base (short)..Stud	15
ACUET	2	J-668	Distributor base (long)...Stud	15
ACUFU	2	J-148	Distributor base stud..Nut	70
ACUGW	1	J-662	Distributor drive..Gear	1 35
ACUHX	1	J-672	Distributor drive gear lock..Pin	10
ACUIY	1	J-673	Distributor drive bearing lock..................................Spring	10
ACUJZ	1	OJ-670	Distributor control shaft bearing..........................Assembly	8 05
			(Includes J-663 to J-674)	
ACULA	1	J-663	Distributor control shaft..Bearing	3 85
ACUMB	1	J-665	Distributor control..Shaft	15
ACUNC	1	J-671	Distributor control shaft..Lever	1 30
ACUOD	1	J-674	Distributor control shaft..Pinion	1 25
ACUPE	3	J-657	Distributor control shaft bearing..............................Screw	30
ACUQF	1	J-664	Distributor control shaft bearing...........................Gasket	05
ACURG	2	J-666	Distributor clamp...Plate	2 60
ACUSH	4	J-656	Distributor clamp plate...Screw	55
ACUTI	1	J-667	Distributor clamp plate...Spring	40
ACUUJ	1	OJ-678	Distributor advance plate......................................Assembly	5 30
			(Includes J-675, J-676)	
ACUVK	1	J-675	Distributor advance..Plate	1 20
ACUWL	1	J-676	Distributor control gear..Segment	2 25
ACUXM	1	J-650	Generator..Assembly	75 00
ACUYN	1	OJ-681	Generator drive shaft..Assembly	47 10
			(Includes J-681, J-553)	
ACUZO	1	J-681	Generator drive...Shaft	39 70
ACVAO	1	J-553	Generator drive shaft...Sprocket	5 90
ACVES	1	J-660	Generator drive shaft front.....................................Bearing	7 10

August 15, 1929

CODE WORD	NO. USED PER CAR	PART NO.	DESCRIPTION	PRICE EACH
ACVIX	1	J-661	Generator drive shaft rear bearing............................Bushing	3 85
ACVJY	1	J-682	Generator drive shaft thrust.................................Washer	75
ACVMA	1	J-683	Generator drive shaft rear oil.............................Slinger	10
ACVOC	1	J-684	Generator drive shaft rear housing............................Cap	3 30
ACVUI	1	J-679	Generator drive shaft rear housing.........................Gasket	05
ACVYM	4	J-680	Generator shaft rear housing cap.............................Screw	45
ACWBO	1	J-685	Generator drive shaft.....................................Coupling	5 40
ACWGU	2	J-654	Generator drive shaft coupling..............................Screw	75
ACWIW	2	J-669	Generator drive shaft coupling................................Nut	15
ACWKY	2	J-677	Generator drive shaft coupling.............................Washer	10
ACWRE	1	OJ-686	Generator drive shaft coupling..........................Assembly	13 25
			(Includes J-687 to J-690)	
ACWUH	1	OJ-687	Generator drive coupling shaft..........................Assembly	6 80
			(Includes J-687, J-688, J-689)	
ACWVI	2	J-689	Generator drive shaft coupling...............................Pilot	55
ACWYL	4	J-654	Generator drive shaft coupling..............................Screw	75
ACXAM	4	J-669	Generator drive shaft coupling................................Nut	45
ACXCO	2	J-677	Generator coupling..Washer	10
ACXER	1	J-692	Generator coupling..Nut	1 15
ACXHU	1	J-693	Generator coupling lock....................................Washer	10
ACXIV	1	J-691	Generator...Coupling	3 30
ACXLY	2	J-654	Generator coupling..Screw	75
ACXOA	2	OJ-694	Generator strap..Assembly	4 85
ACXSE	2	J-696	Generator strap..Pin	1 20
ACXUG	1	J-698	Generator strap...Stud	1 60
ACXWI	1	J-699	Generator strap..Nut	1 35

WATER PUMP

CODE WORD	NO. USED PER CAR	PART NO.	DESCRIPTION	PRICE EACH
ADAQA	1	J-750	Water pump drive shaft...................................Bearing	10 75
ADARB	1	OJ-752	Water pump drive..Shaft	9 25
			(Includes J-752, J-553)	
ADASC	1	J-752	Water pump drive..Shaft	4 80
ADATD	1	J-553	Water pump drive shaft....................................Sprocket	5 90
ADAUE	1	J-563	Water pump shaft sprocket lock.............................Washer	15
ADAVF	1	J-564	Water pump shaft sprocket lock................................Nut	45
ADAWG	1	J-753	Water pump drive shaft thrust..............................Washer	3 10
ADAXH	1	J-754	Water pump thrust...Nut	65
ADAYI	1	J-755AA	Water pump...Coupling	11 50
ADAZJ	1	OJ-751	Water pump..Assembly	73 50

(Includes following to J-776 inc.)
1　OJ-756　Water pump shaft and impeller assembly
1　J-759　Water pump impeller thrust washer
1　J-760　Water pump impeller thrust button
1　J-761　Water pump packing
1　J-762　Water pump packing gland
1　J-763　Water pump packing nut
1　J-764　Water pump body
1　J-765　Water pump body bushing
1　J-1123　Water pump body dowel
1　J-766　Water pump bushing nut
1　J-768　Water pump cover
2　J-773　Water pump body cover screw
4　J-124　Water pump cover screw
1　J-769　Water pump cover gasket
1　J-775　Water pump outlet elbow
2　J-137　Water pump outlet elbow cap (long) screw
2　J-154　Water pump outlet elbow screw
1　J-776　Water pump outlet elbow gasket

CODE WORD	NO. USED PER CAR	PART NO.	DESCRIPTION	EACH
ADBAJ	1	OJ-756	Water pump shaft and impeller................................Assembly (Includes J-757, J-758A)	17 25
ADBEN	1	J-757	Water pump impeller...Shaft	8 25
ADBFO	1	J-758A	Water pump...Impeller	5 50
ADBIS	1	J-773	Water pump body cover (long)...................................Screw	85
ADBKU	4	J-124	Water pump cover...Screw	20
ADBOY	1	J-769	Water pump cover..Gasket	15
ADBRA	1	J-775	Water pump outlet...Elbow	4 90
ADBUD	2	J-137	Water pump outlet elbow cap (long).............................Screw	90
ADBVE	2	J-154	Water pump outlet elbow cap....................................Screw	55
ADBYH	1	J-776	Water pump outlet elbow.......................................Gasket	05
ADBZI	1	OJ-764	Water pump body..Assembly (Includes J-765, J-1123)	42 50
ADCAI	1	J-765	Water pump body...Bushing	50
ADCEM	1	J-1123	Water pump body..Dowel	08
ADCIR	3	J-778	Water pump body...Capscrew	90
ADCLU	1	J-767	Water pump body pilot..Plate	2 20
ADCOX	4	J-680	Water pump body pilot plate.................................Capscrew	45
ADCPY	1	J-770	Water pump connecting..Hose	15
ADCSA	2	J-771	Water pump hose clamp......................................Assembly	10

FAN

CODE WORD	NO. USED PER CAR	PART NO.	DESCRIPTION	EACH
ADGBE	1	J-785	Fan..Assembly (Includes following parts to J-785-21 inc.)	28 50
ADGEH	1	J-785-1	Fan blade..Assembly	3 90
ADFGI	2	J-785-2	Fan blade cap..Screw	06
ADGIM	2	J-785-3	Fan blade..Lockwasher	03
ADGKO	1	J-785-4	Fan blade front..Cap	60
ADGOS	1	J-785-5	Fan hub..Gasket	06
ADGQU	1	J-785-6	Fan blade bearing take-up......................................Spring	15
ADGUY	1	J-785-7	Fan blade bearing take-up spring..............................Retainer	40
ADGXA	1	J-785-8	Fan blade clamp...Washer	15
ADGYB	1	J-785-9	Fan (No. 16 magneto type).....................................Bearing	2 70
ADHAC	1	J-785-10	Fan...Oil Plug	06
ADHCE	1	J-785-11	Fan..Hub	3 75
ADHEG	1	J-785-12	Fan (No. 20 magneto type).....................................Bearing	3 00
ADHIL	1	J-785-13	Fan rear bearing..Gasket	15
ADHLO	1	J-785-14	Fan felt retaining...Washer	20
ADHOR	1	J-785-15	Fan felt...Washer	15
ADHRU	1	J-785-16	Fan felt...Retainer	40
ADHUX	1	J-785-17	Fan..Lockwire	06
ADHVY	1	J-785-18	Fan...Eccentric	90
ADHYA	1	J-785-19	Fan..Spindle	3 30
ADIAB	1	J-785-20	Fan bearing clamp...Nut	10
ADIBC	1	J-785-21	Fan cotter..Pin	03
ADICD	1	J-789	Fan drive...Pulley	3 95
ADIDE	1	J-754	Fan drive pulley...Nut	65
ADIEF	1	J-790	Fan drive pulley lock..Washer	05
ADIFG	1	J-792	Fan...Belt	1 25

CODE WORD	NO. USED PER CAR	PART NO.	DESCRIPTION	PRICE EACH
			OIL PUMP AND OIL RELIEF VALVE	
ADMEB	1	J-850	Oil pump..Body	33 25
ADMGE	1	LYC J-6850	Oil pump body...Assembly	41 35
			(Includes J-866, J-867)	
ADMIG	1	LYC J-7850	Oil pump...Assembly	67 00
			(Includes following to OJ-883)	
			1 J-851 Oil pump cover	
			1 J-852 Oil pump cover gasket	
			1 J-853 Oil pump pressure tube	
			1 J-854 Oil pump pressure tube packing	
			1 J-855 Oil pump pressure tube packing gland	
			1 J-856 Oil pump pressure gear stud	
			1 J-857 Oil pump bearing	
			1 J-858 Oil pump idler gear	
			1 J-865 Oil pump shaft	
			1 J-866 Oil pump shaft (upper) bushing	
			1 J-867 Oil pump shaft (lower) bushing	
			1 J-880 Relief valve	
			1 J-882 Relief valve spring	
			1 OJ-883 Relief valve flexible shaft assembly	
ADMKI	1	J-859	Oil pump body...Screw	10
ADMOM	1	J-877	Oil pump lock...Wire	05
ADMQO	6	J-213	Oil pump cover..Screw	25
ADMUS	1	J-860	Oil pump drive shaft (upper).......................Bushing	3 25
ADMWU	1	J-861	Oil pump drive shaft (lower).......................Bushing	2 35
ADMYW	1	J-862	Oil and fuel pump drive...................................Gear	12 70
ADNAX	1	J-863	Oil pump drive..Shaft	8 10
ADNBY	1	J-864	Oil pump drive shaft...Coupling	1 50
ADNEA	1	J-869	Oil pump pressure tube.......................................Spring	10
ADNHE	1	J-870	Oil pump pressure tube (upper)...................Gasket	05
ADNIF	1	J-871	Oil pump pressure tube (upper)...................Washer	05
ADNLI	1	J-872	Oil pump pressure tube...Nut	05
ADNOL	1	J-873	Oil pump pressure tube (lower)...................Gasket	05
ADNRO	1	J-874	Oil pump pressure tube (lower)...................Washer	05
ADNUR	1	J-880	Oil relief..Valve	95
ADNXU	1	J-882	Oil relief valve..Spring	35
ADNYV	1	OJ-883	Oil relief valve flexible shaft..................Assembly	7 30
			EXHAUST AND INTAKE MANIFOLDS-HOT AIR VALVE- WATER OUTLET MANIFOLD	
ADROH	1	J-1025	Exhaust...Manifold	128 25
ADRPI	1	OJ-61025	Exhaust manifold...Assembly	135 70
			(Includes J-1027 to J-970)	
ADRUN	1	J-1027	Exhaust hot air valve......................................Cover	5 30
ADRVO	1	J-1027X	Exhaust hot air valve....................................Bushing	1 25
ADRYR	1	J-1032	Exhaust hot air valve cover......................Gasket	20
ADSAS	4	J-680	Exhaust hot air valve cover cap................Screw	45
ADSCU	8	J-970	Exhaust manifold...Stud	10
ADSEW	8	J-1003	Exhaust manifold stud...Nut	45
ADSIA	4	J-971	Exhaust manifold...Clamp	1 30
ADSME	4	J-1004	Exhaust manifold clamp......................................Nut	65
ADSOG	4	J-972	Exhaust manifold clamp.....................................Stud	30
ADSQI	1	OJ-1028	Hot air tube...Assembly	4 90
			(Includes J-1030 and J-961AA)	
ADSUM	1	J-1030	Hot air tube...Flange	1 00
ADSWO	1	J-961AA	Hot air..Tube	3 00
ADSYQ	4	J-680	Hot air tube...Capscrew	45

CODE WORD	NO. USED PER CAR	PART NO.	DESCRIPTION	PRICE EACH
ADTAR	1	J-1031	Hot air tube flange..Gasket	15
ADTDU	1	OJ-1035	Exhaust hot air valve..Assembly	3 35
			(Includes J-1026, J-1033, J-1034)	
ADTEV	1	J-1006	Exhaust hot air connection...Gasket	15
ADTGY	1	J-1026	Exhaust hot air...Valve	1 95
ADTJA	1	J-1033	Exhaust hot air control..Shaft	35
ADTNE	1	J-1034	Exhaust hot air pivot...Pin	15
ADTOF	1	J-1048	Hot air valve control..Lever	3 90
ADTRI	1	J-1024	Hot air valve control lever..Key	05
ADTUL	1	J-978	Hot air valve control lever...Screw	45
ADTXO	1	J-957	Hot air valve...Packing	05
ADTYP	1	J-1047	Control bellows..Link	55
ADUAN	1	J-959	Hot air valve control..Bellows	4 60
ADUBR	1	J-962	Hot air (outer)..Tube	2 80
ADUCS	1	J-964	Hot air tube..Gasket	05
ADUDT	1	J-965	Hot air tube pilot..Plate	1 10
ADUEU	4	J-969AA	Exhaust manifold..Gasket	15
ADUFV	1	J-980	Intake...Manifold	114 00
ADUGX	1	LYC	Intake manifold...Assembly	117 00
		J-6980	(Includes J-983, J-989)	
ADUHY	8	J-970	Intake manifold..Stud	10
ADUIZ	8	J-1003	Intake manifold stud (stainless steel)....................................Nut	45
ADUKA	4	J-970	Intake manifold carburetor...Stud	10
ADULB	4	J-1003	Intake manifold carburetor stud (stainless steel)..............Nut	45
ADUMC	4	J-981	Intake manifold..Gasket	10
ADUND	2	J-983	Intake manifold core hole...Plug	1 35
ADUOE	2	J-989	Intake manifold core hole plug..Gasket	10
ADUPF	1	J-1021	Intake hot air...Connection	15 60
ADUQG	4	J-978	Intake hot air connection...Screw	90
ADURH	1	J-988	Intake hot air connection...Gasket	10
ADUSI	1	J-994	Water outlet (with connection)......................................Manifold	40 00
ADUTJ	4	J-995	Water outlet manifold...Gasket	10
ADUUK	8	J-996	Water outlet manifold...Stud	10
ADUVL	8	J-148	Water outlet manifold dowel screw.......................................Nut	75
ADUWM	1	J-990	Carburetor...Assembly	125 00
ADUYO	1	J-984	Intake manifold carburetor..Gasket	10

OIL FILTER

CODE WORD	NO. USED PER CAR	PART NO.	DESCRIPTION	PRICE EACH
ADYRD	1	J-997	Purolator..Assembly	65 00
			(Includes following parts to J-997-15 inc.)	
ADYSE	1	J-997-1	Purolator refill..Element	3 60
ADYTF	1	J-997-2	Purolator case...Gasket	30
ADYUG	1	J-997-3	Purolator retaining nut..Gasket	15
ADYVH	1	J-997-4	Purolator retaining..Nut	3 00
ADYWI	1	J-997-5	Purolator..Case	18 00
ADYXJ	1	J-997-6	Purolator base...Assembly	30 00
ADYYK	1	J-997-7	Purolator..Base	22 50
ADYZL	1	J-997-8	Purolator drain...Plug	3 30
ADZAL	1	J-997-9	Purolator pipe...Plug	1 00
ADZDO	1	J-997-10	Purolator pipe...Plug	50
ADZEP	1	J-997-11	Purolator blow-off cover...Screw	40
ADZIU	1	J-997-12	Purolator blow-off...Ball	15
ADZMY	1	J-997-13	Purolator blow-off...Spring	20
ADZOB	1	J-997-14	Purolator center...Post	3 00
ADZPA	1	J-997-15	Purolator..Gasket	30
ADZTE	1	J-998	Oil filter..Gasket	10
ADZUF	4	J-999	Oil filter...Stud	10
ADZXI	4	J-1000	Oil filter stud (stainless steel)..Nut	60
ADZYJ	2	J-1001	Oil filter sealing...Ring	05

CODE WORD	NO. USED PER CAR	PART NO.	DESCRIPTION	PRICE EACH
			FUEL PUMP-CHASSIS LUBRICATOR-SIGNAL BOX	
AECAJ	1	J-1100	Fuel pump................................Assembly	45 00
AECBK	1	J-1103	Gasoline filter................................Body	2 50
AECCL	1	J-1105	Fuel pump driven................................Gear	1 25
AECDM	1	J-1106	Fuel pump bellows................................Housing	2 75
AECEN	1	J-1107A	Fuel pump drive................................Shaft	11 40
AECFO	1	J-1223	Fuel pump drive shaft................................Plug	20
AECGQ	1	J-1108	Fuel pump drive shaft................................Bearing	2 70
AECHR	1	J-1110	Fuel pump drive................................Housing	12 25
AECIS	1	J-1111	Fuel pump drive housing................................Cover	3 10
AECJT	1	J-1112	Fuel pump housing................................Gasket	10
AECKU	1	J-1113	Fuel pump housing cover................................Gasket	05
AECLV	1	J-1114	Fuel pump bellows................................Assembly	4 80
AECMW	1	J-1115	Fuel pump bellows................................Spring	45
AECNX	1	J-1116	Fuel pump operating................................Shaft	1 90
AECOY	1	J-1117	Fuel pump shaft................................Rod	1 10
AECPZ	1	J-1118	Fuel pump shaft................................Handle	1 60
AECRA	1	J-1119	Fuel pump housing thrust................................Plate	90
AECSB	4	J-1124	Fuel pump housing cover................................Screw	1 20
AECTC	1	J-1130	Fuel pump shaft button................................Nut	15
AECUD	8	J-1122	Fuel pump housing................................Screw	30
AECVE	1	J-1101	Fuel pump to carburetor tube................................Assembly	75
AECWF	1	J-1104	Fuel pump................................Filler Block	2 10
AECXG	1	J-1109	Fuel pump operating shaft................................Spacer	05
AECYH	1	J-1226	Fuel pump intake................................Plug	35
AECZI	1	J-1227	Fuel pump intake................................Valve	10
AEDAI	1	J-1228	Fuel pump outlet................................Valve	10
AEDBJ	2	J-1229	Fuel pump valve................................Spring	10
AEDCK	2	J-1231	Fuel pump valve plug................................Gasket	05
AEDDL	1	J-1151	Chassis lubricator pump and signal box................................Assembly	175 00
AEDEM	1	J-1150	Chassis lubricator pump................................Assembly	38 00
AEDFN	1	J-1143	Chassis lubricator pump operating................................Lever	17 75
AEDGP	1	J-1144	Chassis lubricator pump lever................................Pin	60
AEDHQ	1	J-1148	Chassis lubricator pump piston................................Rod	4 50
AEDIR	1	J-1149	Chassis lubricator pump................................Packing	25
AEDJS	1	J-1152	Chassis lubricator piston................................Spring	15
AEDKT	1	J-1153	Chassis lubricator pump outlet................................Adapter	40
AEDLU	1	J-1155	Chassis lubricator pump packing................................Gland	95
AEDMV	1	J-1156	Chassis lubricator pump................................Housing	24 75
AEDNW	1	J-1157	Chassis lubricator pump housing................................Gasket	80
AEDOX	1	J-1158	Chassis lubricator pump piston................................Assembly	1 80
AEDPY	1	J-1159	Chassis lubricator pump housing................................Cap	4 85
AEDQZ	1	J-1160	Chassis lubricator pump cylinder................................Gasket	05
AEDSA	2	J-1161	Chassis lubricator pump cap................................Stud	10
AEDTB	1	J-1162	Chassis lubricator pump valve................................Spring	20
AEDUC	1	J-1163	Chassis lubricator pump valve spring................................Retainer	45
AEDVD	4	J-1164	Chassis lubricator pump housing................................Screw	50
AEDWE	1	J-1165	Chassis lubricator signal switch................................Felt	05
AEDXF	1	J-1166	Chassis lubricator pump................................Cylinder	45
AEDYG	1	J-1167	Chassis lubricator strainer felt................................Retainer	15
AEDZH	1	J-1168	Chassis lubricator strainer................................Felt	15
AEEAH	1	J-1169	Chassis lubricator strainer felt................................Support	10
AEEBI	1	J-1180	Chassis lubricator pump regulator guide................................Screw	70
AEECJ	1	J-1181	Chassis lubricator pump regulator stop................................Pin	55
AEEDK	1	J-1184	Chassis lubricator pump regulator stop................................Spring	10
AEEFM	1	J-1183	Chassis lubricator pump regulator spring................................Cap	70
AEEGO	1	J-1193	Chassis lubricator pump regulator spring................................Assembly	2 80
AEEHP	1	J-1214	Chassis lubricator pump piston rod................................Pin	15
AEEIQ	1	J-6483	Chassis lubricator pump................................Switch	50
AEEJR	1	J-1146	Signal box................................Assembly	135 00

CODE WORD	NO. USED PER CAR	PART NO.	DESCRIPTION	EACH
AEEKS	1	J-1127	Signal box cover..Gasket	10
AEELT	2	J-1128	Signal box long...Stud	80
AEEMU	2	J-1129	Signal box cover...Stud	30
AEENV	5	J-1130	Signal box stud...Nut	15
AEEOW	1	J-1131	Signal box driven...Gear	1 10
AEEPX	1	J-1132	Signal box driven gear...Pin	15
AEEQY	1	J-1133	Signal box drive...Shaft	2 50
AEERZ	1	J-1134	Signal box drive shaft..Bearing	2 75
AEETA	1	J-1135	Signal box drive shaft..Washer	1 10
AEEUB	2	J-996	Signal box to fuel pump housing......................................Stud	10
AEEVC	2	J-148	Signal box to fuel pump housing stud..................................Nut	30
AEEWD	3	J-1185	Signal box terminal post..Washer	20
AEEXE	1	J-1188	Signal box cap...Gasket	10
AEEYF	1	J-1300	Fuel pump (Autopulse)...Assembly	47 50

CLUTCH-CLUTCH AND BRAKE PEDALS

CODE WORD	NO. USED PER CAR	PART NO.	DESCRIPTION	EACH
AEGWA	1	J-1500	Clutch..Assembly (Includes J-1501 and J-1502)	60 50
AEGXB	1	J-1501	Clutch driven member..Assembly J-1501 supplied in assembly only Part not furnished separate. The old assembly will be reworked at the factory for $11.50.	36 50
AEGYC	1	J-1502	Clutch cover plate...Assembly J-1502 supplied in assembly only Part not furnished separate. The old assembly will be reworked at the factory for $10.00.	27 50
AEGZD	1	J-1505	Clutch release...Bearing	4 95
AEHAD	1	J-1506	Clutch release..Sleeve	2 00
AEHBE	1	J-1503	Release sleeve oil..Wick	10
AEHCF	1	J-1504	Release sleeve spring..Post	20
AEHDG	1	J-1507	Clutch pilot...Bearing	1 00
AEHEH	1	J-1508	Clutch pilot bearing..Retainer	1 40
AEHFI	6	J-1509	Clutch driving...Stud	15
AEHGK	2	J-1510	Clutch throwout bearing..Spring	10
AEHHL	1	J-1564	Clutch release shaft key...Washer	25
AEHIM	1	A-1008	Clutch release shaft...Washer	05
AEHJN	1	J-1569	Brake pedal..Pad	1 75
AEHKO	1	J-1507	Clutch pedal...Assembly (Includes J-1572, J-1585, J-1587)	13 25
AEHLP	1	J-1572	Clutch...Pedal	12 50
AEHMQ	1	J-1585	Clutch pedal stop (L. H.)...Pad	60
AEHNR	1	J-1587	Clutch pedal stop (R. H.)...Pad	20
AEHOS	1	J-1571	Brake pedal...Assembly (Includes J-1573, J-1581, J-1584, J-1586)	18 75
AEHQU	1	J-1573	Brake...Pedal	16 50
AEHRV	1	J-1581	Brade pedal...Spacer	1 35
AEHSW	1	J-1584	Brake pedal stop (R. H.)...Pad	60
AEHTX	1	J-1586	Brake Pedal stop (L. H.)...Pad	20
AEHUY	1	J-1574	Clutch pedal...Pad	1 95
AEHVZ	2	J-1575	Clutch Pedal pad...Cover	30
AEHXA	2	J-1576	Clutch and brake pedal slot..Grommet	15
AEHYB	2	J-1577	Clutch and brake pedal spring...Pin	20
AEHZC	2	J-1578	Clutch and brake pedal...Spring	10
AEIAC	2	J-1579	Clutch and brake pedal spring..Clip	05
AEIBD	1	J-1582	Brake pedal spacer..Sleeve	35
AEICE	1	J-1583	Clutch pedal adjuster...Lever	4 25

CODE WORD	NO. USED PER CAR	PART NO.	DESCRIPTION	PRICE EACH	

TRANSMISSION

CODE WORD	NO. USED PER CAR	PART NO.	DESCRIPTION	PRICE EACH	
AEKDD	1	J-1950	Transmission..Assembly	525	00
			(Includes following parts to J-2033 inc.)		
AEKEE	1	J-1951	Transmission..Case	86	00
AEKFF	1	J-1998	Transmission case pan...Gasket		25
AEKGH	1	J-1956	Transmission case..Pan	8	50
AEKHI	1	J-1966	Main drive..Gear	17	25
AEKIJ	1	J-2040	Main drive gear (No. 1211)....................................Bearing	6	75
AEKJK	1	J-1955	Main drive gear bearing..Retainer	7	75
AEKKL	6	J-2034	Main drive gear bearing retainer.............................Gasket		10
AEKLM	1	J-1968	Second speed drive..Gear	5	00
AEKMN	1	J-1961	Eccentric..Gear	25	25
AEKNO	2	J-2027	Eccentric gear (No. NC-212)..................................Bearing	5	75
AEKOP	2	J-2023	Eccentric gear bearing race..................................Lock Screw		10
AEKPQ	1	J-1965	Direct and second speed clutch.................................Gear	9	65
AEKQR	1	J-2030	Clutch gear shift..Collar	5	25
AEKRS	3	J-2031	Clutch gear shift collar..Pin		35
AEKST	1	J-2032	Clutch gear shift collar..Ring	2	25
AEKTU	2	J-1999	Eccentric gear snap...Ring		30
AEKUV	1	J-1952	Main...Shaft	26	50
AEKVW	1	J-2047	Main shaft front (No. 211).....................................Bearing	8	00
AEKWX	1	J-2028	Main shaft bearing..Washer		15
AEKXY	1	J-1969	Main shaft snap..Ring		30
AEKYZ	1	J-1962	Main shaft oil retainer (Rear)...............................Washer		15
AELBA	1	J-2043	Main shaft rear (No. 1308)....................................Bearing	6	00
AELCB	1	J-1959	Main shaft rear bearing...Adapter	1	60
AELDC	1	J-1970	Main shaft rear bearing..Retainer	5	25
AELED	1	J-1971	Main shaft rear bearing retainer.............................Gasket		10
AELFE	1	J-2036	Main shaft..Nut		15
AELGG	1	J-1981	Main shaft low and reverse...Gear	11	50
AELHH	1	J-2035	Main shaft pilot..Bushing		35
AELII	1	J-2022	Main shaft front bearing......................................Lock Screw		10
AELJJ	1	J-1973	Speedometer driver gear..Bushing		10
AELKK	1	J-1982	....Countershaft	3	75
AELLL	1	J-2026	Countershaft lock...Plate		10
AELMM	1	J-1958	Countershaft...Gears	55	50
AELOO	2	J-1977	Countershaft gear...Bearing	6	50
AELPP	1	J-1997	Countershaft gear bearing..Spacer		75
AELQQ	1	J-2025	Reverse idler gear...Shaft		75
AELRR	1	J-2026	Reverse idler gear shaft lock......................................Plate		10
AELSS	1	J-1960	Reverse idler...Gear	6	50
AELTT	1	J-1967	Reverse idler gear..Bushing		50
AELUU	2	J-2033	Clutch throwout shaft...Bushing		40
AELVV	1	J-2048	Universal joint companion..Flange	17	50
AELWW	1	J-2037	Universal joint companion flange.............................Washer		25
AELXN	1	J-1921	Speedometer 5T drive (14-53 axle 3.78-1)................Gear	2	00
AELYY	1	J-1923	Speedometer 12T driven (14-53 axle 3.78-1)............Gear	1	00
AELZZ	1	J-1921	Speedometer 5T drive (14-53 axle 4.07-1)................Gear	2	00
AEMAZ	1	J-1922	Speedometer 13T driven (13-53 axle 4.07-1)............Gear	1	00
AEMCA	1	J-1920	Speedometer 6T drive (13-56 axle 4.30-1)................Gear	2	00
AEMDB	1	J-1911	Speedometer 16T driven (13-56 axle 4.30-1)............Gear	1	00
AEMEC	1	J-1429A	Speedometer drive pinion.......................................Bushing		65
AEMFD	1	J-2011	Gear shift...Bracket	17	70
AEMGF	1	J-1988	Gear shift bracket dust..Felt		10
AEMHG	1	J-2007	Gear shift..Lever	12	75
AEMIH	1	J-1978	Gear shift lever (lower end of lever)...........................Ball	3	60
AEMJI	1	J-2013	Gear shift lever fulcrum...Pin		75
AEMKJ	1	J-2012	Gear shift lever..Socket	9	50
AEMLK	2	J-1979	Gear shift lever socket..Pin		10
AEMML	1	J-1986	Gear shift lever support...Spring		15
AEMNM	1	JA-1647	Gear shift lever spring...Washer		10

CODE WORD	NO. USED PER CAR	PART NO.	DESCRIPTION	PRICE EACH
AEMON	1	J-2019	Gear shift lever socket..Nut	3 15
AEMPO	1	J-7219	Gear shift lever socket nut...Screw	10
AEMQP	1	J-1824	Gear shift lever knob and adapter.............................Assembly	1 75
AEMRQ	1	J-2055	Gear shift lever...Assembly	18 00
			(Includes J-1978, J-2007, J-2013)	
AEMSR	1	J-1953	Shift...Frame	21 25
AEMTS	1	J-1964	Shift frame..Gasket	15
AEMUT	1	J-2039	Shift frame vent..Plug	10
AEMVU	1	J-1993	Shift (high and second)...Rail	10 25
AEMWV	1	J-1994	Shift (low and reverse)...Rail	14 25
AEMXW	2	J-1995	Shift rail interlock..Plunger	75
AEMYX	1	J-1996	Shift rail poppet...Spring	10
AEMZY	1	J-1976	Back up switch..Plunger	85
AENAY	1	J-1990	Shifter (high and intermediate)..Fork	9 90
AENBZ	1	J-1991	Shifter (low and reverse)..Fork	4 75
AENDA	1	J-1992	Shifter fork..Screw	25
AENEB	1	J-1957	Clutch throwout..Yoke	18 25
AENFC	1	J-1564	Clutch throwout yoke key..Washer	25
AENGE	1	J-2044	Clutch throwout (R. H.)..Shaft	90
AENHF	1	J-2046	Clutch throwout shaft...Screw	65
AENIG	1	J-2045	Clutch throwout (L. H.)..Shaft	3 00
AENJH	1	J-6037	Clutch throwout oil...Line	20
AENKI	1	J-6017	Clutch throwout oil line...Drip Plug	30
AENLJ	2	J-6029	Clutch throwout oil line...Adapter	05
AENMK	1	J-2024	Clutch throwout oil hole...Filler	35
AENNL	1	JA-2009	Transmission case filler..Plug	60
AENOM	1	JA-2010	Transmission case filler plug...Gasket	10

HAND BRAKE

CODE WORD	NO. USED PER CAR	PART NO.	DESCRIPTION	PRICE EACH
AEPNJ	1	J-2000	Hand brake lever..Assembly	62 50
			(Includes following parts to J-2016 inc.)	
AEPOK	1	J-2001	Hand brake..Lever	41 25
AEPPL	1	J-2002	Hand brake lever fulcrum..Pin	1 75
AEPQM	1	J-2003	Hand brake latch...Spoon	3 50
AEPRN	1	A-1390	Hand brake pawl rod lever...Screw	25
AEPSO	1	A-1397	Hand brake lever..Plunger	40
AEPTP	1	A-1398	Hand brake lever plunger...Spring	10
AEPUQ	1	A-1399	Hand brake lever...Plug	05
AEPVR	1	J-2005	Hand brake upper pawl...Rod	60
AEPWS	1	J-2006	Hand brake upper pawl rod...End	1 60
AEPXT	1	A-1390	Hand brake upper pawl rod end...Screw	25
AEPYU	1	J-2008	Hand brake pawl rod lever bell..Crank	1 20
AEPZV	1	J-2009	Hand brake pawl rod lever bell crank...................................Screw	25
AEQAV	1	J-2010	Hand brake lower pawl..Rod	4 95
AEQBW	1	J-2014	Hand brake...Pawl	9 75
AEQCX	1	J-2015	Hand brake pawl fulcrum...Pin	60
AEQDY	1	J-2016	Hand brake pawl..Spring	10
AEQEZ	1	J-2017	Hand brake lever...Ratchet	4 00
AEQGB	1	J-2018	Hand brake lever stop...Pin	15
AEQHC	1	J-1963	Hand brake anchor...Bracket	7 90
AEQID	1	J-2049	Hand brake link...Assembly	1 95
AEQJE	2	J-2228	Hand brake link end...Pin	30
AEQKF	2	J-2210	Hand brake..Shoe	4 95
AEQLG	2	J-2222	Hand brake shoe pivot...Sleeve	1 00
AEQMH	2	J-2004	Hand brake shoe anchor...Bolt	45
AEQNI	1	J-2230	Hand brake shoe anchor...Plate	70
AEQOJ	2	J-2214	Hand brake shoe...Lining	1 60
AEQPK	20	A-960	Hand brake shoe lining..Rivet	02

CODE WORD	NO. USED PER CAR	PART NO.	DESCRIPTION	PRICE EACH
AEQQL	1	J-2212	Hand brake..Drum	20 50
AEQRM	1	J-2213	Hand brake drum heat................................Insulator	25
AEQSN	1	J-2215	Hand brake..Screw	11 25
AEQTO	1	J-2216	Hand brake splined..Screw	3 25
AEQUP	1	J-2218	Hand brake screw...Lever	3 95
AEQVQ	1	J-2227	Hand brake adjusting..Nut	1 10
AEQWR	2	J-2231	Hand brake..Spring	10
AEQXS	2	J-2232	Hand brake spring retainer...........................Washer	03
AEQYT	1	J-2236	Hand brake screw (R. H.)................................Nut	60
AEQZU	1	J-2237	Hand brake screw (L. H.)................................Nut	60
AERAU	1	J-2220	Hand brake equalizer....................................Bracket	16 25
AERBV	2	J-2201	Hand brake shoe and lining.........................Assembly	7 75
AERCW	1	J-2229	Hand brake anchor plate center.........................Bolt	15
AERDX	1	J-2238	Hand brake shoe equalizer............................Sleeve	11 50
AEREY	1	J-2239	Hand brake equalizer bracket......................Bushing	60
AERFZ	1	J-2240	Hand brake lever..Spring	10
AERGA	1	J-2241	Hand brake lever spring..Pin	15
			FRONT AXLE	
AETGZ	1	J-2500	Front axle..Assembly (Includes following parts to JA-1654 inc.)	485 00
AETIA	1	J-2507	Front axle..I Beam	61 25
AETJB	1	J-2503	Front brake cover (R. H.).........................Assembly (Includes J-680, J-2519, J-2520, J-2565, J-2567, J-2568, J-2570)	20 50
AETKC	1	J-2504	Front brake cover (L. H.).........................Assembly (Includes J-680, J-2519, J-2521, J-2566, J-2567, J-2568, J-2570)	20 50
AETLD	4	J-2502	Brake shoe and lining..............................Assembly (Includes J-2517, J-2571, J-2572)	13 75
AETME	4	J-2517	Brake..Shoe	6 75
AETNF	2	J-2519	Front brake (lower half)..................................Cover	6 50
AETOG	1	J-2520	Front brake (upper half) (R. H.)................Cover	8 25
AETPH	1	J-2521	Front brake (upper half) (L. H.)................Cover	8 25
AETQI	2	J-2526	Front brake..Drum	45 00
AETRJ	24	J-2527	Front brake drum..Screw	10
AETSK	2	J-2540	Front brake shoe (lower).............................Support	12 25
AETTL	1	J-2541	Front brake toggle (R. H.)..........................Support	2 25
AETUM	1	J-2542	Front brake toggle (L. H.)..........................Support	2 25
AETVN	2	J-2544	Front brake toggle..Arm	4 60
AETWO	2	J-2545	Front brake cylinder..Boot	75
AETXP	2	J-2549	Front brake toggle adjusting............................Link	3 40
AETYQ	2	J-2551	Front brake toggle..Link	2 20
AETZR	4	J-2552	Front brake upper cover......................................Stud	4 95
AEUAR	2	J-2554	Front brake toggle support friction..........Washer	25
AEUBS	2	J-2555	Front brake toggle support..........................Bushing	30
AEUCT	6	J-2556	Front brake toggle..Pin	45
AEUDU	4	J-2557	Front brake shoe anchor..Pin	65
AEUEV	2	J-2558	Front brake hydraulic..Piston	1 05
AEUFW	2	J-2560	Front brake lower cover..Felt	10
AEUGY	2	J-2561	Brake piston cup washer..................................Insert	60
AEUHZ	2	J-2562	Brake cylinder piston seal....................................Cup	75
AEUJA	2	J-2563	Brake cylinder piston seal cup spreader............Spring	10
AEUKB	4	J-2564	Brake shoe..Spring	10
AEULC	1	J-2565	Front brake adjustment (R. H.)................Cover	90
AEUMD	1	J-2566	Front brake adjustment (L. H.)................Cover	90
AEUNE	2	J-2567	Front brake bleeder..Cover	1 00
AEUOF	4	J-2568	Front brake adjustment cover hinge..............Screw	10
AEUPG	2	J-2569	Front brake cover (upper)....................................Felt	10
AEUQH	4	J-2570	Front brake bleeder and adj. cover................Washer	05

CODE WORD	NO. USED PER CAR	PART NO.	DESCRIPTION	EACH	
AEURI	4	J-680	Front brake bleeder and adj. cover...........................Screw		10
AEUSJ	4	J-2571	Brake..Lining	2	65
AEUTK	40	J-2572	Brake lining..Rivet		03
AEUUL	2	J-2578	Front brake toggle arm..Pad		75
AEUVM	4	J-2579	Front brake toggle arm pad..Rivet		03
AEUWN	1	J-2580	Front brake toggle adj. link (R. H.).............................Guide	1	90
AEUXO	1	J-2581	Front brake toggle adj. link (L. H.)..............................Guide	1	90
AEUYP	2	JA-1585	Front brake piston...Disc		10
AEUZQ	2	JA-1592A	Front brake hydraulic air bleeder................................Screw		40
AEVAN	4	JA-1595	Front brake toggle arm friction..Disc		05
AEVBR	2	JA-1601A	Front brake toggle support..Spring		15
AEVCS	4	JA-1605	Brake shoe pin (upper)...Washer		02
AEVDT	2	JA-1613	Brake toggle adjusting...Block	2	25
AEVEU	2	JA-1617	Brake toggle adjusting...Locknut		10
AEVFV	4	JA-1627	Brake shoe (upper)..Pin		45
AEVGX	4	JA-1629	Brake shoe pin (lower)..Washer		04
AEVHY	2	J-2501	Steering knuckle pivot pin..Assembly	24	50
			(Includes brake cylinder insert)		
AEVKA	2	J-2506	Steering knuckle pivot pin..Lock		20
AEVLB	2	J-2508	Steering knuckle pivot pin hydraulic ....Packing		65
AEVMC	2	J-2509	Steering knuckle pivot pin hydraulic packing............Screw	1	20
AEVND	1	J-2512	Steering (R. H.)..Knuckle	40	00
AEVOE	1	J-2513	Steering (L. H.)..Knuckle	40	00
AEVPF	1	J-2515	Steering (double)...Arm	12	75
AEVQG	1	J-2516	Steering (single)...Arm	7	25
AEVRH	2	J-2528	Steering pivot pin thrust ball......................................Bearing	10	25
AEVSI	2	J-2529	Steering pivot pin thrust bearing.................................Cover		80
AEVTJ	2	J-2530	Steering pivot pin thrust bearing cover...........................Felt		05
AEVUK	2	J-2531	Steering pivot pin thrust bearing retainer.....................Nut	2	50
AEVVL	2	J-2532	Steering pivot pin thrust bearing retainer nut..........Shim		95
AEVWM	2	J-2533	Steering pivot pin..Nut	3	15
AEVYO	2	J-2534	Steering knuckle radial ball...Bearing	10	25
AEVZP	2	J-2535	Steering knuckle radial bearing....................................Cover	1	00
AEWAP	2	J-2536	Steering knuckle radial bearing...Felt		10
AEWBQ	2	J-2538	Steering knuckle radial bearing felt............................Retainer		10
AEWCR	4	J-2539	Steering arm...Bolt	1	00
AEWDS	1	J-2574	Steering arm...Ball	1	50
AEWET	1	J-2575	Steering arm ball...Nut		15
AEWFU	1	J-1123	Steering arm ball...Dowel		10
AEWGW	1	J-2537	Steering tie rod..Assembly	32	50
			(Includes following parts to J-2537-11 inc.)		
AEWHX	1	J-2537-1	Steering tie..Rod	3	50
AEWIY	1	J-2537-10	Steering tie rod socket and stud (R. H.).............Assembly	4	75
AEWJZ	1	J-2537-11	Steering tie rod socket and stud (L. H.)..............Assembly	4	75
AEWLA	1	J-2537-12	Tie rod socket dust..Cover		25
AEWMB	1	J-2537-13	Tie rod socket dust cover...Shield		15
AEWNC	1	J-2576	Tie rod ball stud..Washer		10
AEWOD	2	J-2505	Front wheel (inner)..Bearing	12	25
AEWPE	2	J-2518	Front wheel hub bearing...Spacer	2	75
AEWQF	12	J-2522	Front hub locating..Pin		25
AEWRG	1	J-2523	Front wire wheel (R. H.)..Hub	37	40
AEWSH	1	J-2524	Front wire wheel (L. H.)..Hub	37	40
AEWTI	2	J-2525	Front hub bearing...Retainer	6	60
AEWUJ	2	J-2546	Front hub bearing retainer..Felt		10
AEWVK	2	J-2548	Thrust bearing retainer nut...Lock		15
AEWWL	1	JA-1644	Front wheel (R. H.)..Nut		35
AEWXM	1	JA-1645	Front wheel (L. H)...Nut		35
AEWYN	2	JA-1647	Front wheel nut...Washer		15
AEWZO	2	JA-1654	Front wheel (outer)...Bearing	10	25

CODE WORD	NO. USED PER CAR	PART NO.	DESCRIPTION	PRICE EACH
			REAR AXLE	
AEZFS	1	J-3000	Rear axle..Assembly	750 00
AEZGT	1	J-3001	Rear axle housing (parts welded in assembly)............Assembly	160 25
AEZHU	12	J-3012	Differential carrier..Stud	10
AEZIV	2	J-3013	Rear brake (upper)..Cover	4 60
AEZJW	2	J-3014	Rear brake (lower)...Cover	5 25
AEZKX	1	J-3015	Rear axle wheel bearing (R. H.)..Nut	1 70
AEZLY	1	J-3016	Rear axle wheel bearing (L. H.)..Nut	1 70
AEZMZ	2	J-3017	Rear axle wheel bearing..Retainer	7 95
AEZOA	2	J-3019	Rear axle...Packing	85
AEZPC	2	J-3020	Rear axle packing...Retainer	30
AEZQB	1	J-3021	Rear axle (R. H.)...Shaft	70 40
AEZRD	1	J-3022	Rear axle (L. H.)...Shaft	70 40
AEZSE	1	J-3023	Wire wheel (R. H. rear)...Hub	37 40
AEZTF	1	J-3024	Wire wheel (L. H. rear)...Hub	37 40
AEZUG	16	J-3025	Wheel bearing retainer...Bolt	10
AEZVH	2	J-3027	Differential carrier..Gasket	20
AEZWI	1	J-3035	Differential gear...Cover	11 30
AEZXJ	1	J-3037	Rear axle wheel bearing (R. H.)................................Lock Nut	1 25
AEZYK	1	J-3038	Rear axle wheel bearing (L. H.)................................Lock Nut	1 25
AEZZL	12	J-3045	Differential gear cover...Stud	08
AFAAM	2	J-3050	Rear brake...Cylinder	8 25
AFACO	2	J-3053	Rear brake toggle..Support	2 10
AFAER	2	J-3055	Rear brake drum..Pilot	3 75
AFAFS	12	J-3056	Rear brake cover..Bolt	08
AFAGT	4	J-3057	Rear brake cover..Stud	15
AFAHU	12	J-3061	Rear hub locating...Pin	25
AFAIV	1	J-3064	Rear brake toggle adjusting link (R. H.)....................Guide	1 60
AFAJW	1	J-3065	Rear brake toggle adjusting link (L. H.)....................Guide	1 60
AFAKX	4	J-2517	Brake...Shoe	6 75
AFALY	4	J-2502	Brake shoe and lining..Assembly	13 75
			(Includes J-2517, J-2571, J-2572)	
AFAMZ	2	J-2526	Brake..Drum	45 00
AFAOA	24	J-2527	Brake drum..Screw	07
AFAPC	2	J-2544	Brake toggle..Arm	3 60
AFAQB	2	J-2545	Brake cylinder..Boot	70
AFARD	2	J-2549	Brake toggle adjusting..Link	3 00
AFASE	2	J-2551	Brake toggle..Link	2 25
AFATF	2	J-2554	Toggle support friction...Washer	25
AFAUG	2	J-2555	Brake toggle support...Bushing	30
AFAVH	6	J-2556	Brake toggle...Pin	45
AFAWI	4	J-2557	Brake shoe lower..Pin	65
AFAXJ	2	J-2558	Hydraulic brake..Piston	1 10
AFAYK	2	J-2561	Brake piston cup washer...Insert	45
AFAZL	2	J-2562	Brake cylinder piston seal..Cup	50
AFBAL	2	J-2563	Piston seal cup spreader..Spring	10
AFBDO	4	J-2564	Brake shoe...Spring	15
AFBEP	4	J-2571	Brake..Lining	2 65
AFBIU	40	J-2572	Brake lining..Rivet	03
AFBMY	2	J-2578	Brake toggle arm...Pad	75
AFBOB	4	J-2579	Brake toggle arm pad...Rivet	03
AFBPA	2	JA-1585	Brake piston..Disc	10
AFBTE	2	JA-1592A	Hydraulic air bleeder..Screw	40
AFBUF	4	JA-1595	Toggle arm friction...Disc	05
AFBXI	2	JA-1601A	Brake toggle support...Spring	15
AFBYJ	4	JA-1605	Brake shoe upper pin..Washer	02
AFCAK	2	JA-1613	Brake toggle adjusting..Block	25
AFCEO	2	JA-1616	Brake toggle adjusting..Nut	40
AFCIT	2	JA-1617	Brake toggle adjusting lock...Nut	10
AFCJU	4	JA-1627	Brake shoe (upper)..Pin	45
AFCNY	4	JA-1629	Brake shoe pin (lower)...Washer	04
AFCOZ	2	JX-1908	Rear axle wheel bearing nut lock...................................Washer	08
AFCQA	1	J-3066	Differential carrier..Assembly	375 60
			(Includes following parts to JX-2087 inc.)	
AFCYI	4	J-3002	Differential bevel..Pinion	3 50
AFDAJ	2	J-3003	Differential side..Gear	12 50
AFDEN	8	J-3004	Differential case...Bolt	65

CODE WORD	NO. USED PER CAR	PART NO.	DESCRIPTION	PRICE EACH
AFDFO	1	J-3007	Bevel pinion nut..Lock washer	03
AFDIS	2	J-3008	Differential bearing nut..Lock Washer	10
AFDKU	2	J-3009	Differential carrier (R. H.).......................................Stud Nut	10
AFDOY	1	J-3018	Differential carrier bearing..Insert	12 50
AFDRA	1	J-3026	Differential...Carrier	85 70
AFDUD	1	J-3067	Differential case...Assembly	84 75
AFDYH	1	J-3030	Differential carrier (L. H.)..Cap	2 50
AFDZI	1	J-3031	Differential carrier (R. H.)...Cap	5 25
AFEAI	1	J-3032	Rear axle (Hypoid 14-53)...Pinion	37 25
AFEBJ	1	J-3033	Rear axle (Hypoid 14-53)..Gear	58 40
AFECK	1	J-3034	Differential ball (R. H.)..Bearing	22 50
AFEDL	16	J-3036	Differential ring gear...Bolt	20
AFEEM	1	J-3039	Drive pinion bearing...Retainer	10 90
AFEFN	1	J-3040	Drive pinion bearing retainer...Shim	1 60
AFEGP	1	J-3041	Bevel drive pinion bearing...Spacer	2 75
AFEHQ	1	J-3044	Differential bearing retainer..Lock	10
AFEIR	2	J-3048	Differential carrier (Right side).....................................Stud	1 90
AFEJS	2	J-3049	Differential carrier (Left side)..Stud	2 30
AFEKT	1	J-3051	Differential..Assembly	175 00
AFELU	2	J-3052	Differential bearing...Nut	1 20
AFEMV	1	J-3058	Rear axle (13-53)..Pinion	37 25
AFENW	1	J-3059	Rear axle (13-53)...Gear	58 40
AFEOX	4	J-3060	Drive pinion bearing retainer..Screw	20
AFEPY	1	J-3062	Rear axle (13-56)..Pinion	37 25
AFEQZ	1	J-3063	Rear axle (13-56)...Gear	58 40
AFESA	3	JX-1901	Rear axle wheel and pinion.......................................Bearing	17 60
AFETB	1	JA-2009	Differential oil..Plug	1 65
AFEUC	1	JA-2010	Differential oil Plug..Gasket	05
AFEVD	1	JX-2017	Differential spider..Arm	12 25
AFEWE	1	JX-2042	Differential (L. H.)...Bearing	13 25
AFEXF	1	JX-2045	Differential bearing lock..Screw	05
AFEYG	1	JX-2064	Drive pinion front (double row)................................Bearing	17 75
AFEZH	1	JX-2069	Pinion bearing retainer...Nut	4 50
AFFAH	2	JX-2081	Bevel pinion..Nut	60
AFFBI	1	JX-2087	Bevel drive pinion..Washer	1 20

PROPELLER SHAFT-TORQUE TUBE-UNIVERSAL JOINT

CODE WORD	NO. USED PER CAR	PART NO.	DESCRIPTION	PRICE EACH
AFIXA	1	J-3452	Torque tube...Assembly	45 30
AFIYB	1	J-3474	Torque tube bearing...Cap	7 25
AFIZC	1	J-3475	Torque yoke bearing spacer..Ring	20
AFJAC	1	J-3477	Torque yoke bearing...Retainer	5 25
AFJCE	1	J-3478	Torque yoke bearing retainer...Shim	1 50
AFJEG	1	J-3480	Torque tube...Yoke	23 80
AFJIL	1	J-3481	Torque tube yoke...Cap	9 50
AFJLO	2	J-3482	Torque yoke shock...Insulator	1 90
AFJOR	1	J-3483	Torque yoke insulator (R. H.) (142½ W. B.)..............Bracket	5 75
AFJRU	1	J-3484	Torque yoke insulator (L. H.) (142½ W. B.)...............Bracket	5 75
AFJUX	2	J-3485	Torque yoke insulator bracket...Cap	2 25
AFJVY	1	J-3486	Torque yoke insulator (R. H.) (153½ W. B.)..............Bracket	6 20
AFJYA	1	J-3487	Torque yoke insulator (L. H.) (153½ W. B.)...............Bracket	6 20
AFKAB	8	J-3492	Torque tube to axle...Bolt	10
AFKDE	8	J-3493	Torque tube yoke insulator cap....................................Screw	05
AFKEF	4	J-3494	Torque tube yoke and cap...Bolt	10
AFKGI	2	J-3495	Torque tube yoke and cap...Stud	35
AFKMO	1	J-3455	Propeller shaft..Assembly	45 50
AFKOQ	1	J-3456	Propeller shaft..Bearing	7 50
AFKSU	1	J-3503	Universal joint (142½ W. B.)....................................Assembly	100 50
			(Includes following parts to J-3548 inc.)	

CODE WORD	NO. USED PER CAR	PART NO.	DESCRIPTION	EACH
AFKUW	1	J-3506	Universal joint companion................................Flange	12 50
AFKWY	1	J-3507	Universal joint flange......................................Yoke	5 75
AFKZA	4	J-3508	Universal joint spacer....................................Block	3 50
AFLAA	1	J-3509	Universal joint sleeve.....................................Yoke	7 00
AFLEE	1	J-3510	Universal joint..Cross	15 65
AFLHI	1	J-3511	Universal joint..Journal	6 25
AFLIJ	4	J-3512	Universal joint...Bushing	40
AFLNO	2	J-3513	Universal joint bushing...............................Retainer	15
AFLOP	1	J-3514	Universal joint inner casing.........................Assembly	2 00
AFLTU	1	J-3515	Universal joint outer casing.........................Assembly	1 00
AFLUV	1	J-3516	Universal joint casing.................................Packing	25
AFLXY	1	J-3517	Universal joint casing..................................Spring	20
AFLYZ	1	J-3518	Universal joint dust.......................................Cap	45
AFMBA	1	J-3528	Universal joint steel....................................Washer	15
AFMED	1	J-3529	Universal joint felt.....................................Washer	20
AFMFE	1	J-3530	Universal joint...Key	35
AFMII	1	J-3531	Universal joint shaft...................................Cotter	15
AFMOO	8	J-3532	Universal joint flange.....................................Bolt	20
AFMUU	4	J-3533	Universal joint flange.....................................Bolt	30
AFMYY	8	J-3534	Universal joing flange bolt................................Nut	15
AFNAZ	1	J-3535	Universal joint shaft......................................Nut	60
AFNCA	8	J-3536	Universal joint flange bolt..........................Lockwasher	60
AFNEC	1	J-3537	Universal joint spring.................................Retainer	25
AFNIH	1	J-3538	Universal joint retainer lock..............................Ring	20
AFNJI	1	J-3539	Universal joint..Gasket	20
AFNON	1	J-3540	Universal joint tubular shaft (142½ W. B.).............Assembly	24 25
AFNPO	1	J-3542	Universal joint casing lock..............................Screw	15
AFNUT	1	J-3543	Universal joint outer.....................................Casing	3 25
AFNVU	8	J-3544	Universal joint rubber......................................Ball	75
AFNYX	4	J-3545	Universal joint flange.....................................Nut	15
AFNZY	4	J-3546	Universal joint cotter......................................Pin	15
AFOAY	2	J-3547	Universal joint oil..Pipe	2 00
AFOBZ	1	J-3548	Universal joint oil....................................Retainer	6 65
AFODA	1	J-3504	Universal joint (153½ W. B.)..........................Assembly	103 50
			(Same as J-3503 except tubular shaft assembly)	
AFOEB	1	J-3541	Universal joint tubular shaft (153½ W. B.)...........Assembly	20 50
AFOFC	1	J-3520	Radius rod...Assembly	3 50
AFOGE	4	J-3524	Radius rod..Bolt	15

FRAME

CODE WORD	NO. USED PER CAR	PART NO.	DESCRIPTION	EACH
AFSAU	1	J-3760	Frame (142½ W. B.)...................................Assembly	360 00
AFSEY	1	J-3772	Frame (R. H.) side (142½ W. B.).......................Member	70 50
AFSGA	1	J-3773	Frame (L. H.) side (142½ W. B.).......................Member	70 50
AFSIC	1	J-3774	Frame (153½ W. B.)...................................Assembly	380 40
AFSKE	1	J-3775	Frame (R. H.) side (153½ W. B.).......................Member	74 50
AFSOI	1	J-3776	Frame (L. H.) side (153½ W. B.).......................Member	74 50
AFSUO	1	J-3753	Front frame cross member............................Assembly	29 50
AFSYS	1	J-3761	Rear spring support cross member....................Assembly	28 50
AFTAT	1	J-3767	Rear body cross member..............................Assembly	29 60
AFTBU	1	J-3768	Rear frame cross member.............................Assembly	34 75
AFTEX	2	J-3769	Rear spring front....................................Pivot Pin	3 00
AFTFY	1	J-3770	Rear engine (R. H.)....................................Hanger	12 50
AFTHA	1	J-3771	Rear engine (L. H.)....................................Hanger	12 50
AFTIB	1	J-3779	Radiator cross member...............................Assembly	31 50
AFTLE	1	J-3780	Center cross member................................Assembly	43 75
AFTOH	1	J-3787	Gas tank frame...Bracket	95
AFTPI	6	X-2519	Intermediate and front body...........................Bracket	80
AFTUN	2	J-3791	Rear body...Bracket	55

August 15, 1929

CODE WORD	NO. USED PER CAR	PART NO.	DESCRIPTION	PRICE EACH
AFTVO	1	J-3795	Front engine (and spring rear) (R. H.)................................Support	22 25
AFTYR	1	J-3796	Front engine (and spring rear) (L. H.)................................Support	22 25
AFUAS	2	J-3798	Running board rear................................Hanger	1 95
AFUBT	2	J-3799	Running board center hanger (142½ W. B.)................Assembly	7 25
AFUCU	2	J-3809	Fender to head lamp bolt................................Clip	90
AFUDV	6	J-3810	Offset shackle pivot pin................................Bushing	45
AFUEW	2	J-3811	Offset shackle front pin outer................................Bushing	65
AFUFX	2	J-3812	Rear spring front shackle inner thrust................Washer	60
AFUGZ	2	J-3813	Rear spring front pivot pin................................Dowel	03
AFUIA	2	J-5730	Rear spring front pivot pin................................Nut	15

RADIATOR

CODE WORD	NO. USED PER CAR	PART NO.	DESCRIPTION	PRICE EACH
AFYCQ	1	J-4200	Radiator shell and core................................Assembly	285 00
AFYDR	1	J-4210	Radiator................................Shell	50 00
AFYES	1	J-4211	Radiator core................................Assembly	210 40
AFYFT	1	J-4214	Radiator filler (for first 12 cars)................................Cap	2 25
AFYGV	1	J-4215	Radiator filler cap (for first 12 cars)................Flange	1 20
AFYHW	1	J-4216	Radiator filler cap (for first 12 cars)................Spring	35
AFYIX	1	J-4217	Radiator filler cap (for first 12 cars)................Gasket	20
AFYJY	1	J-4218	Radiator filler cap hinge (for first 12 cars)................Pin	20
AFYKZ	10	J-4219	Radiator shell to core cup................................Washer	02
AFYMA	1	J-4220	Radiator filler cap short (for first 12 cars)................Spring	30
AFYNB	1	J-4221	Radiator inlet................................Hose	1 20
AFYOC	1	J-4222	Radiator thermostat................................Housing	4 25
AFYPD	1	J-4224	Radiator thermostat housing................................Gasket	20
AFYQE	1	J-4225	Radiator sylphon................................Assembly	3 30
AFYRF	1	J-4228	Radiator outlet hose................................Pipe	2 15
AFYSG	1	J-770	Radiator outlet to pipe................................Hose	10
AFYTH	1	J-4229	Radiator outlet pipe to pump................................Hose	70
AFYUI	1	J-4230	Radiator thermostat................................Gasket	05
AFYVJ	2	J-4231	Radiator footing................................Stud	25
AFYWK	2	J-4233	Radiator footing................................Pad	05
AFYXL	4	J-4237	Radiator elbow hose (chrome)................................Clamp	30
AFYYM	2	J-4238	Radiator hose (plain)................................Clamp	05
AFYZN	1	J-4239	Radiator crank bearing cover................................Assembly	2 25
AFZBO	1	J-4242	Radiator tie rod................................Assembly	11 25
AFZGU	1	J-4249	Radiator drain................................Cock	35
AFZIW	1	J-4256	Radiator filler cap................................Gasket	20
AFZKY	1	J-4275	Radiator filler cap................................Assembly	7 50
AFZNA	1	J-4271	Radiator filler cap and stud................................Assembly	2 40
AFZRE	1	J-4272	Radiator filler cap................................Spider	1 30
AFZUH	1	J-4273	Radiator filler cap seal................................Disc	1 25
AFZVI	1	J-4274	Radiator filler cap seal................................Washer	05
AFZYL	1	J-4265	Radiator filler cap lock retainer................................Pin	08
AGAAO	1	J-4276	Radiator diagonal tie rod................................Assembly	5 00
AGABP	2	J-4279	Radiator diagonal tie rod eye................................Bolt	40
AGACQ	1	J-4232	Radiator heat indicator................................Flange	1 25

STEERING GEAR

CODE WORD	NO. USED PER CAR	PART NO.	DESCRIPTION	PRICE EACH
AGBKY	1	J-4462	Steering gear (less steering wheel)................................Assembly	60 00
AGBNA	1	J-4460	Steering gear (with steering wheel)..............................Assembly	75 00
AGBRE	1	J-4461	Steering (3 spoke)..Wheel	22 75
AGBVI	1	J-4520	Steering gear drag...Link	5 50
AGBYL	2	J-4522	Steering column plate (for first 6 cars)........................Stud	03
AGCAM	1	J-4523	Steering column plate clamp (for first 6 cars)...............Bar	20
AGCCO	1	J-4524	Steering column inst. board (med. pos.) (for first 6 cars)....Plate	7 25
AGCER	1	J-4525	Steering column upper...Bracket	6 75
AGCHU	1	J-4526	Steering column upper bracket..Cap	2 50
AGCIV	1	J-4527	Steering column upper bracket.......................................Clamp	90
AGCLY	1	J-4529	Steering column lower (R. H.).......................................Bracket	2 50
AGCOA	1	J-4530	Steering column lower (L. H.)..Bracket	2 50
AGCSE	2	J-4531	Steering column bracket...Rubber	15
AGCUG	1	J-4532	Steering column toe board..Plate	3 25
AGCWI	1	J-4533	Steering column Inst. board (low pos.) (for first 6 cars)....Plate	8 95
AGCYK	1	J-4534	Steering column upper bracket (top)..............................Cover	8 10
AGDAL	1	J-4535	Steering column upper bracker (lower)..........................Cover	7 90
AGDDO	1	J-4541	Steering gear to distributor rod..................................Assembly	35
AGDEP	1	J-4542	Steering gear to carburetor rod...................................Assembly	30
AGDIU	1	J-4460-1	Housings and bushings...Assembly	18 50
AGDMY	1	J-4460-2	Cam and wheel tube and bearings...............................Assembly	24 25
AGDOB	1	J-4460-3	Adj. plug, jacket tube and bushing..............................Assembly	15 75
AGDPA	1	J-4460-4	Lever shaft..Assembly	16 25
AGDTE	1	J-4460-5	Steering arm and ball..Assembly	10 25
AGDUF	1	J-4460-7	Lower (on ½″ tube)..Lever	70
AGDXI	1	J-4460-8	Lower (on ⅜″ tube)..Lever	70
AGDYJ	1	J-4460-9	Steering wheel..Nut	30
AGEAK	1	J-4460-10	Side cover..Assembly	6 50
AGEBL	1	J-4460-11	Adjusting...Screw	1 75
AGECM	1	J-4460-12	Adjusting screw hexagon...Nut	90
AGEDN	1	J-4460-13	Housing side..Cover	2 50
AGEEO	2	J-4460-14	Side cover..Gasket	04
AGEFP	1	J-4460-15	Adjusting plug..Lock	05
AGEGR	*	J-4460-16	Adjusting plug .003...Shim	05
AGEHS	*	J-4460-17	Adjusting plug .007...Shim	05
AGEIT	1	J-4460-18	Wheel (No. 9 modified woodruff).......................................Key	04
AGEJU	1	J-4460-20	Lever shaft (outer)...Bushing	1 50
AGEKV	1	J-4460-21	Lever shaft (inner)...Bushing	1 15
AGELW	1	J-4460-22	Cam, tube and wheel nut...Assembly	19 35
AGEMX	1	J-4460-23	Wheel (plain)...Nut	70
AGENY	2	J-4460-24	Ball..Race	1 50
AGEOZ	2	J-4460-25	Ball race retaining..Ring	04
AGEQA	1	J-4460-26	Jacket tube and bushing..Assembly	11 75
AGERB	1	J-4460-27	Jacket tube...Bushing	1 15
AGESC	1	J-4460-28	Adjusting..Plug	4 10
AGETD	1	J-4460-30	Lever shaft castle...Nut	45
AGEUE	1	J-4460-31	End cover..Assembly	50
AGEVF	1	J-4460-32	Clamping (upper)...Plate	25
AGEWG	1	J-4460-33	Clamping (lower)..Plate	25
AGEXH	1	J-4460-34	Switch..Support	35
AGEYI	1	J-4460-35	End..Plate	25
AGEZJ	1	J-4460-36	Felt...Washer	04
AGFAJ	1	J-4460-37	⅝″ control mounting (with base and bushings)...............Tube	5 75
AGFEN	1	J-4460-38	Spring..Bushing	15
AGFFO	1	J-4460-39	Silencer (⅝″ tube)..Bushing	20
AGFIS	1	J-4460-40	½″ control tube and silencer......................................Assembly	3 50
AGFKU	1	J-4460-41	Silencer (½″ tube)..Bushing	04
AGFOY	1	J-4460-42	⅜″ control tube and silencer......................................Assembly	3 25
AGFRA	1	J-4460-43	Silencer (⅜″ tube)..Bushing	04
AGFUD	1	J-4460-44	9/32″ control tube and silencer..................................Assembly	3 75
AGFVE	1	J-4460-45	Silencer (9/32″ tube)..Bushing	20
AGFYH	1	J-4460-46	Gas control lever, stud and ball..................................Assembly	3 50
AGFZI	1	J-4460-48	Spark control lever, stud and ball...............................Assembly	3 50
AGGAH	1	J-4460-50	Lighting switch control lever stud and ball................Assembly	3 50
AGGBI	1	J-4460-54	Friction (between base and disc for ½″ tube)..............Washer	04
AGGEL	1	J-4460-55	Friction (between discs for ½″ and ⅜″ tubes)..............Washer	04

CODE WORD	NO. USED PER CAR	PART NO.	DESCRIPTION	PRICE EACH
AGGGO	1	J-4460-56	Friction (between discs for 3/8″ and 9/32″ tubes)..............Washer	04
AGGIQ	1	J-4460-57	Friction (on 9/32″ tube)...............Washer	20
AGGMU	1	J-4460-58	Friction (below control cap)...............Spring	10
AGGOW	3	J-4460-59	Friction washer...............Spacer	10
AGGQY	1	J-4460-60	Cable (with insulating and contact washers)...............Assembly	80
AGGTA	1	J-4464	Horn button and control cap...............Assembly	8 50
AGGUB	1	J-4465	Horn button complete...............Assembly	4 00
AGGXE	1	J-4466	Horn button (the button itself)...............Cap	2 75
AGGYF	1	J-4467	Horn button...............Stem	20
AGHAG	1	J-4468	Horn button stem...............Retainer	25
AGHCI	1	J-4469	Horn button stem...............Spring	15
AGHEK	1	J-4470	Horn button stem spring...............Washer	20
AGHHO	1	J-4471	Horn button stem unit...............Assembly	75
AGHIP	1	J-4472	Horn button stem and cap...............Assembly	3 50
AGHNU	1	J-4473	Horn button...............Eyelet	35
AGHOV	1	J-4474	Horn button spring...............Washer	15
AGHRY	1	J-4475	Horn button insulating...............Washer	20
AGHUA	1	J-4476	Horn button (brass)...............Washer	25
AGHYE	1	J-4477	Horn button contact...............Spring	20
AGIAF	1	J-4478	Horn button small...............Spring	25
AGIBG	1	J-4479	Horn button large...............Spring	60
AGICH	1	J-4480	Horn button wire contact...............Washer	10
AGIDI	1	J-4481	Horn button wire insulating...............Washer	10
AGIEJ	1	J-4482	Horn button...............Insulator	25
AGIFK	1	J-4483	Control...............Cap	4 25
AGIGM	1	J-4484	Steering wheel control...............Ring	3 50

MASTER CYLINDER ASSEMBLY

CODE WORD	NO. USED PER CAR	PART NO.	DESCRIPTION	PRICE EACH
AGIJP	1	J-4801	Master cylinder...............Assembly	27 75
AGIKQ	1	J-4801-1	Master cylinder supply...............Tank	12 00
AGILR	3	J-4801-2	Master cylinder outlet fitting...............Gasket	05
AGIMS	1	J-4858	Master cylinder outlet...............Fitting	40
AGINT	2	J-4801-4	Master cylinder outlet...............Plug	40
AGIOU	1	J-4801-5	Master cylinder filler plug...............Gasket	10
AGIPV	1	J-4801-6	Master cylinder supply tank...............Cover	1 50
AGIQW	1	J-4801-7	Master cylinder head...............Gasket	10
AGIRX	1	J-4801-8	Master cylinder brake shaft welch...............Plug	10
AGISY	1	J-4801-9	Master cylinder (with internals)...............Head and Barrel	9 75
AGITZ	1	J-4801-10	Master cylinder piston...............Assembly	90
AGIVA	1	J-4801-11	Master cylinder valve...............Assembly	1 30
AGIWB	1	J-4801-12	Master cylinder piston...............Stop	10
AGIXC	1	J-4801-13	Master cylinder piston return spring...............Retainer	25
AGIYD	1	J-4801-14	Master cylinder shaft oil seal...............Cup	25
AGIZE	1	J-4801-15	Master cylinder piston...............Cup	55
AGJAE	1	J-4801-16	Master cylinder brake...............Shaft	3 75
AGJEI	1	J-4801-17	Master cylinder piston return...............Spring	25
AGJIN	1	J-4801-18	Master cylinder brake shaft...............Lever	2 75
AGJJO	1	J-4801-19	Master cylinder brake shaft lever...............Bolt	15
AGJOT	1	J-4801-20	Master cylinder cover...............Gasket	15
AGJPU	1	J-4801-21	Master cylinder (without terminals)...............Head and Barrel	6 75
AGJTY	6	J-4801-22	Master cylinder cover bolt...............Lockwasher	03
AGJUZ	4	J-4801-23	Master cylinder head...............Lockwasher	03
AGJWA	6	J-4801-24	Master cylinder cover...............Bolt	10
AGJYC	4	J-4801-25	Master cylinder head fastening...............Bolt	10
AGKAD	1	J-4801-26	Master cylinder filler plug...............Assembly	2 60
AGKBE	1	J-4802	Master cylinder...............Bracket	40
AGKEH	1	J-4803	Master cylinder...............Lever	5 60
AGKFI	4	J-4804	Master cylinder lever...............Link	10

CODE WORD	NO. USED PER CAR	PART NO.	DESCRIPTION	EACH
AGKIM	4	J-4805	Master cylinder lever link..Pin	05
AGKKO	1	J-4808	Master cylinder lever adjusting..Plate	5 25

HYDRAULIC BRAKE PIPES AND FITTINGS

CODE WORD	NO. USED PER CAR	PART NO.	DESCRIPTION	EACH
AGMZA	1	J-4806	Hydraulic brake line frame tee..Assembly	45
AGNAA	2	J-3215	Hydraulic two way valve end..Assembly	65
AGNEE	1	J-4807	Hydraulic oil line frame...Tee	2 25
AGNHI	1	J-4815	Hydraulic brake line torque tube (for first 6 cars)..........Connection	80
AGNIJ	1	J-4816	Hydraulic brake line torque tube (after 6 cars)...............Connection	4 70
AGNNO	1	J-4820	Frame tee to master cylinder tube...Assembly	60
AGNOP	1	J-4825	Frame tee to torque tube hose (142½ W. B.)......................Assembly	70
AGNTU	1	J-4930	Frame to torque tube brake hose..Assembly	2 75
AGNUV	4	J-4833	Radiator rod brake line clamp..Screw	08
AGNXY	4	J-4834	Radius rod brake line..Clamp	35
AGNYZ	1	J-4835	Torque tube connection to R. H. rear brake cylinder tube..Assembly	75
AGOCB	1	J-4840	Torque tube connection to L. H. brake cylinder tube........Assembly	75
AGODC	1	J-4845	Frame tee to front axle fitting tube......................................Assembly	1 65
AGOED	1	J-4854	Front axle hydraulic brake hose..Connection	6 25
AGOFE	1	J-4855	Frame to front axle brake hose...Assembly	4 25
AGOGG	1	J-4856	Hydraulic torque tube hose union jam...Nut	20
AGOHH	1	J-4857	Brake hose (for ⅜ tube)..Union	60
AGOII	1	J-4858	Union connection master cylinder to brake...............................Line	30
AGOJJ	1	J-4859	Hydraulic brake frame to rear hose.......................................Bracket	10
AGOKK	1	J-4860	Front axle brake line frame..Bracket	5 40
AGOLL	1	J-4862	Hydraulic brake hose front axle frame..................................Bracket	5 40
AGOMM	1	J-4863	Hydraulic brake hose front axle..Union	60
AGOOO	1	J-4864	Hydraulic brake hose front axle union.......................................Elbow	30
AGOPP	1	J-4865	Hydraulic brake hose front axle...Spring	15
AGOQQ	1	J-4866	Front brake hose spring..Clip	10
AGORR	1	J-4867	Front brake hose spring..Stud	15
AGOSS	1	J-4868	Front brake hose support clip..Liner	05
AGOTT	1	J-4870	Front axle brake line tube (R. H.)..Assembly	1 05
AGOUU	1	J-4872	Front axle brake line tube (L. H.)...Assembly	1 05
AGOVV	1	J-4873	Front axle brake line tube..Clip	05
AGOWW	1	J-4880	Frame tee to torque tube hose tube (153½ W. B.)..............Assembly	1 05
AGOXN		J-4818	Hydraulic brake..Liquid	5 75
			(½ gal. required—furnished in 1-gal. cans only) per Gal.	

MUFFLER AND EXHAUST PIPES

CODE WORD	NO. USED PER CAR	PART NO.	DESCRIPTION	EACH
AGQYW	1	J-5201	Muffler...Assembly	60 40
AGRAX	1	J-5203	Muffler cutout control handle..Screw	1 25
AGRBY	8	J-5206	Exhaust pipe flange..Nut	20
AGREA	2	J-5207	Exhaust pipe...Flange	4 50
ARGHE	2	J-5208	Exhaust pipe...Gasket	10
AGRIF	1	J-5221	Muffler shield and extension..Assembly	4 30
AGRLI	1	J-5225	Muffler cutout bell crank..Washer	45
AGROL	1	J-5227	Muffler cutout bell..Crank	1 75
AGRRO	1	J-5228	Muffler cutout control bottom...Lever	2 70
AGRUR	1	J-5229	Muffler cutout control..Shaft	1 70

CODE WORD	NO. USED PER CAR	PART NO.	DESCRIPTION	PRICE EACH
AGRXU	1	J-5230	Muffler cutout control frame................................Bracket	3|00
AGRYV	1	J-5231	Muffler cutout control................................Lever	5|50
AGSAW	3	J-5232	Muffler cutout control clevis................................Pin	|45
AGSCY	1	J-5233	Muffler tail pipe (R. H.)................................Assembly	4|75
AGSFA	1	J-5234	Muffler tail pipe (L. H.)................................Assembly	4|75
AGSIE	1	J-5236	Muffler tail pipe rear................................End	8|30
AGSMI	1	J-5237	Muffler tail pipe end................................Support	1|50
AGSOK	2	J-5238	Muffler tail pipe wedge................................Plug	|90
AGSSO	1	J-5241	Tail pipe middle support................................Rod	|35
AGSUQ	1	J-5243	Tail pipe middle support................................Spacer	|15
AGSYU	1	J-5244	Muffler tail pipe shield (use J-5221)................................Assembly	6|50
AGTAV	1	J-5247	Muffler cutout control................................Link	3|90
AGTDY	1	J-5248	Muffler cutout control cross................................Link	3|75
AGTEZ	1	J-5249	Muffler cutout control spring................................Anchor	|45
AGTID	1	J-5250	Muffler tail pipe (R. H.) (153½ W. B.)................................Assembly	5|10
AGTJE	1	J-5251	Muffler tail pipe (L. H.) (153½ W. B.)................................Assembly	5|10
AGTNI	1	J-5253	Muffler cutout control link................................Assembly (Includes J-5256, J-5247)	4|50
AGTOJ	1	J-5254	Cutout bell crank (153½ W. B.)................................Bracket	1|25
AGTTO	1	J-5255	Tail pipe middle support................................Bolt	|08
AGTUP	1	J-5256	Muffler cutout control link ball................................Joint	|20
AGTYT	1	J-5260	Muffler cutout control shaft................................Pin	|08
AGTZU	1	J-5261	Intake heater outlet................................Pipe	10|80
AGUAU	1	J-5264	Intake heater muffler and pipe (142½ W. B.)................................Assembly	14|25
AGUBV	1	J-5265	Intake heater muffler and pipe (153½ W. B.)................................Assembly	14|75
AGUCW	1	J-5267	Intake heater exhaust pipe................................Clamp	|30
AGUDX	1	J-5272	Intake heater exhaust valve................................Body	2|50
AGUEY	1	J-5273	Muffler outlet................................Body	17|50
AGUFZ	2	J-5276	Intake heater exhaust pipe flange................................Gasket	|10
AGUGA	1	J-5277	Intake heater exhaust valve................................Assembly	|35
AGUHB	1	J-5278	Exhaust................................Pipe	30|75
AGUIC	1	J-5279	Front muffler................................Bracket	8|10
AGUJD	1	J-5280	Intake heater exhaust valve control link................................Assembly	|85
AGUKE	1	J-5281	Intake heater exhaust valve control................................Yoke	|35
AGULF	1	J-5282	Intake heater exhaust valve controll ball................................Joint	|15
AGUMG	1	J-5283	Intake heater exhaust valve control................................Stud	|20
AGUNH	1	J-5285	Muffler cutout................................Valve	1|40
AGUOI	1	J-5287	Muffler cutout valve shaft................................Lever	1|55
AGUPJ	1	J-5288	Muffler cutout valve................................Shaft	|65
AGUQK	1	J-5289	Muffler rear (142½ W. B.)................................Support	2|20
AGURL	1	J-5290	Muffler rear (153½ W. B.)................................Support	2|40
AGUSM	1	J-5291	Muffler cutout valve................................Spring	|30
AGUTN	1	J-5292	Exhaust pipe asbestos wire woven................................Covering	10|60
AGUUO	1	J-5293	Muffler cutout valve body................................Assembly (Includes J-5273, J-5285, J-5287, J-5288)	22|50
AGUVP	1	J-5266	Muffler outlet body................................Gasket	|30
AGUWQ	1	J-5294	Muffler front shield (142½ W. B.)................................Assembly	8|50
AGUXR	1	J-5298	Exhaust pipe covering................................Clamp	|10
AGUYS	1	J-5299	Exhaust pipe................................Assembly	5|50
AGUZT	1	J-5300	Muffler rear shield................................Assembly	8|95
AGVAT	1	J-5310	Muffler front shield 153½ W. B.)................................Assembly	11|25

INSTRUMENT BOARD AND DASH

CODE WORD	NO. USED PER CAR	PART NO.	DESCRIPTION	PRICE EACH
AGYTJ	1	J-5401	Instrument................................Board	27|50
AGYUK	1	J-5402	Instrument board front finish................................Plate	44|25
AGYVL	1	J-5404	Gasoline (U. S. gallons) (complete)................................Gauge	6|75
AGYWM	1	J-5601	Gasoline (imp. gallons) (complete)................................Gauge	7|95
AGYYO	1	J-5602	Gasoline (liters) (complete)................................Gauge	7|95
AGYZP	1	J-5606	Gasoline (U. S. gallons) gauge................................Head	3|50

CODE WORD	NO. USED PER CAR	PART NO.	DESCRIPTION	PRICE EACH
AGZAP	1	J-5608	Gasoline (imp. gallons) gauge..........................Head	4 75
AGZET	1	J-5607	Gasoline (liters) gauge..........................Head	4 75
AGZFU	1	J-5609	Gasoline gauge (142½ W. B.)..........................Line	1 00
AGZIY	1	J-5610	Gasoline gauge (153½ W. B.)..........................Line	1 25
AGZLA	1	J-5611	Gasoline tank..........................Unit	2 00
AGZOD	1	J-5612	Gasoline tank unit..........................Gasket	10
AGZPE	1	J-5405	Oil pressure (lbs. per sq. in.)..........................Gauge	1 95
AGZTI	1	J-5604	Oil pressure (kilogram per sq. ct.)..........................Gauge	3 75
AGZUJ	1	J-5406	Brake pressure (lbs. per sq. in.)..........................Gauge	1 95
AGZYN	1	J-5603	Brake pressure (kilogram per sq. ct.)..........................Gauge	3 75
AGZZO	1	J-5407	..........................Ammeter	1 95
AHAAP	1	J-5408	(U. S. miles)..........................Speedometer	3C 25
AHABQ	1	J-5600	(Kilo)..........................Speedometer	32 50
AHACR	1	J-5409	Speedometer..........................Shaft	5 50
AHADS	1	J-5410	..........................Tachometer	4C 00
AHAET	1	J-5411	Tachometer..........................Shaft	2 25
AHAFU	1	J-5412	..........................Chronograph	82 30
AHAGW	1	J-5413	(Feet)..........................Altimeter	72 15
AHAHX	1	J-5605	(Metric)..........................Altimeter	75 25
AHAIY	1	J-5415	Heat..........................Indicator	6 00
AHAJZ	2	J-5511	Heat indicator tube dash..........................Grommet	05
AHALA	2	J-5416	Instrument board..........................Light	1 40
AHAMB	1	J-5450	Instrument board light..........................Switch	1 00
AHANC	1	J-5417	Speedometer cable..........................Clip	08
AHAOD	1	J-5418	..........................Dash	135 00
AHAPE	1	J-5419	Dash..........................Moulding	31 40
AHAQF	1	J-5620	Dash cover..........................Assembly	3 25
AHARG	1	J-5420	Dash tachometer shaft..........................Plate	1 60
AHASH	1	J-5421	Dash wire..........................Cover	3 75
AHATI	6	J-5510	Dash wire cover..........................Screw	25
AHAUJ	1	J-5422	Speedometer shaft..........................Grommet	10
AHAVK	1	J-5423	Speedometer shaft grommet..........................Clamp	60
AHAWL	1	J-2545	Dash tachometer shaft..........................Grommet	40
AHAXM	1	J-5426	Coil lock (first 12 cars)..........................Bezel	1 25
AHAYN	1	J-5428	Instrument board..........................Moulding	9 20
AHAZO	1	J-5429	Instrument board (R. H.)..........................Support	9 60
AHBAO	1	J-5430	Instrument board (L. H.)..........................Support	11 30
AHBES	1	J-5431	Choke..........................Control	60
AHBIX	1	J-5432	Starter..........................Control	45
AHBMA	1	J-5433	Starter control wire loop..........................Clip	30
AHBOC	2	J-5434	Signal light (first 12 cars)..........................Body	3 00
AHBQE	4	J-5435	Signal light (first 12 cars)..........................Bezel	1 10
AHBUI	1	J-5436	Signal light (battery) (first 12 cars)..........................Lens	60
AHBYM	2	J-5437	Signal light (oil) (first 12 cars)..........................Lens	60
AHCBO	1	J-5438	Signal light (chassis lub.) (first 12 cars)..........................Lens	60
AHCGU	4	J-5439	Signal light lens (first 12 cars)..........................Retainer	03
AHCIW	4	J-5440	Signal light (first 12 cars)..........................Stud	08
AHCKY	2	J-5441	Signal light (first 12 cars)..........................Gasket	15
AHCNA	1	A-3054	Oil pressure gauge dash..........................Elbow	1 90
AHCRE	1	A-3055	Hydraulic brake gauge dash..........................Elbow	2 90
AHCUH	8	J-5453	Signal lamp socket (first 12 cars)..........................Insulator	10
AHCVI	4	J-5454	Signal lamp socket (first 12 cars)..........................Connector	05
AHCYL	1	J-5456	Engine to dash oil gauge tube..........................Assembly	1 10
AHDAM	1	J-5458	Engine oil and brake gauge to dash tube..........................Assembly	1 60
AHDCO	1	J-5460	Frame tee to dash-brake gauge tube..........................Assembly	1 00
AHDER	1	J-5472	Brake gauge dash elbow bleeder..........................Screw	30
AHDHU	1	J-5486	Toe..........................Board	3 75
AHDIV	2	J-5487	Instrument board light..........................Flange	05
AHDLY	4	J-5488	Signal light (after 12 cars)..........................Stud	08
AHDOA	4	J-5489	Signal light stud (after 12 cars)..........................Nut	15
AHDSE	4	J-5490	Signal light lens retainer (after 12 cars)..........................Wire	05
AHDUG	2	J-5491	Signal light (after 12 cars)..........................Body	2 25
AHDWI	4	J-5492	Signal light (after 12 cars)..........................Bezel	60
AHDYK	1	J-5493	Coil lock (after 12 cars)..........................Bezel	60
AHEAL	4	J-5494	Signal lamp (after 12 cars)..........................Socket	25
AHEBM	8	J-5495	Signal lamp socket (after 12 cars)..........................Insulator	74
AHECN	4	J-5496	Signal lamp socket (after 12 cars)..........................Connection	70
AHEDO	1	J-5497	Signal light (chassis lub.) (after 12 cars)..........................Lens	60

CODE WORD	NO. USED PER CAR	PART NO.	DESCRIPTION	PRICE EACH
AHEEP	1	J-5498	Signal light (battery) (after 12 cars)................................Lens	60
AHEFR	2	J-5499	Signal light (oil) (after 12 cars)................................Lens	60
AHEGS	1	J-5512	Body light 3-way push pull................................Switch	1 60
AHEHT	6	A-3126	Ignition wire................................Grommet	05
AHEIU	1	A-3127	Switch wire (on dash)................................Grommet	05
AHEJV	1	J-5515	Instrument board hand brake lever................................Rest	2 75
AHEKW	1	J-5528	Dash wire harness................................Grommet	20

ACCELERATOR

CODE WORD	NO. USED PER CAR	PART NO.	DESCRIPTION	PRICE EACH
AHIFL	1	A-3815	Accelerator pedal leather................................Washer	05
AHIGN	1	A-3817	Accelerator pedal pivot................................Pin	10
AHIHO	1	A-3818	Accelerator pedal................................Spring	05
AHIIP	1	J-5466	Accelerator (first 51 cars)................................Pedal	1 25
AHIJQ	1	J-5467	Accelerator pedal toe board................................Bracket	2 75
AHIKR	1	J-5468	Accelerator pedal spring................................Washer	05
AHILS	1	J-5469	Accelerator pedal................................Felt	05
AHIMT	1	J-5470	Accelerator pedal felt................................Retainer	20
AHINU	1	J-5473	Accelerator cam................................Lever	4 10
AHIOV	1	J-5474	Accelerator cam lever dash................................Bracket	3 25
AHIPW	1	J-5475	Accelerator cam lever................................Pin	25
AHIQX	1	J-5478	Accelerator pedal pad (first 51 cars)................................Assembly	50
AHIRY	1	J-5479	Accelerator rod clamp (first 51 cars)................................Cap	70
AHISZ	1	J-5480	Accelerator rod (first 51 cars)................................Clamp	75
AHIUA	1	J-5481	Accelerator pedal rod................................Assembly	7 50
AHIVB	1	J-5482	Accelerator pedal and bracket................................Assembly	5 50
AHIWC	1	J-5483	Accelerator................................Pedal	2 25
AHIXD	1	J-1578	Accelerator rod................................Spring	10
AHIYE	1	J-1579	Accelerator rod spring................................Clip	05
AHIZF	1	J-5502	Accelerator rod end (pedal end)................................Pin	08
AHJAF	1	J-5504	Accelerator rod rear yoke................................End	35
AHJDI	1	J-5506	Accelerator pedal and rubber................................Assembly	1 50

CHASSIS SPRINGS-SHACKLES-BUMPERS-ENGINE SUPPORT CUSHIONS-SHOCK ABSORBERS-WHEELS-HUBS

CODE WORD	NO. USED PER CAR	PART NO.	DESCRIPTION	PRICE EACH
AHOCC	2	J-5700	Front chassis spring................................Assembly	18 00
AHODD	2	J-5706	Rear chassis spring (roadster)................................Assembly	25 00
AHOEE	2	J-5707	Rear chassis spring (5-pass. sedan)................................Assembly	26 00
AHOFF	2	J-5708	Rear chassis spring (7-pass. sedan)................................Assembly	28 00
AHOGH	10	J-5709	Offset shackle pivot pin filler................................Plug	60
AHOHI	4	J-5710	Offset spring................................Shackle	11 50
AHOIJ	4	J-5711	Offset shackle side................................Arm	6 40
AHOJK	4	J-5712	Offset shackle pivot................................Pin	80
AHOKL	4	J-5713	Offset shackle adjusting................................Shim	10
AHOLM	16	J-5714	Offset shackle................................Packing	05
AHOMN	2	J-5715	Front spring front pivot pin filler................................Plug	10
AHONO	2	J-5716	Front spring front pivot pin clamp................................Screw	05
AHOOP	2	J-5717	Front spring front pivot................................Pin	75
AHOPQ	2	J-5718	Front spring front pivot pin................................Nut	70

CODE WORD	NO. USED PER CAR	PART NO.	DESCRIPTION	EACH	
AHOQR	2	J-5719	Front spring front eye..Bushing		60
AHORS	2	J-5720	Rear spring front..Shackle	11	50
AHOST	2	J-5723	Rear spring front shackle outer thrust..................Washer		50
AHOTU	2	J-5724	Rear spring front shackle adjusting........................Shim		15
AHOUV	2	J-5725	Rear spring clip...Plate	5	50
AHOVW	16	J-110	Front and rear spring clip..Nut		15
AHOWX	2	J-5728	Rear spring front shackle..Cap	8	25
AHOXY	6	J-5729	Spring shackle..Bolt		75
AHOYZ	12	J-5730	Shackle bolt..Nut		15
AHPBA	12	J-5731	Spring eye..Bushing		75
AHPED	6	J-5732	Spring eye bushing...Packing		50
AHPFE	4	J-5734	Spring seat..Pad		10
AHPII	2	J-5735	Rear spring front pivot pin.......................................Plug		15
AHPOO	2	J-5736	Rear spring front pivot pin filler...............................Plug		30
AHPUU	2	J-5738	Front axle caster adjusting......................................Shim		55
AHPYY	4	J-5739	Front spring (short)...Clip		95
AHQAZ	4	J-5742	Rear spring (medium)...U-Bolt		75
AGQCA	2	J-5755	Front engine support...Cushion		30
AHQEC	4	J-5756	Rear engine support...Cushion		35
AHQIH	10	J-5757	Engine support disc..Cushion		10
AHQJI	2	J-5759	Front engine support cushion..............................Washer		08
AHQON	8	J-5760	Rear engine support cushion...............................Washer		08
AHQPO	2	J-5761	Front engine support...Spring		10
AHQUT	2	J-5762	Front engine support spring................................Washer		08
AHQVU	2	J-5763	Front engine support..Bolt		20
AHQYX	8	J-5764	Rear engine support...Bolt		10
AHQZY	1	J-5852	Front shock absorber (R. H.) (Lovejoy).............Assembly	22	50
AHRAY	1	J-5853	Front shock absorber (L. H.) (Lovejoy).............Assembly	22	50
AHRDA	1	J-5854	Rear shock absorber (R. H.) (Lovejoy).............Assembly	22	50
AHREB	1	J-5855	Rear shock absorber (L. H.) (Lovejoy).............Assembly	22	50
AHRGE	2	J-5856	Rear shock absorber front......................................Spacer		30
AHRIG	1	J-5858	Rear shock absorber connecting link (R. H.).......Bracket	3	25
AHRKI	1	J-5859	Rear shock absorber connecting link (L. H.).......Bracket	3	20
AHROM	2	J-5863	Rear shock absorber rear..Spacer		70
AHRQO	1	J-5865	Front bumper..Assembly	38	40
AHRUS	1	J-5866	Rear bumper...Assembly	38	40
AHRWU	4	J-5867	Bumper...Clip		70
AHRYW	8	J-5868	Bumper clip..Bolt		20
AHSAX	6	J-5869	Bumper clip bolt...Nut		15
AHSBY	2	J-5872	Front spring rubber bumper...............................Assembly		30
AHSEA	2	J-5873	Rear spring rubber bumper................................Assembly		35
AHSHE	1	J-5876	License plate bar..Bracket	2	00
AHSIF	1	J-5897	Front shock absorber link (R. H.).....................Assembly	4	25
AHSLI	1	J-5898	Front shock absorber link (L. H.).....................Assembly	4	25
AHSOL	2	J-5899	Rear shock absorber link..................................Assembly	4	25
AHSRO	4	J-5815	Gas line..Clip		03
AHSUR	2	J-5870	Car bumper...Spacer	4	50
AHSXU	2	J-5875	License plate...Bar		50
AHSYV	6	J-6300	Wire..Wheel	90	00
AHTAW	2	J-6307	Houk C 6 R. H. hub..Cap	15	30
AHTCY	2	J-6308	Houk C 6 L. H. hub..Cap	15	30

SPARE WHEEL CARRIER

CODE WORD	NO. USED PER CAR	PART NO.	DESCRIPTION	EACH	
AHWVO	2	J-5877	Spare wheel hub cap lock..Bar		60
AHWYR	1	J-5878	Spare wheel (R. H.)..Support	49	75
AHXAS	1	J-5879	Spare wheel (L. H.)..Support	49	75
AHXCU	2	J-5880	Spare wheel hub (first 51 cars)..................................Cap	23	50
AHXEW	2	J-5881	Spare wheel hub cap (first 51 cars).................Assembly	48	25

CODE WORD	NO. USED PER CAR	PART NO.	DESCRIPTION	PRICE EACH
AHXIA	2	J-5882	Spare wheel support (first 51 cars)..................................Hub	11 20
AHXME	2	J-5883	Spare wheel carrier (first 51 cars)..................................Pilot	5 65
AHXOG	2	J-5884	Spare wheel hub cap pilot (first 51 cars)........................Pin	30
AHXQI	2	J-5885	Spare wheel hub cap (first 51 cars)..............................Pilot	1 25
AHXUM	2	J-5886	Spare wheel support bolt..Plate	75
AHXWO	2	J-5887	Spare wheel hub cap (first 51 cars)..............................Lock	6 50
AHXYQ	2	J-5888	Spare wheel hub cap..Assembly	16 25
AHYAR	2	J-5889	Spare wheel hub...Cap	9 50
AHYBS	2	J-5892	Spare wheel hub..Pilot	2 25
AHYCT	2	J-5893	Spare wheel support...Hub	5 75
AHYDU	2	J-5894	Spare wheel hub cap..Lock	3 25
AHYEV	2	J-5895	Spare wheel hub cap lock......................................Pin	20
AHYFW	2	J-5896	Spare wheel hub cap lock..................................Spring	15

GAS TANK

CODE WORD	NO. USED PER CAR	PART NO.	DESCRIPTION	PRICE EACH
AIAUK	1	J-5800	Gasoline tank (first 51 cars).........................Assembly	35 80
AIAVL	1	J-5805	Gasoline tank filler..Vent	5 30
AIAWM	1	J-5808	Gasoline tank gauge..Assembly	1 10
AIAYO	1	J-5809	Gasoline tank filler cap......................................Assembly	2 75
AIAZP	1	J-5810	Gasoline tank filler...Gasket	05
AIBAP	1	J-5811	Gasoline tank filler vent....................................Gasket	05
AIBBQ	1	J-5812	Gasoline tank filler vent cap hinge........................Pin	95
AIBCR	1	J-5813	Gasoline gauge tank...Gasket	05
AIBDS	6	J-1122	Gasoline tank filler vent....................................Screw	30
AIBET	1	J-5817	Gasoline tank supply pipe.................................Assembly	2 25
			(Consists of J-5818, J-5819, J-5822)	
AIBFU	1	J-5826	Gasoline tank (after 51 cars)...........................Assembly	35 80
AIBGW	1	J-5827	Gasoline tank to fuel pump tube (142½ W. B.)....Assembly	5 50
AIBHX	6	J-5829	Gasoline oil tube clamp......................................Block	15
AIBIY	1	J-5830	Gasoline tank front bracket.................................Bolt	10
AIBJZ	2	J-5831	Gasoline tank end bracket..................................Bolt	10
AIBLA	3	J-5832	Gasoline tank bracket leather..........................Washer	05
AIBMB	1	J-5833	Gasoline tank to fuel pump tube (153½ W. B.)....Assembly	6 50
AIBNC	1	J-5835	Gasoline tank filler cap and vent.....................Assembly	8 50
AIBOD	1	J-5840	Gasoline tank filler cap.....................................Gasket	15

CHASSIS LUBRICATION SYSTEM

CODE WORD	NO. USED PER CAR	PART NO.	DESCRIPTION	PRICE EACH
AIDQD	1	J-6010	Supply..Tank	15 50
AIDRE	2	J-6012	Front spring front shackle connection and.............Drip Plug	30
AIDSF	2	J-6013	Rear spring rear shackle connection and...............Drip Plug	30
AIDTG	1	J-6014	Frame to torque tube yoke connection and............Drip Plug	45
AIDUH	2	J-6014	Frame to front shock absorber connection and.......Drip Plug	45
AIDVI	1	J-6014	R. H. Front spring rear shackle connection and......Drip Plug	45
AIDWJ	2	J-6015	Rear spring front shackle connection and..............Drip Plug	45
AIDXK	1	J-6017	Clutch throwout bearing connection and...............Drip Plug	30
AIDYL	1	J-6018	L. H. Front spring rear shackle connection and......Drip Plug	30
AIDZM	1	J-6019	L. H. Front spring rear shackle and shock absorber connection and ....Drip Plug	60

August 15, 1929

CODE WORD	NO. USED PER CAR	PART NO.	DESCRIPTION	PRICE EACH
AIEAM	8	J-6038	Drip plug..Nuts	05
AIEBN	2	J-6023	Frame to rear shock absorber (3-way)........Junction	50
AIECO	1	J-6024	Frame to clutch throwout (4-way)...............Junction	25
AIEDP	1	J-6026	Frame to torque tube yoke (3-way)............Junction	25
AIEER	37	J-6039	Junction threaded......................................Bushing	05
AIEFS	2	J-6027	Drag link and torque tube yoke elbow.........Adapter	15
AIEGT	2	J-6028	Rear spring rear shackle elbow...................Adapter	15
AIEHU	*	J-6030	Lubricating system copper...........................Tubing (This number is for bulk tube. When ordering specify amount required by feet and inches.)	20 Per Ft.
AIEIV	1	J-6032	Tank to pump tube.................................Assembly	2 75
AIEJW	1	J-6034	Chassis lubricating pump to frame tube....Assembly	75
AIEKX	45	J-6040	Compression...Sleeves	02
AIELY	1	J-6041	Torque tube hose...................................Assembly	2 75
AIEMZ	1	J-6042	Drag link hose......................................Assembly	2 75
AIEOA	1	J-6043	Drag link hose frame..................................Fitting	45
AIEPC	1	J-6044	Drag link hose to frame.............................Bushing	08
AIEQB	1	J-6045	Drag link hose to frame..............................Sleeve	05
AIERD	2	J-6054	Front shock absorber frame.........................Fitting	30
AIESE	4	J-6055	Shock absorber arm swivel......................Assembly	90
AIETF	*	J-6060	Lubricating system steel...............................Tubing (This number is for bulk tube. When ordering specify amount required by feet and inches.)	40 Per Ft.
AIEUG	1	J-6096	Drag link lubricator tube..................................Clip	30
AIEVH	2	J-6097	Chassis lubricator tank to pump tube................Clip	05
AIEWI	11	J-6098	Chassis lubricator tubing (7/32 bolt hole)......Clamp	05
AIEXJ	4	J-6099	Chassis lubricator tubing (9/32 bolt hole)......Clamp	08

LAMPS

CODE WORD	NO. USED PER CAR	PART NO.	DESCRIPTION	PRICE EACH
AIGVE	2	J-6460	Head lamp...Assembly	47 25
AIGWF	2	J-6460-1	Head lamp body....................................Assembly	30 00
AIGXG	2	J-6460-2	Head lamp electrical..............................Assembly	1 35
AIGYH	2	J-6460-3	Head lamp door (less lens)....................Assembly	10 50
AIGZI	2	J-6460-4	Head lamp...Reflector	3 60
AIHAI	2	J-6460-5	Head lamp reflector...................................Gasket	15
AIHBJ	4	J-6460-6	Head lamp reflector...................................Screws	03
AIHCK	2	J-6460-7	Head lamp socket retaining...........................Spring	15
AIHDL	2	J-6460-8	Head lamp prop bolt..Nut	10
AIHEM	2	J-6460-9	Head lamp prop bolt...........................Lockwasher	04
AIHFN	2	J-6460-10	Head lamp prop...Washer	15
AIHGP	2	J-6460-11	Head lamp door..Screw	15
AIHHQ	2	J-6460-12	Head lamp door screw........................Lockwasher	03
AIHIR	2	J-6460-13	Head lamp door screw.............................Retainer	03
AIHJS	8	J-6460-14	Head lamp lens retaining...............................Wire	06
AIHKT	2	J-6460-15	Head lamp (twilite)..Lens	2 50
AIHLU	2	J-6460-16	Head lamp (6-8 V-21-32 C P)........................Bulbs	75
AIHMV	1	J-6461	Head lamp (R. H.)....................................Bracket	30 70
AIHNW	1	J-6462	Head lamp (L. H.)....................................Bracket	30 70
AIHOX	1	J-6463	Head lamp tie...Rod	11 50
AIHPY	2	J-6464	Head lamp bracket terminal.........................Cover	1 30
AIHQZ	2	J-6465	Head lamp bolt...Washer	15
AIHSA	2	J-6466	Head lamp junction..Stud	30
AIHTB	2	J-6467	Head lamp junction...Nut	30
AIHUC	2	J-6468	Head lamp junction.....................................Sleeve	1 45
AIHVD	4	J-6469	Head lamp junction....................................Spacer	15
AIHWE	4	J-154	Head lamp bracket......................................Screw	20
AIHXF	1	J-6475	Tail lamp...Assembly	27 40
AIHYG	1	J-6475-1	Tail lamp body...................................Assembly	16 80

CODE WORD	NO. USED PER CAR	PART NO.	DESCRIPTION	PRICE EACH
AIHZH	1	J-6475-2	Tail lamp door..Assembly	6 75
AIIAH	1	J-6475-3	Tail lamp reflector..Assembly	5 10
AIIBI	1	J-6475-4	Tail lamp bulb support...Assembly	55
AIICJ	1	J-6475-5	Tail lamp electrical (less bulbs)..................................Assembly	2 10
AIIDK	5	J-6475-6	Tail lamp square (6-32 x ¼ Brass).......................................Nut	05
AIIEL	1	J-6475-7	Tail lamp (No. 6 std.)......................................Lockwasher	03
AIIFM	1	J-6475-8	Tail lamp door..Screw	10
AIIGO	2	J-6475-9	Tail lamp bulb support...Screw	03
AIIHP	2	J-6475-10	Tail lamp license bracket and crossbar........................Screw	03
AIIIQ	5	J-6475-11	Tail lamp shield retaining...Screw	03
AIIJR	1	J-6475-12	Tail lamp plug retaining headless set...........................Screw	04
AIIKS	1	J-6475-13	Tail lamp hex (¼-20 steel)...Nut	05
AIILT	1	J-6475-14	Tail lamp lower lens..Gasket	05
AIIMU	1	J-6475-15	Tail lamp lower (License plate lens-clear)...................Lens	55
AIINV	1	J-6475-16	Tail lamp lens...Gasket	15
AIIOW	3	J-6475-17	Tail lamp lens..Clip	05
AIIPX	2	J-6475-18	Tail lamp lower lens...Retainer	05
AIIQY	1	J-6475-19	Tail lamp door screw...Retainer	03
AIIRZ	1	J-6475-20	Tail lamp door screw...Lockwasher	03
AIITA	3	J-6475-21	Tail lamp socket retaining...Spring	10
AIIUB	1	J-6475-22	Tail lamp shield (includes lense)..............................Assembly	3 60
AIIVC	1	J-5875	Tail lamp license cross..Bar	50
AIIWD	1	J-6475-24	Tail lamp (clear-special)...Lense	2 10
AIIXE	1	J-6475-25	Tail lamp body connector...Assembly	1 35
AIIYF	1	J-6479	Tail lamp bracket plug..Assembly	1 80
AIIZG	1	J-6475-27	Tail lamp (red pyrolin stop lens)..................................Lens	2 40
AIJAG	1	J-6475-28	Tail lamp (6/8 V 3 C. P.)...Bulb	35
AIJBH	2	J-6475-29	Stop and back-up light (6/8 V 21 C. P.).........................Bulb	50
AIJCI	1	J-6476	Tail lamp...Bracket	9 75
AIJDJ	1	J-6477	Tail lamp bracket clamp...Screw	60
AIJEK	2	J-6478	Tail lamp bracket clamp..Sleeve	25
AIJFL	1	J-6479	Tail lamp bracket 3 way wire................................Connection	1 80
AIJGN	1	J-6480	Tail lamp connection pilot...Screw	04
AIJHO	1	J-6490	Cowl lamp (R. H.)..Assembly	17 50
AIJIP	1	J-6491	Cowl lamp (L. H.)..Assembly	17 50
AIJJQ	1	J-6490-1	Cowl lamp body (R. H.)...Assembly	4 20
AIJKR	1	J-6491-1	Cowl lamp body (L. H.)...Assembly	4 20
AIJLS	2	J-6490-3	Cowl lamp...Lens	60
AIJMT	2	J-6490-4	Cowl lamp socket...Screw	15
AIJNU	2	J-6490-5	Cowl lamp...Socket	45
AIJOV	2	J-6490-6	Cowl lamp...Reflector	1 20
AIJPW	2	J-6490-7	Cowl lamp...Gasket	10
AIJQX	2	J-6490-8	Cowl lamp lens and reflector retaining...........................Wire	25
AIJRY	2	J-6490-9	Cowl lamp..Lockwasher	04
AIJSZ	2	J-6490-10	Cowl lamp mounting..Bolt	45
AIJUA	2	J-6490-11	Cowl lamp body..Connector	40
AIJVB	2	J-6490-12	Cowl lamp door (less lens).......................................Assembly	3 60
AIJWC	2	J-6490-13	Cowl lamp lead wire...Assembly	60
AIJXD	2	J-6490-14	Cowl lamp light (6-8 V-3 CP)...Bulb	35
AIJYE	2	J-6494	Cowl lamp bushing..Screw	04
AIJZF	2	J-6495	Cowl lamp connector..Plug	30
AIKAF	2	J-6496	Cowl lamp dash connector...Plug	35

ELECTRICAL UNITS AND WIRING

CODE WORD	NO. USED PER CAR	PART NO.	DESCRIPTION	PRICE EACH
AIMAD	1	J-6483	Chassis oil light..Switch	40
AIMBE	1	J-6484	Stop light...Switch	40
AIMCF	1	J-6485	Stop light switch..Adapter	1 25
AIMDG	1	J-6486	Back up light..Switch	60

CODE WORD	NO. USED PER CAR	PART NO.	DESCRIPTION	EACH
AIMEH	1	J-6556	Current limit..Relay	6 00
AIMFI	1	J-6557	Steering gear lighting................................Switch	1 75
AIMGK	1	J-6558	Electric...Horn	37 50
AIMHL	2	J-6559	Horn..Terminal	15
AIMIM	1	J-6560	Exide 3x CR-21-2G..............................Battery	60 00
AIMJN	1	J-6561	Battery ground..Strap	45
AIMKO	1	J-6562	Engine ground..Strap	10
AIMLP	1	J-6568	Starter switch lower lever..............................Pin	20
AIMMQ	1	J-6569	Starter switch...Lever	1 25
AIMNR	1	J-6570	Horn wire (thru. strg. column)............Terminal	05
AIMOS	1	J-6571	Horn..Bracket	6 50
AIMPT	1	J-6572	Horn bracket nut.....................................Washer	40
AIMQU	1	J-6573	Steering gear lighting switch..................Cover	20
AIMRV	1	J-6574	Steering gear lighting switch terminal....Plate	15
AIMSW	1	J-6575	Junction..Block	85
AIMTX	8	J-6576	Spark plug wire....................................Terminal	15
AIMUY	1	J-1122	Horn to bracket..Screw	30
AIMVZ	1	J-6578	Distributor to coil wire & term. (L.T.) (35 inches long)......Assembly	15
AIMXA	1	J-6579	Distributor to coil wire & term. (L.T.) (41 inches long)......Assembly	20
AIMYB	2	J-6580	Distributor to coil wire & term. (H.T.) (39 inches long).....Assembly	30
AIMZC	1	J-6581	Spark plug (No. 1 and 8 cylinder)..............Wire	30
AINAC	1	J-6582	Spark plug (No. 2 and 7 cylinder)..............Wire	30
AINBD	1	J-6583	Spark plug (No. 3 and 6 cylinder)..............Wire	25
AINCE	1	J-6584	Spark plug (No. 4 and 5 cylinder)..............Wire	25
AINDF	1	J-6607	Inst. panel light (pos.)..................................Wire	05
AINEG	1	J-6608	Inst. panel light (ground)............................Wire	10
AINFH	1	J-719	Signal lamp feed wire...........................Terminal	02
AINGJ	1	J-6611	Signal lamp harness wire.....................Assembly	1 25
AINHK	1	J-6612	Inst. panel and cowl lamp wiring harness....Assembly	1 95
AINIL	1	J-6613	Headlamp harness wire........................Assembly	1 25
AINJM	1	J-6614	Stop, back-up and tail light harness (142½ W.B.).......Assembly	1 75
AINKN	1	J-6615	Stop, back-up and tail light harness (153½ W.B.).......Assembly	1 80
AINLO	1	J-6616	Battery to starting switch cable (Pos.)....Assembly	2 25

TOOLS

CODE WORD	NO. USED PER CAR	PART NO.	DESCRIPTION	EACH
AIPKL	1	J-6951	Tool..Equipment (Includes following to A-4820 inc.)	69 75
AIPLM	1	J-6950	Tool kit..Assembly (Includes the following to J-6994 inc.)	22 25
AIPMN	1	J-6970	Tool (Waterproof with leather insert straps)...Case	6 95
AIPNO	1	J-6971	....Hammer	1 00
AIPOP	1	J-6972	Combination N. P..Plier	65
AIPPQ	1	J-6973	Cotter pin..Puller	15
AIPQR	1	J-6974	Large screw...Drive	60
AIPRS	1	J-6975	Small screw..Driver	40
AIPST	1	J-6976	Pin drift..Punch	35
AIPTU	1	J-6977	Cold..Chisel	35
AIPUV	1	J-6978	Adjustable...Wrench	1 65
AIPVW	1	J-6979	Check nut...Wrench	2 65
AIPWX	1	J-6980	⅛ pipe plug (Allen type)........................Wrench	15
AIPXY	1	J-6981	¼ pipe plug (Allen type)........................Wrench	20
AIPZY	1	J-6982	⅜ pipe plug (Allen type).......................Wrench	25
AIQBA	1	J-6983	Brake bleeder...Wrench	65
AIQCB	1	J-6984	Spark plug..Wrench	1 05
AIQDC	1	J-6985	Water pump gland....................................Wrench	45
AIQED	1	J-6986	7/16 T handle socket (without handle)....Wrench	1 20
AIQFE	1	J-6987	⅝ T handle socket (without handle)......Wrench	1 10
AIQGG	1	J-6988	9/16 offset handle socket.......................Wrench	1 00

CODE WORD	NO. USED PER CAR	PART NO.	DESCRIPTION	PRICE EACH
AIQHH	1	J-6989	Double end (5/16 and ⅜)..Wrench	20
AIQII	1	J-6990	Double end (7/16 and ½)..Wrench	25
AIQJJ	1	J-6991	Double end (9/16 and 11/16)..Wrench	25
AIQKK	1	J-6992	Double end (⅝ and ¾)..Wrench	35
AIQLL	1	J-6993	Double end (13/16 and ⅞)..Wrench	40
AIQMM	1	J-6994	Double end (1″ and 1⅛)..Wrench	65
AIQOO	1	J-6954	Hub cap..Wrench	7 50
AIQPP	1	J-6955	Hand starting..Crank	2 75
AIQRR	1	J-6956	Key (Orkey ring)..Chain	30
AIQSS	1	J-6957	Floor board latch..Key	35
AIQTT	1	J-6959	Cam cover..Wrench	35
AIQUU	1	J-6961	Tire..Gauge	2 00
AIQVV	1	J-6962	Tire..Pump	2 50
AIQWW	1	J-6963	(And handle)..Jack	4 50
AIQXN	1	J-6964	Alemite grease..Gun	2 50
AIQYY	1	A-4804	Lead..Hammer	1 50
AIQZZ	1	A-4820	Brake bleeder (rubber)..Tube	25
AIRAZ	1	J-6965	Distributor breaker sychronizing....................................Gauge	2 00
AIRCA	1	J-7001	Valve timer..Assembly	22 20 Net
AIRDB	2	J-7009	Valve timer hook..Bolt	1 50 Net
AIREC	2	J-7010	Valve timer hook bolt..Nut	50 Net

RUNNING BOARDS-FENDERS-APRONS-SHIELDS-UNDERPANS-HOOD

CODE WORD	NO. USED PER CAR	PART NO.	DESCRIPTION	PRICE EACH
AITFB	1	J-7100	Front fender and bracket (R. H. in prime)....................Assembly (Front fender finished for $15.00 net additional)	75 25
AITGD	1	J-7101	Front fender and bracket (L. H.) in prime....................Assembly (Front fender finished for $15.00 net additional)	75 25
AITHE	1	J-7108	Battery and tool box (R. H.)..Cover	7 30
AITIF	1	J-7109	Battery and tool box (L. H.)..Cover	7 30
AITJG	1	J-7115	Rear (R. H.) (in prime)..Fender (Rear fender finished for $10.00 net additional)	49 50
AITKH	1	J-7116	Rear (L. H.) (in prime)..Fender (Rear fender finished for $10.00 net additional)	49 50
AITLI	2	J-7118	Fender tire well..Moulding	11 75
AITMJ	36	J-7147	Rear fender trim bar..Bolt	03
AITNK	2	J-7193	Rear fender trim (18¾ long)..Bar	1 00
AITOL	4	J-7194	Rear fender trim (14¾ long)..Bar	90
AITPM	4	J-7195	Rear fender trim (11¾ long)..Bar	75
AITQN	2	J-7196	Rear fender trim (7″ long)..Bar	75
AITRO	1	J-7120	Gas tank..Cover	40 50
AITSP	2	J-7121	Battery and tool box..Tray	1 25
AITTQ	1	J-7124	Front running board splash (R. H.)................................Apron	1 70
AITUR	1	J-7125	Front running board splash (L. H.)................................Apron	1 70
AITVS	1	J-7126	Rear running board (R. H.) splash (142½ WB)............Apron	2 20
AITWT	1	J-7127	Rear running board (L. H.) splash (142½ WB)............Apron	2 20
AITXU	1	J-7128	Rear running board (R. H.) splash (153½ WB)............Apron	2 70
AITYV	1	J-7129	Rear running board (L. H.) splash (153½ WB)............Apron	2 70
AITZW	1	J-7130	Radiator splash..Apron	12 50
AIUAW	2	A-8047	Front dust reflector..Screw	15
AIUBX	1	J-7150	Engine (R. H.) (front)..Underpan	4 25
AIUCY	1	J-7151	Engine (L. H.) (front)..Underpan	4 25
AIUDZ	1	J-7152	Engine right rear side..Pan	1 50
AIUFA	1	J-7153	Engine left front side..Pan	1 50
AIUGC	1	J-7154	Engine left center side..Pan	1 50

CODE WORD	NO. USED PER CAR	PART NO.	DESCRIPTION	PRICE EACH
AIUHD	1	J-7155	Engine left rear side..........Pan	1 50
AIUIE	2	J-7156	Radiator hood..........Lacing	50
AIUJF	2	J-7157	Dash hood..........Lacing	60
AIUKG	1	J-7250	Running board (R. H.) (142½ W. B.)..........Assembly	84 75
AIULH	1	J-7251	Running board (L. H.) (142½ W. B.)..........Assembly	84 75
AIUMI	1	J-7252	Running board (R. H.) (153½ W. B.)..........Assembly	97 50
AIUNJ	1	J-7253	Running board (L. H.) (153½ W. B.)..........Assembly	97 50
AIUOK	1	J-7180	Running (142½ W. B.) (R. H.)..........Board	49 70
AIUPL	1	J-7181	Running (142½ W. B.) (L. H.)..........Board	49 70
AIUQM	1	J-7182	Running (153½ W. B.) (R. H.)..........Board	61 20
AIURN	1	J-7183	Running (153½ W. B.) (L. H.)..........Board	61 20
AIUSO	1	J-7184	Running board front bolt (R. H.)..........Plate	2 65
AIUTP	1	J-7185	Running board front bolt (L. H.)..........Plate	2 65
AIUUQ	1	J-7186	Running board rear bolt (R. H.)..........Plate	2 80
AIUVR	1	J-7187	Running board rear bolt (L. H.)..........Plate	2 80
AIUWS	1	J-7188	Running board (142½ W. B.) (large outside)..........Trim	10 20
AIUXT	2	J-7189	Running board (153½ W. B.) (Large outside)..........Trim	12 55
AIUYU	2	J-7190	Running board (142½ W. B.) (Trim)..........Support	1 25
AIUZV	2	J-7191	Running board (153½ W. B.) Trim..........Support	1 25
AIVAV		J-7192	Running board (for J-7180-1-2-3)..........Bolt	70
			(12 required for 142½ W. B.)	
			(16 required for 153½ W. B.)	
AIVBW	1	J-7202	Battery and tool box cover and lock (R. H.)..........Assembly	21 50
AIVCX	1	J-7203	Battery and tool box cover and lock (L. H.)..........Assembly	21 50
AIVDY	2	J-7204	Battery and tool box cover lock..........Handle	1 10
AIVEZ	2	J-7205	Battery and tool box cover lock..........Bracket	3 20
AIVGB	2	J-7206	Battery and tool box cover lock oper...........Hub	3 30
AIVHC	4	J-7207	Battery and tool box cover lock forked..........Bar	10
AIVID	4	J-7208	Battery and tool box cover lock straight..........Bar	02
AIVJE	4	J-7209	Battery and tool box cover lock bar..........Plate	70
AIVKF	2	J-7211	Battery and tool box cover lock handle..........Nut	15
AIVLG	4	J-7212	Battery and tool box cover lock operating..........Rod	30
AIVMH	4	J-7213	Battery and tool box cover lock bar..........Pivot	45
AIVNI	4	J-7214	Battery and tool box hood..........Lock	1 00
AIVOJ	2	J-6522	Battery support...........Strips	10
AIVPK	1	J-6523	Battery tilt..........Strap	35
AIVQL	2	J-6524	Battery hold down clamp lever..........Spacer	50
AIVRM	2	J-6525	Battery hold down clamp lever pivot..........Bolt	05
AIVSN	4	J-6526	Battery hold down clamp guide..........Pin	10
AIVTO	2	J-6527	Battery hold down hook..........Assembly	85
AIVUP	2	J-6529	Battery clamp stop..........Pin	08
AIVVQ	1	J-6531	Battery clamp rear..........Lever	25
AIVWR	1	J-6532	Battery clamp front..........Lever	25
AIVXS	1	J-6533	Battery box guide (front)..........Block	1 00
AIVYT	1	J-6534	Battery box guide (rear)..........Block	1 10
AIVZU	1	J-7160	Hood (complete) (in prime)..........Assembly	135 00
			(Hood assembly will be finished for $25.00 net additional)	
AIWAU	3	J-7219	Hood lock cyl. spring..........Screw	10
AIWBV	4	J-7222	Hood hook eye bolt..........Assembly	3 95
AIWCW	2	J-7225	Hood center support bracket..........Assembly	25
AIWDX	2	J-7226	Hood center bracket rubber..........Bumper	10
AIWEY	4	J-7227	Hood hook eye bolt..........Spring	05
AIWFZ	4	J-7228	Hood lock eye bolt..........Washer	04
AIWGA	2	J-7229	Hood operating..........Handle	1 60
AIWHB	2	J-7231	Hood lock cylinder ejector..........Spring	05
AIWIC	2	J-7232	Hood lock cylinder retaining..........Plate	05
AIWJD	2	J-7233	Hood lock center..........Bracket	5 20
AIWKE	2	J-7234	Hood lock operating..........Lever	3 00
AIWLF	4	J-7238	Hood hook..........Bracket	3 95
AIWMG	2	J-7240	Hood (R. H.)..........Hook	1 40
AIWNH	2	J-7241	Hood (L. H.)..........Hook	1 40
AIWOI	4	J-7242	Hood hook eye bolt..........Bracket	2 30
AIWPJ	2	J-7243	Hood lock eye bolt bracket front..........Support	2 20
AIWQK	5	J-7244	Hood hook pivot..........Bushing	10
AIWRL	5	J-7245	Hood hook retaining..........Washer	04
AIWSM	4	J-7246	Hood latch eye..........Bolt	1 50
AIWTN	4	J-7247	Hood lock operating rod..........Assembly	1 10
AIWUO	2	JA-1601A	Hood lock lever spring..........Washer	10

CODE WORD	NO. USED PER CAR	PART NO.	DESCRIPTION	PRICE EACH
AIWVP	1	J-7165	Hood (front)..Bracket	95
AIWWQ	1	J-7168	Hood (R. H.)...Ledge	9 75
AIWXR	1	J-7169	Hood (L. H.)...Ledge	9 75
AIWYS	16	A-8048	Hood ledge...Screw	20
AIWZT	1	J-7171	Hood...Rest	1 20
AIXAT	8	A-8046	Hood ledge large..Spacer	55
AIXBU	8	J-7173	Hood ledge small..Spacer	15
AIXCV	2	J-124	Hood ledge small..Screw	40
AIXDW	4	J-7217	Hood hook pivot..Stud	15
AIXEX	4	J-7218	Hood hook..Bracket	95
AIXFY	2	J-7665	Floor board latch strike..Plate	25
AIXHA	2	A-4985	Floor board..Lock	35
AIXIB	1	J-7670	Rumble seat fender upper...Step	6 75
AIXJC	2	J-7755	Trunk rack...Arm	4 25
AIXKD	1	J-7756	Trunk rack frame (R. H.)..Bracket	6 50
AIXLE	1	J-7757	Trunk rack frame (L. H.)..Bracket	6 50
AIXMF	2	J-7758	Trunk rack hinge..Pin	15
AIXNG	2	J-7759	Trunk rack...Plunger	80
AIXOH	2	J-1996	Trunk rack plunger..Spring	10
AIXPI	2	J-7761	Trunk rack arm strap...Pin	10

CODE WORD	PART NO.	DESCRIPTION	SIZE	MAT'L	FINISH	AMT. USED	WHERE USED	PRICE EACH
AIZPG	0146	Ball	5/16 dia.	Steel		1	J-1150	05
AIZQH	0283	Sq. hd. M. bolt	3/16-24 U.S.F.x ½	Steel	Udylite	192	J-7133	04
						48	J-7131	
AIZRI	0312	C. bolt less nut	¼-20x¼ 9/16 hd. dia.	Steel	Udylite	64	J-7175	03
						16	J-7176	
						80	J-7177	
						20	J-7178	
AIZSJ	0252	Lamp bulb	3 C. P.			4	J-5494	25
						2	J-5416	
AIZTK	0219	Connection	⅜ tube ¼ pipe thd	Brass		1	J-4807	35
AIZUL	0254	Connection	¼ dia tub ⅛ pipe thd.	Brass		2	J-4826-RH	15
						2	J-4841-LH	
						1	J-4807	
AIZVM	0258	Connection	⅜ tube x ¼ pipe thd	Brass	Nickel	1	J-1100	30
AIZWN	0261	Pipe coupling	⅛" I. P.	Iron		1	J-3751	12
						1	J-3752	
AIZXO	0307	Connection	¼ tube x ⅛ pipe thd	Brass	Nickel	1	J-100	20
AIZYP	0308	Connection	5/16 tube x ⅛ pipe thd	Brass	Nickel	1	J-1150	20
						1	J-6010	
AIZZQ	0257	90° Elbow	⅜ tube x ¼ pipe thd	Brass	Nickel	1	J-1100	45
						1	J-990	
AJAAR	0221	90° Elbow	¼ tube x ⅛ pipe thd	Brass		2	J-3050	25
AJABS	0281	Pl. yoke end	No. 10 (3/16")	Steel		1	J-5481	20
AJACT	0316	Adj. yoke end.	⅜-24 std.	Steel	Cyanide	1	JR-4811	25
AJADU	0182	Zerk fitting	⅛ pipe thd.	Steel		2	J-2500	10
AJAEV	0334	Alemite fitting	⅛ pipe thd. 67½° elbow	Steel		2	J-2500	18
AJAFW	0185	Gasket	57/64 I. D. 1⅛ O. D. 3/32 th.	Cop-Abs		1	J-5819	05
AJAGY	0128	Woodruff key	No. 3 (½ x ⅛)	Steel		1	J-758	05
						1	J-1105	
						1	J-1131	
						1	J-1974	
AJAHZ	0129	Woodruff key	No. 5 (⅝ x ⅛)	Steel		2	J-857	05
AJAJA	0130	Woodruff key	No. 11 (⅞ x 3/16)	Steel		2	J-553	05
						1	J-1583	
						1	JR-1592	
AJAKB	0132	Woodruff key	No. 6 (⅝ x 5/32)	Steel		1	J-650	05
AJALC	0131	Woodruff key	No. A (⅞ x ¼)	Steel		2	J-551	05
AJAMD	0330	Woodruff key	No. 4 (⅝ x 3/32)	Steel		1	JR-5522	05
AJANE	0260	Pipe nipple	⅛" I. P. 3"	Iron		1	J-3751	10
						1	J-3752	
AJAOF	0106	C-Nut	7/16-20	Steel	Udylite	1	J-125	03
						2	J-3035	
						1	J-5800	
						2	J-5763	
						1	J-5250-51	
						1	J-5233-34	
AJAPG	0107	C. Nut	⅝-18	Steel	Udylite	1	J-685	03
						2	J-2573	
						2	LEN-1589	
AJAQH	0144	C. Nut	⅜-24	Steel		1	J-1105	02
AJARI	0147	C. Nut	⅜-24	Steel	Udylite	12	J-3026	03
						6	J-3481	
						2	J-7158	
						12	J-3452	
						4	J-7246	
						8	J-5764	
						2	J-7234	
						12	J-1975	
AJASJ	0148	C. Nut	½-20	Steel		2	J-3030	02
AJATK	0164	C. Nut	½-20	Steel	Udylite	2	J-5800	03
						4	J-5857	
						4	J-5862	
AJAUL	0169	C. Nut	9/16-18	Steel	Udylite	4	J-3520	03
						1	J-1583	
AJAVM	0186	C. Nut	5/16-24	Steel	Udylite	2	J-6525	03
						1	J-5236	

CODE WORD	PART NO.	DESCRIPTION	SIZE	MAT'L	FINISH	AMT. USED	WHERE USED	PRICE EACH
AJAWN	0244	Compression nut	5/16 3-URoll ball	Brass		2	J-8454	04
AJAXO	0108	High nut	5/8-18	Steel		2	J-342	05
AJAYP	0142	Jam nut	3/8-24 x 1/4	Steel		12	J-3012	04
						12	J-3045	
AJAZQ	0222	Jam nut	1/4-28	Steel	Udylite	1	J-5247	03
						1	J-1047	
						1	J-5481	
AJBAN	0239	Jam nut	7/16-24 x 5/16	Steel	Udylite	1	J-2044	03
AJBEU	0240	Jam nut	5/16-24 x 3/16	Steel	Udylite	1	J-2009	03
AJBHY	0251	Jam nut	9/16-18 x 5/16	Steel	Udylite	4	J-5861	03
AJBIZ	0271	Jam nut	1/2-30 x 5/16	Steel	Udylite	4	J-5861	03
AJBKA	0277	Jam nut	5/8-18 x 5/16	Steel	Udylite	1	J-4857	03
AJBOE	0285	Jam nut	7/16-20 x 1/4	Steel		1	A-3054	02
						1	A-3055	
						1	JR-1590	
AJBSI	0282	Knurled nut	8-32 x 7/16 dia.	Brass	Udylite	3	J-1177	05
AJBUK	0100	P. Hex nut	5/16-24	Steel		32	J-417	02
						6	J-552	
						6	J-556	
						8	J-450	
						8	J-451	
						4	J-452	
						4	J-453	
						2	J-659	
						1	J-4859	
						4	J-5244	
						2	J-5222	
						2	J-5254	
						2	J-5290	
AJBYO	0101	P. Hex nut	5/16-24	Steel	Udylite	12	J-208	03
						2	J-2506	
						2	J-2520	
						2	J-2521	
						4	J-3013	
						1	J-5238	
						3	J-4529	
						3	J-4530	
						4	J-4532	
						6	J-5429	
						6	J-5430	
						1	A-3817	
						8	J-7242	
						12	J-5418	
						2	J-1159	
						4	J-4802	
						3	J-6010	
						6	J-5878	
						6	J-5879	
						2	J-4808	
						2	JR-4517	
						2	JR-4518	
						4	JR-4516	
						4	J-4222	
AJCAP	0102	P. Hex nut	3/8-24	Steel		7	J-555	02
						4	JR-4537	
						2	JR-4876	
						1	JR-4811	
AJCET	0103	P. Hex nut	3/8-24	Steel	Udylite	1	J-785	03
						12	J-3035	
						2	J-3053	
						2	J-3054	
						1	J-2541	
						1	J-2542	
						2	J-2543	
						5	J-3483	
						5	J-3484	
						2	J-7234	
						4	J-4460	
						1	J-1572	

CODE WORD	PART NO.	DESCRIPTION	SIZE	MAT'L	FINISH	AMT. USED	WHERE USED	PRICE EACH
						8	J-5418	
						1	J-5264	
						1	J-5265	
						4	J-5279	
						2	J-4276	
AJCFU	0104	P. Hex nut	7/16-20	Steel		12	J-318	02
AJCIY	0105	P. Hex nut	10-32	Steel	Udylite	20	J-5428	03
						2	J-4524	
						3	J-5467	
						1	J-2010	
						6	J-5462	
						1	J-6096	
						1	J-5280	
						24	J-7118	
						2	J-5515	
AJCLA	0173	P. Hex nut	7/16-20	Steel	Udylite	4	J-5867	03
						1	J-5241	
						4	J-5711	
						4	J-5878	
						4	J-5879	
						2	J-4276	
						2	J-4211	
AJCOD	0194	P. Hex nut	1/4-28	Steel	Udylite	18	J-5419	03
						1	J-6041	
						1	J-4866	
						2	J-5266	
						4	J-6054	
						2	J-6043	
						2	J-6023	
						1	J-6024	
						1	J-6026	
						1	J-6042	
						2	J-6527	
						3	J-5829	
						1	JR-5522	
						2	JR-4507	
						1	JR-5544	
						4	JR-5530	
AJCPE	0250	P. Hex nut	14-24 A. S. M. E.	Steel	Udylite	1	J-1579	03
						11	J-4210	
						2	J-5875	
AJCTI	0265	P. Hex nut	9/16-18 S. A. E.	Steel		2	J-5852	02
						2	J-5853	
						2	J-5854	
						2	J-5855	
AJCUJ	0266	P. Hex nut	10-24 A. S. M. E.	Steel		1	J-1173	02
AJCYN	0267	P. Hex nut	8-32 A. S. M. E.	Brass	Nickel	3	J-1177	03
AJCZO	0280	P. Hex nut	10-32	Steel	Chrome	1	J-4542	03
						1	J-4541	
						2	J-2003	
AJDAO	0294	P. Hex nut	7/16-20 S. A. E.	Steel	Chrome	2	J-4276	06
AJDES	0327	P. Hex nut	1/2-20 S. A. E.	Steel	Udylite	1	JR-4459	06
AJDIX	0335	P. Hex nut	1/4-20 A. S. M. E.	Steel	Udylite	1	J-1584-86	06
						1	J-1585-87	
						10	J-7100-01	
						6	J-7115-16	
AJDJY	0284	Sq. nut	3/16-24 for mach. bolt 0283	Steel	Udylite	192	J-7139	04
						48	J-7140	
AJDMA	0313	Sq. nut	1/4-20 U. S.	Steel	Udylite	64	J-7175	04
						16	J-7176	
						80	J-7177	
						20	J-7178	
						8	J-7193	
						16	J-7194	
						12	J-7195 2-3-4-6 Pass	
						6	J-7195 5 & 7 Pass	

CODE WORD	PART NO.	DESCRIPTION	SIZE	MAT'L	FINISH	AMT. USED	WHERE USED	PRICE EACH
						4	J-7196	
							5 & 7 Pass	
AJDOC	0189	Tube union nut	3/8 dia. tube 1-5/16 lg.	Brass		1	J-5834	15
						2	J-4821	
						2	J-4826	
						2	J-4881	
						2	J-4846	
AJDQE	0253	Tube union nut	1/4 dia. tube	Brass		4	J-5457	15
						4	J-4836	
						4	J-4841	
AJDUI	0255	Tube union nut	3/8 dia. tube	Brass	Nickel	1	J-5833	20
						2	J-1101	
						1	J-5827	
AJDYM	0256	Tube union nut	5/16 dia. tube	Brass		2	J-4870	15
						2	J-4872	
AJEBO	0269	Tube union nut	5/16 tube	Brass	Nickel	2	J-6032	20
AJECP	0270	Tube union nut	1/4 tube	Brass	Nickel	2	J-5456	18
						2	J-5459	
AJEGU	0127	Clevis pin	3/16	Steel	Chrome	1	J-4541	05
						1	J-5481	
						1	J-4545	
AJEHV	0275	Clevis pin	3/16 S. A. E.	Steel	Udylite	2	J-2010	05
						2	JR-4508	
AJEIW	0305	Clevis pin	1/4 S. A. E.	Steel	Udylite	1	J-5253	05
						2	J-5248	
AJEJX	0317	Clevis pin	3/8 S. A. E. Std.	Steel	Cyanide	2	JR-4811	05
AJEKY	0263	Clevis pin	5/16 S. A. E. Std.	Steel	Udylite	4	J-6569	05
AJELZ	0120	Cotter pin	3/32 x 3/4	Steel	Udylite	4	J-696	05
						12	J-3026	
						6	J-3480-01	
						2	J-7158	
						12	J-3452	
						2	J-7234	
						12	J-1975	
AJENA	0121	Cotter pin	3/32 x 1	Steel		16	J-309	01
						1	J-125	
						1	J-1105	
						2	J-3030	
						2	J-5862	
						2	J-5857	
AJEPB	0122	Cotter pin	1/8 x 1 1/4	Steel		2	J-342	01
						4	J-101	
						2	J-102	
						4	J-103	
						4	J-104	
						1	J-685	
						1	J-1583	
AJEQD	0123	Cotter pin	1/16 x 3/8	Steel		1	J-959	01
						1	J-1143	
						3	J-5232	
						4	J-7212	
						2	J-2010	
						1	J-5280	
						2	JR-4508	
AJERE	0149	Cotter pin	3/32 x 1	Steel	Udylite	2	J-3035	02
						2	J-5800	
						2	J-5763	
						8	J-5764	
AJESF	0150	Cotter pin	3/32 x 5/8	Steel		1	JX-2069	01
						4	JA-1613	
						12	J-2544	
						4	JA-2551	
						1	J-5800	
						1	J-5250-51	
						1	J-5233-34	
						2	J-2049	
						4	J-7246	
						2	J-6569	
						2	JR-4811	

CODE WORD	PART NO.	DESCRIPTION	SIZE	MAT'L	FINISH	AMT. USED	WHERE USED	PRICE EACH
AJETG	0152	Cotter pin	⅛ x ⅞	Steel		8	J-2517	01
AJEUH	0155	Cotter pin	⅛ x 1½	Steel		2	J-2514	01
						1	JA-1644	
						1	JA-1645	
						1	J-2036	
AJEVI	0170	Cotter pin	⅛ x 1¼	Steel	Udylite	4	J-3520	02
						6	J-5729	
						4	J-5712	
						4	J-3769	
AJEWJ	0171	Cotter pin	3/32 x 1⅛	Steel	Udylite	2	J-5800	02
						4	J-5857	
							J-5862	
AJEXK	0180	Cotter pin	1/16 x ¾	Steel	Udylite	8	J-690	02
						2	J-6525	
						1	J-5236	
AJEYL	0309	Cotter pin	5/32 x ¾	Steel	Udylite	1	J-2240	02
AJEZM	0137	Escutcheon pin	No. 12 (.109) x 2″	Brass		4	J-158	02
AJFAM	0124	Taper pin	No. 000 000 x ⅜	Steel		1	J-163	10
AJFCO	0125	Taper pin	No. 00 00 x ½	Steel		1	J-674	10
AJFER	0126	Taper pin	No. 00 00 x ⅝	Steel		1	J-671	10
AJFHU	0310	Taper pin	No. 4 x 1	Steel		2	J-7758	15
AJFIV	0329	Taper pin	No. 0 x ¾	Steel		1	J-5287	15
						1	JR-5521	
AJFLY	0268	Escutcheon pin	No. 15 (.072) x ½	Brass		2	J-1174	01
AJFOQ	0133	Plug (Allen)	⅛ Briggs std.	Steel		4	J-100	12
						1	J-681	
						2	J-1150	
						4	J-5712	
						2	J-5717	
						6	J-5729	
AJFSE	0134	Plug (Allen)	¼ Briggs std.	Steel		2	J-400	12
						1	J-1156	
						1	J-5826	
AJFUG	0135	Plug (Allen)	½ Briggs std.	Steel		2	J-100	12
AJFWI	0141	Plug (Allen)	⅜ Briggs std.	Steel		1	J-3035	12
						1	J-3010	
						1	J-993	
AJFYK	0225	Plug (Hdless)	¾ Briggs std. ⅝ long 17/32 sq. hole	Iron		1	J-1956	15
AJGAK	0139	R. Hd. rivet	⅛ x 7/16	Iron		2	J-143	02
AJGEO	0176	Button Hd. rivet	.187 x 7/16	Aluminum		4	J-7238	03
						6	J-7171	
AJGIT	0138	Co'sunk Hd. rivet	⅛ x ¼	Iron		2	J-678	02
AJGJU	0174	Co'sunk Hd. rivet	.187 x 7/16	Aluminum		16	J-7238	03
						12	J-7233	
AJGNY	0175	Co'sunk Hd. rivet	3/16 x 5/16	Steel		12	J-7209	02
						10	J-7205	
AJGOZ	0296	Co'sunk Hd. rivet	.250 dia. x ¾	Aluminum		1	J-6534	03
AJGQA	0297	Co'sunk Hd. rivet	.250 dia. x 1	Aluminum		1	J-6533	03
AJGUE	0202	Fl. Hd. rivet	¼ x 5/16	Steel		4	J-7208	04
AJGYI	0209	Fl. Hd. split rivet	9/64 x ½	Steel	Japann'd	4	J-6522	01
						2	J-6523	
						18	J-7156	
AJHAJ	0151	R. Hd. rivet	¼ x ¾	Steel		10	J-3023	02
						10	J-3024	
						4	J-3787	
						2	J-7236	
AJHEN	0159	R. Hd. rivet	¼ x ⅝	Steel		16	J-3804	02
AJHFO	0167	R. Hd. rivet	5/16 x 1	Steel		8	J-3791	02
AJHIS	0181	R. Hd. rivet	5/16 x ⅞	Steel		28	J-3797-8	02
							153½ W.B.	
						36	J-3797-8	
							142½ W.B.	
AJHKU	0200	R. Hd. rivet	5/16 x 1¼	Steel		4	J-3797-8	03
							153½ W.B.	
						2	J-3798	
							142½ W.B.	

CODE WORD	PART NO.	DESCRIPTION	SIZE	MAT'L	FINISH	AMT. USED	WHERE USED	PRICE EACH
						4	J-5915	
AJHOY	0216	R. Hd. rivet	3/16 x ¼	Steel		12	J-695	02
AJHRA	0217	R. Hd. rivet	3/16 x 5/16	Steel		4	J-695	02
						5	J-5294	
						7	J-5310	
						7	JR-5314	
AJHUD	0321	R. Hd. rivet	3/16 x ½	Steel		8	J-7121	02
AJHVE	0322	R. Hd. rivet	5/32 x ¼	Steel		4	J-5249	02
AJHYH	0145	Trunk rivet	No. 12 x ⅝	Copper		2	J-1119	01
AJHZI	0301	Fil. hd. C. screw	5/16-24 x 1	Steel	Udylite	2	J-4534-35	05
AJIAI	0311	Fil. hd. C. screw	5/16-24 x ¾	Steel		2	J-1066	04
AJIBJ	0109	Hex. hd. C. screw	5/16-24 x ⅝	Steel	Udylite	3	J-1100	05
						4	J-323	
						4	J-325	
						2	J-2520	
						2	J-2521	
						2	J-5290	
AJICK	0110	Hex. hd. C. screw	5/16-24 x ⅞	Steel		3	J-660	04
						3	J-750	
AJIDL	0111	Hex. hd. C. screw	⅜-24 x 1⅛	Steel	Udylite	30	J-200	05
						6	J-5401	
						6	J-5418	
						4	J-4460	
						4	J-4461	
						4	J-6462	
						4	JR-4537	
AJIEM	0112	Hex. hd. C. screw	⅜-24 x 2½	Steel	Udylite	1	J-785	05
AJIFN	0113	Hex. hd. C. screw	½-20 x 1¼	Steel		1	J-551	04
AJIGP	0140	Hex. hd. C. screw	5/16-24 x 1½	Steel		2	J-2519	04
						2	J-4526	
AJIHQ	0153	Hex. hd. C. screw	5/16 x ¾	Steel	Udylite	4	J-3050	05
						4	J-2520	
						4	J-2521	
						1	J-4859	
						4	J-5244	
						2	J-5254	
						4	J-4802	
AJIIR	0154	Hex. hd. C. screw	⅜-24 x 1¼	Steel	Udylite	2	J-3953	05
						2	J-3054	
						2	J-4276	
AJIJS	0156	Hex. hd. C. screw	5/16-24 x 1¼	Steel	Udylite	4	J-2519	05
						2	J-5200	
						2	J-4854	
						6	J-5430	
						2	JR-4877	
AJIKT	0160	Hex. hd. C. screw	5/16-24 x ½	Steel	Udylite	2	J-2548	05
AJILU	0161	Hex. hd. C. screw	5/16-24 x 1¾	Steel	Udylite	6	J-3474	05
						2	J-652	
AJIMV	0162	Hex. hd. C. screw	5/16-24 x 1¼	Steel	Chrome	6	J-5429	05
AJINW	0163	Hex. hd. C. screw	⅜-24 x 4¾	Steel	Udylite	2	J-3483	05
						2	J-3484	
						2	J-3486	
						2	J-3487	
AJIOX	0165	Hex. hd. C. screw	5/16-24 x ⅞	Steel	Udylite	12	J-5200	05
						2	J-5423	
						2	J-1021	
						8	J-7242	
						1	J-5226	
						1	J-5228	
						1	J-2215	
						8	J-5883	
						8	J-5892	
AJIPY	0168	Hex. hd. C. screw	⅜-24 x 1	Steel	Udylite	2	J-6571	05
AJIQZ	0177	Hex. hd. C. screw	5/16 x ⅜	Steel	Udylite	4	J-3791	05
AJISA	0178	Hex. hd. C. screw	⅜-24 x ⅞	Steel	Udylite	1	J-5227	05
						6	J-1500	
						1	J-5264	
						1	J-5265	

CODE WORD	PART NO.	DESCRIPTION	SIZE	MAT'L	FINISH	AMT. USED	WHERE USED	PRICE EACH
						3	J-5279	
						2	JR-4876	
AJITB	0187	Hex. hd. C. screw	7/16-20 x 1½	Steel	Udylite	2	J-2220	05
AJIUC	0188	Hex. hd. C. screw	¼-28 x ¾	Steel	Udylite	2	J-5856	05
						2	J-5863	
						3	J-6041	
						6	J-7243	
						6	J-7237	
						4	J-6054	
						2	J-6043	
						2	JR-4507	
AJIVD	0191	Hex. hd. C. screw	⅜-24 x 3	Steel	Udylite	2	J-4527	05
						2	J-5279	
AJIWE	0195	Hex. hd. C. screw	5/16-18 x 1¾	Steel	Udylite	1	J-5413	05
AJIXF	0204	Hex. hd. C. screw	5/16-24 x 1⅞	Steel	Udylite	1	J-4529	05
						1	J-4530	
						2	J-6492	
						2	J-6493	
AJIYG	0210	Hex. hd. C. screw	⅜-24 x 1⅜	Steel	Udylite	2	J-5418	05
						1	J-1572	
AJIZH	0211	Hex. hd. C. screw	9/16-18 x 3½	Steel	Udylite	1	J-5852	05
						1	J-5853	
						1	J-5854	
						1	J-5855	
AJJAH	0212	Hex. hd. C. screw	9/16-18 x 3¾	Steel	Udylite	1	J-5852	05
						1	J-5853	
						1	J-5854	
						1	J-5855	
AJJBI	0218	Hex. hd. C. screw	5/16-24 x 2¾	Steel	Udylite	2	J-5222	05
AJJEL	0227	Hex. hd. C. screw	5/16-18 x ¾	Steel	Udylite	24	J-1956	05
						2	J-4210	
AJJGO	0230	Hex. hd. C. screw	⅜-16 x ⅞	Steel	Udylite	4	J-1955	05
						2	J-2026	
						2	J-2017	
						3	J-1970	
AJJIQ	0233	Hex. hd. C. screw	⅜-16 x ¾	Steel	Udylite	4	J-1854	05
AJJMU	0234	Hex. hd. C. screw	5/16-18 x ⅞	Steel	Udylite	6	J-1953	05
						9	J-7115	
						9	J-7116	
AJJOW	0235	Hex. hd. C. screw	5/16-18 x 2¼	Steel	Udylite	2	J-1953	05
AJJQY	0236	Hex. hd. C. screw	5/16-18 x 2⅜	Steel	Udylite	1	J-1953	05
AJJTA	0238	Hex. hd. C. screw	7/16-20 x 1¼	Steel		2	J-1957	04
AJJUB	0241	Hex. hd. C. screw	⅜-16 x 1⅛	Steel	Udylite	3	J-1963	05
AJJXE	0242	Hex. hd. C. screw	⅜-24 x ¾	Steel	Udylite	4	J-2212	05
AJJYF	0246	Hex. hd. C. screw	5/16-24 x 2¼	Steel	Chrome	10	J-5418	05
						1	J-5238	
AJKAG	0247	Hex. hd. C. screw	5/16-24 x 2½	Steel	Chrome	2	J-5418	05
AJKCI	0249	Hex. hd. C. screw	¼-28 x ⅜	Steel		1	J-4873	04
						2	J-5244	
						7	J-5314	
AJKEK	0264	Hex. hd. C. screw	⅜-16 x ⅝ U. S.	Steel	Udylite	6	J-4801	05
						5	JR-4810	
						2	JR-4877	
AJKHO	0273	Hex. hd. C. screw	¼-28 x ½	Steel	Udylite	1	J-4866	05
						2	J-5266	
						4	J-7670	
						1	JR-6555	
AJKIP	0287	Hex. hd. C. screw	¼-28 x 1¼	Steel	Udylite	1	J-6024	05
						1	J-6026	
						1	J-6042	
						3	J-5829	
AJKNU	0288	Hex. hd. C. screw	5/16-24 x ⅝	Steel	Chrome	2	J-6010	05
AJKOV	0289	Hex. hd. C. screw	⅜-24 x 1½	Steel	Udylite	8	J-5728	05
AJKRY	0292	Hex. hd. C. screw	7/16-20 x 1½	Steel	Udylite	3	J-5878	05
						3	J-5879	
						1	JR-1590	
AJKUA	0298	Hex. hd. C. screw	7/16-20 x 1¾	Steel	Udylite	1	J-5878	05
						1	J-5879	
AJKYE	0300	Hex. hd. C. screw	5/16-24 x 1	Steel	Udylite	2	J-4808	05

CODE WORD	PART NO.	DESCRIPTION	SIZE	MAT'L	FINISH	AMT. USED	WHERE USED	PRICE EACH
AJLAF	0325	Hex. hd. C. screw	3/8-16 x 1¾	Steel		2	JR-4459	04
AJLDI	0326	Hex. hd. C. screw	½-20 x 1-½	Steel	Udylite	1	JR-4459	05
AJLEJ	0328	Hex. hd. C. screw	5/16-18 x 1-⅛	Steel	Udylite	2	JR-4517	05
AJLIO	0331	Hex. hd. C. screw	¼-28 x 1	Steel	Udylite	1	JR-5522	05
AJLOU	0333	Hex. hd. C. screw	½-20 x 1-⅛	Steel	Udylite	2	J-5858	05
						2	J-5859	
AJLSY	0314	Hex. hd. C. screw	5/16-24 x 1-¼	Steel	Chrome	6	J-5429	05
AJLVA	0318	Hex. hd. C. screw	3/8-24 x 5	Steel	Udylite	3	J-3483	05
						3	J-3484	
						3	J-3486	
						3	J-3487	
AJLYD	0319	Hex. hd. C. screw	¼-28 x 1-3/8	Steel	Udylite	2	J-6025	05
AJLZE	0117	Fil. hd. M. screw	12-24 x 3/8	Brass		2	J-118	04
AJMAE	0179	Fil. hd. M. screw	8-32 x ¾	Steel	Udylite	2	J-6575	05
AJMEI	0183	Fil. hd. M. screw	10-24 x ¼	Steel	Udylite	6	J-5808	05
AJMIN	0196	Fil. hd. M. screw	10-24 x 7/16	Steel	Udylite	4	J-5420	05
						1	J-5808	
AJMJO	0197	Fil. hd. M. screw	12-24 x 5/8	Steel	Udylite	2	J-6556	05
AJMOT	0213	Fil. hd. M. screw	10-24 x ¾	Steel	Udylite	2	J-4524	05
						2	J-4533	
AJMPU	0214	Fil. hd. M. screw	10-24 x 1	Steel	Udylite	2	J-4524	05
AJMTY	0215	Fil. hd. M. screw	12-24 x 1½	Steel	Chrome	4	J-1170	05
AJMUZ	0224	Fil. hd. M. screw	8-32 x ½	Steel	Udylite	3	J-6612	05
AJMWA	0229	Fil. hd. M. screw	12-24 U.S.F. x½	Steel	Udylite	3	J-4816	05
						1	J-2238	
AJMYC	0115	Fil. hd. M. screw	10-24 x ½	Brass		2	J-454	04
						4	J-455	
						1	J-456	
						1	J-457	
						1	J-473	
AJNAD	0116	Fil. hd. M. screw	12-24 x 5/8	Brass		5	J-105	04
							J-108	
AJNBE	0201	Fil. hd. M. screw	10-32 x 1¼	Steel	Udylite	3	J-5467	05
						6	J-5462	
AJNEH	0208	Fil. hd. M. screw	¼-28 x ⅞	Steel	Udylite	18	J-5419	05
AJNFI	0248	Fil. hd. M. screw	14-24 x 5/8	Steel	Udylite	1	J-1579	05
						11	J-4210	
						2	J-5875	
AJNIM	0320	Fil. hd. M. screw	¼-20 x 1	Steel	Udylite	1	J-1584-86	05
						1	J-1585-87	
AJNKO	0199	Fr. hd. M. screw	5/16-24 x ⅞	Steel	Udylite	2	J-5474	05
						2	J-4529	
						2	J-4530	
						2	JR-4517	
						2	JR-5519	
AJNOS	0205	Fr. hd. M. screw	5/16-24 x 1¾	Steel	Udylite	1	J-4529	05
						1	J-4530	
AJNQU	0206	Fr. hd. M. screw	5/16-24 x 1⅛	Steel	Udylite	2	J-4532	05
						2	JR-4516	
AJNUY	0207	Fr. hd. M. screw	5/16-24 x 1½	Steel	Udylite	2	J-4532	05
						2	JR-4518	
						2	JR-4516	
AJNXA	0276	Fr. hd. M. screw	8-32 x ¼	Brass	Chrome	4	J-6464	05
AJNYB	0290	Fr. hd. M. screw	5/16-24 x 5/8	Steel	Chrome	3	J-5878	05
						3	J-5879	
AJOAC	0291	Fr. hd. M. screw	5/16-24 x 1¼	Steel	Chrome	6	J-5886	05
						3	J-5878-79	
AJOBD	0323	Fr. hd. M. screw	10-32 x ½	Steel	Chrome	3	J-5879	05
						24	J-7118	
AJOCE	0114	R. hd. M. screw	10-24 x 3/8	Steel		5	J-212	04
							J-6486	
AJODF	0192	R. hd. M. screw	10-32 x ½	Brass	Nickel	20	J-5429	05
						1	J-6096	
AJOEG	0293	R. hd. M. screw	8-32 x 1-1/7	Steel	Udylite	2	J-7226	05
AJOFH	0303	R. hd. M. screw	12-24 x ½	Steel	Udylite	12	J-7150	05
						12	J-7151	
						4	J-7152	
						7	J-7153	
						3	J-7154	

CODE WORD	PART NO.	DESCRIPTION	SIZE	MAT'L	FINISH	AMT. USED	WHERE USED	PRICE EACH
						4	J-7155	
						5	JR-7166	
						4	JR-7167	
						5	JR-7169	
AJOGJ	0332	R. hd. M. screw	1-32 x ½	Steel	Udylite	10	Chassis Lub. Line Clip	05
AJOHK	0223	Sq. hd. set screw	¼-20 x ½	Steel	Udylite	2	J-7314	05
AJOIL	0203	R. hd. wood screw	No. 8 x ⅝	Steel	Udylite	3	J-5470	03
						4	J-5487	
						30	J-Body as Req'd Seat Pan	
						8	J-7126-27	
						12	J-7128-29	
AJOJM	0220	Fl. hd. wood screw	No. 8 x ⅝	Steel		72	J-7190	02
						20	J-7184	
						20	J-7185	
						20	J-7186	
						20	J-7187	
AJOKN	0259	Fl. hd. wood screw	No. 6 x ¾	Steel		4	J-5484	02
AJOLO	0245	Compression sleeve	5/16 3-U roll ball	Brass		2	J-4854	03
AJOMP	0272	Wire terminal	Sherman No. 4 x .032 th.	Copper		2	J-5416	05
AJONQ	0228	L. washer	¼ x 3/32 x 3/64	Steel		24	J-1956	01
						1	J-2019	
AJOOR	0232	L. washer	⅜ x ⅛ x 3/32	Steel	Udylite	4	J-1955	02
						2	J-2026	
						2	J-2017	
						3	J-1963	
						4	J-1954	
						4	J-1970	
AJOPS	0237	L. washer	5/16 x ⅛ x 3/32	Steel	Udylite	9	J-1953	02
						1	J-2008	
						4	J-4222	
						2	J-1066	
AJOQT	0243	L. washer	7/16 x 5/32 x ⅛	Steel	Udylite	2	J-2220	02
						2	J-4211	
AJORU	0274	L. washer	⅜ x ⅛ x ⅛	Steel	Udylite	6	J-1500	02
						2	J-5279	
AJOSV	0278	L. washer	⅝ x 13/64 x 3/32	Steel	Udylite	1	J-4857	02
AJOTW	0302	L. washer	9/16 x 3/32 x ⅛	Steel	Udylite	2	J-5852	02
						2	J-5853	
						2	J-5854	
						2	J-5855	
AJOUX	0315	L. washer	¼ x 3/32 x 1/16	Steel	Udylite	64	J-7175	02
						12	J-7176	
						80	J-7177	
						20	J-7178	
						8	J-7193	
						16	J-7194	
						12	J-7195 2-3-4-6-Pass	
						6	J-7195 5 & 7 Pass	
						4	J-7196	
						10	J-7100-01	
						6	J-7115-16	
AJOVY	0324	L. washer	No. 10 x 1/16 x 3/64	Steel		24	J-7118	01
						2	J-6486	
AJOWZ	0118	P. washer	7/64 I. D. 5/16 O. D. 120th	Brass		4	J-158	02
AJOYA	0119	P. washer	15/32 I. D. 15/16 O. D. 1/16th	Steel		1	J-125	02
AJOZB	0143	P. washer	13/32 I. D. 13/16 O. D. 1/16th	Steel		1	J-1105	02
						2	J-4460	
						1	J-1572	
AJPAB	0157	P. washer	9/32 I. D. ⅝ O. D. 1/16th	Steel	Udylite	2	J-2565	02

CODE WORD	PART NO.	DESCRIPTION	SIZE	MAT'L	FINISH	AMT. USED	WHERE USED	PRICE EACH
						2	J-2567	
						2	J-7168	
						1	J-7169	
						4	J-7207	
						1	J-1579	
						2	J-7236	
						2	J-6527	
						4	J-7670	
						64	J-7175	
						16	J-7176	
						80	J-7177	
						20	J-7178	
AJPEF	0190	P. washer	7/32 I. D. ½ O. D. 1/16th	Steel	Udylite	2	J-6449	02
						10	J-7205	
AJPGI	0295	P. washer	15/32 I. D. 15/16 O. D. 1/16 th	Steel	Chrome	2	J-4276	03
AJPIK	0299	P. washer	11/32 I. D. 11/16 O. D. x 1/16 th	Steel	Udylite	2	J-5236	03
						2	J-4529	
						2	J-4530	
						2	JR-4517	
						2	JR-4518	
						4	J-3057	
AJPMO	0304	P. washer	¼ I. D. 9/16 O. D. 1/16 th	Steel	Udylite	12	J-7150	02
						12	J-7151	
AJPOQ	0158	Wire	No. 18 (.049) B.W.G	Iron		23 ¾″	J-112	03 Per ft.
						41″	J-321	
						24″	J-557	
						6′— ⅝″	J-850	
						3″	J-3044	
						28″	J-3028	
						56″	J-3017	
						48″	J-3013-14	
						7″	J-2029	
						10″	J-1992	
						9″	J-2004	
						20″	J-2212	
AJPSU	0136	Adj. yoke	No. 10-32 std.	Steel		1	J-2010	25
AJPUW	0279	Adj. yoke	No. 10-32 std.	Steel	Chrome	1	J-4542	30
						1	J-4541	

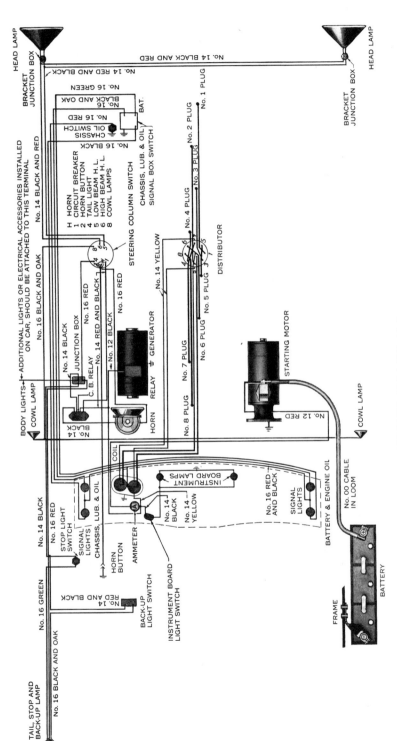

WIRING DIAGRAM

Printed in U. S. A.

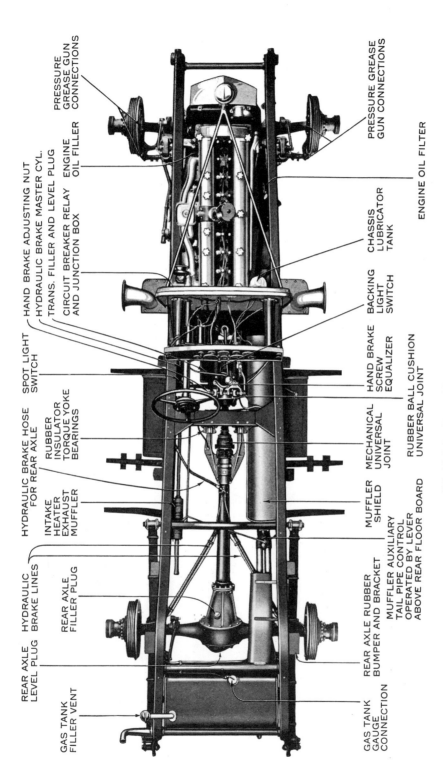

PLAN VIEW OF CHASSIS

PRESSURE GREASE GUN CONNECTIONS

PRESSURE GREASE GUN CONNECTIONS

ENGINE OIL FILTER

CHASSIS LUBRICATOR TANK

BACKING LIGHT SWITCH

HAND BRAKE SCREW EQUALIZER

RUBBER BALL CUSHION UNIVERSAL JOINT

MECHANICAL UNIVERSAL JOINT

MUFFLER SHIELD

MUFFLER AUXILIARY TAIL PIPE CONTROL OPERATED BY LEVER ABOVE REAR FLOOR BOARD

REAR AXLE RUBBER BUMPER AND BRACKET

GAS TANK GAUGE CONNECTION

HAND BRAKE ADJUSTING NUT

HYDRAULIC BRAKE MASTER CYL.

TRANS. FILLER AND LEVEL PLUG

ENGINE OIL FILLER

CIRCUIT BREAKER RELAY AND JUNCTION BOX

SPOT LIGHT SWITCH

HYDRAULIC BRAKE HOSE FOR REAR AXLE

RUBBER INSULATOR TORQUE YOKE BEARINGS

INTAKE HEATER EXHAUST MUFFLER

HYDRAULIC BRAKE LINES

REAR AXLE FILLER PLUG

REAR AXLE LEVEL PLUG

GAS TANK FILLER VENT

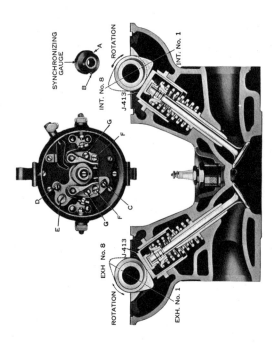

SYNCHRONIZING GAUGE

ROTATION

INT. No. 8

INT. No. 1

J-413

EXH No. 8

J-413

ROTATION

EXH. No. 1

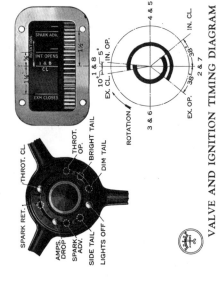

SPARK ADV.

ROTATION

INT. OPENS

1 & 8

CL

EXH CLOSES

1½

1¼

SPARK RET.

THROT. CL.

THROT. OP.

BRIGHT TAIL

DIM TAIL

AMPS. DROP

SPARK ADV.

SIDE TAIL

LIGHTS OFF

1 & 8   5°   4 & 5

10°   IN. OP.

EX. CL.   38°

38°   IN. CL.

EX. OP.   2 & 7

3 & 6

ROTATION

VALVE AND IGNITION TIMING DIAGRAM

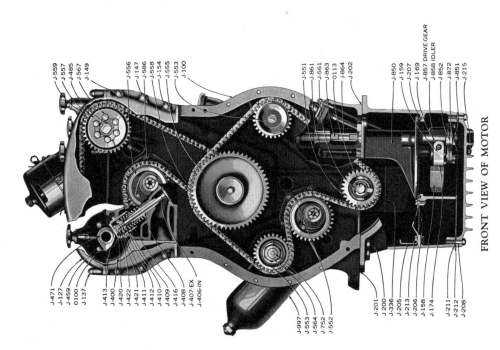

J-559
J-557
J-485
J-567
J-149

J-556
J-147
J-586
J-558
J-154
J-555
J-553
J-100

J-551
J-861
J-561
J-863
O113
J-864
J-202

J-850
J-159
J-207
J-169
J-857 DRIVE GEAR
J-858 IDLER
J-852
J-872
J-851
J-215

J-471
J-127
J-459
O100
J-137

J-413
J-400
J-420
J-422
J-411
J-412
J-410
J-409
J-416
J-408
J-407-EX
J-406-IN

J-997
J-553
J-564
J-752
J-552

J-201
J-200
J-336
J-205
J-213
J-206
J-174
J-158
J-211
J-212
J-208

FRONT VIEW OF MOTOR

49

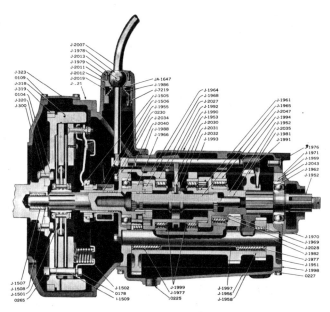

CLUTCH AND TRANSMISSION

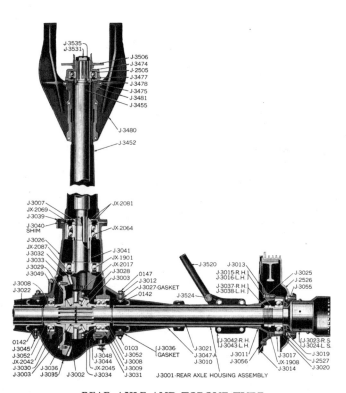

REAR AXLE AND TORQUE TUBE

Printed in U. S. A.

50

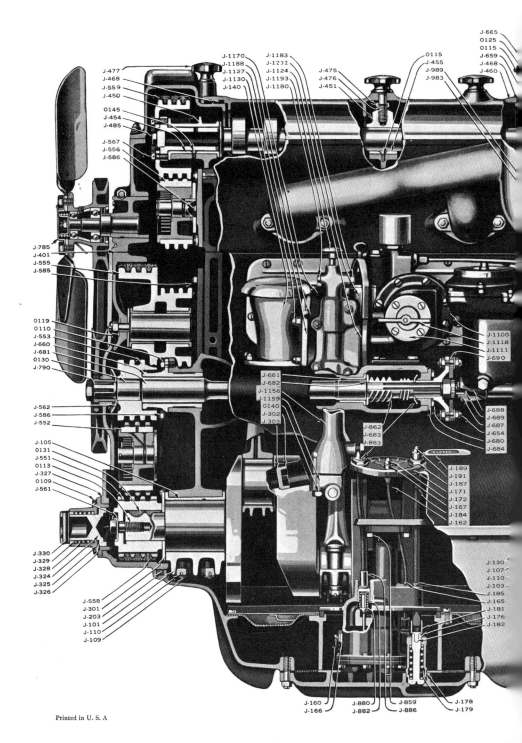

Printed in U. S. A

J-472
J-461
J-465

J-474
J-476
J-475
J-469
J-458
J-453
J-490
J-489
J-467

J-124
J-316
J-317
J-306
J-313
J-315
J-314
J-699
J-698
J-695
J-154
J-153
J-150
J-151
J-138
J-323
J-318
J-319
J-321

J-691
J-309
J-311
J-310
J-312
J-300

J-121
J-112
J-146

J-1507
J-1508
J-320

J-108
J-130
J-104

J-110
J-204
J-331

SIDE VIEW OF MOTOR

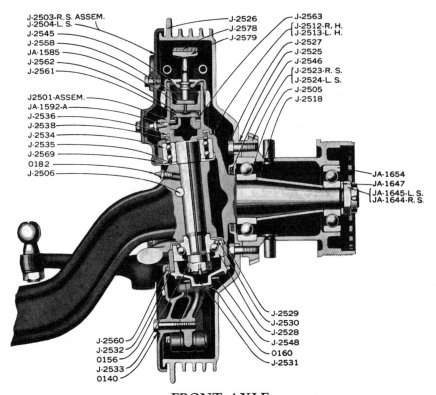

J-2503-R. S. ASSEM.
J-2504-L. S.
J-2545
J-2558
JA-1585
J-2562
J-2561

J2501-ASSEM.
JA-1592-A
J-2536
J-2538
J-2534
J-2535
J-2569
0182
J-2506

J-2526
J-2578
J-2579

J-2563
J-2512-R. H.
J-2513-L. H.
J-2527
J-2525
J-2546
J-2523-R. S.
J-2524-L. S.
J-2505
J-2518

JA-1654
JA-1647
JA-1645-L. S.
JA-1644-R. S.

J-2560
J-2532
0156
J-2533
0140

J-2529
J-2530
J-2528
J-2548
0160
J-2531

FRONT AXLE

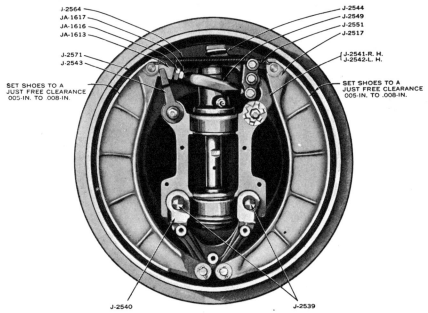

J-2564
JA-1617
JA-1616
JA-1613

J-2571
J-2543

SET SHOES TO A
JUST FREE CLEARANCE
.005-IN. TO .008-IN.

J-2544
J-2549
J-2551
J-2517

J-2541-R. H.
J-2542-L. H.

SET SHOES TO A
JUST FREE CLEARANCE
.005-IN. TO .008-IN.

J-2540

J-2539

EXTERNAL VIEW BRAKE ASSEMBLY

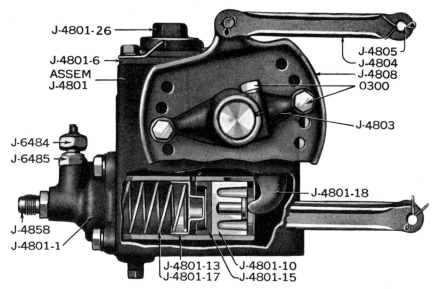

MASTER CYLINDER

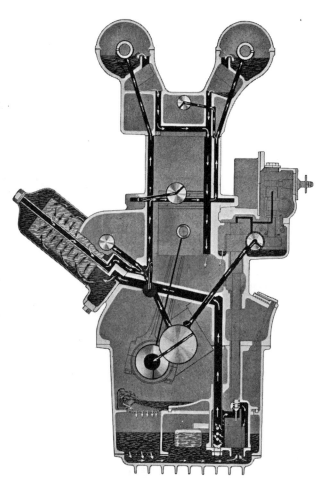

LUBRICATING SYSTEM OF MOTOR

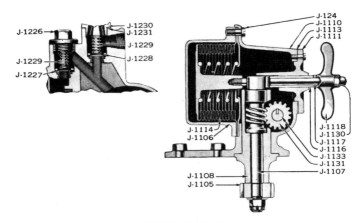

FUEL PUMP

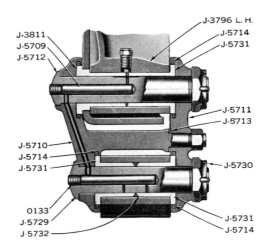

FRONT SPRING REAR SHACKLE

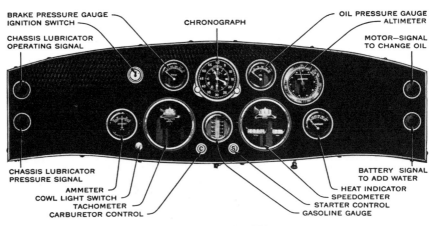

INSTRUMENTS

PART NO.	DESCRIPTION	PAGE
0100	Plain hex nut **5/16-24** S. A. E. med. thd.	37
0101	Plain hex nut **5/16-24** S. A. E. med. thd.	37
0102	Plain hex nut **⅜-24** S. A. E. med. thd.	37
0103	Plain hex nut **⅜-24** S. A. E. med. thd.	37
0104	Plain hex nut **7/16-20** S. A. E. med. thd.	38
0105	Plain hex nut No. **10-32** S. A. E. med. thd.	38
0106	Castle nut **7/16-20** S. A. E. med. thd.	36
0107	Castle nut **⅝-18** S. A. E. med. thd.	36
0108	High nut **5/18-18** S. A. E. med thd.	37
0109	Hex hd. cap screw **5/16-24** x ⅝ S. A. E. med. thd.	41
0110	Hex hd. cap screw **5/16-24** x ⅞ S. A. E. med. thd.	41
0111	Hex. hd. cap screw **⅜-24** x 1⅛ S. A. E. med. thd.	41
0112	Hex. hd. cap screw **⅜-24** x 2½ S. A. E. med. thd.	41
0113	Hex. hd. cap screw **½-20** x 1¼ S. A. E. med. thd.	41
0114	Round head mach. screw No. **10-24** x ⅜	43
0115	Flat head mach. screw No. **10-24** x ½	43
0116	Flat head mach. screw No. **12-24** x ⅝	43
0117	Fillister head mach. screw No. **12-24** x ⅜	43
0118	Plain cut washer **7/64 ID 5/16 OD 120''** thick	44
0119	Plain cut washer **15/32 ID 15/16 OD 1/16** thick	44
0120	Cotter pin **3/32** x ¾	39
0121	Cotter pin **3/32** x 1	39
0122	Cotter pin **⅛** x 1¼	39
0123	Copper pin **1/16** x ⅜	39
0124	Taper pin No. **000 000** x ⅜	40
0125	Taper pin No. **00 00** x ½	40
0126	Taper pin No. **00 00** x ⅝	40
0127	Rod end pin **3/16** S. A. E. std.	39
0128	Woodruff key No. **3** (½ x ⅛)	36
0129	Woodruff key No. **5** (⅝ x ⅛)	36
0130	Woodruff key No. **11** (⅞ x 3/16)	36
0131	Woodruff key No. **A** (⅞ x ¼)	36
0132	Woodruff key No. **6** (⅝ x 5/32)	36
0133	Pipe plug (Allen) **⅛** Briggs std.	40
0134	Pipe plug (Allen) **¼** Briggs std.	40
0135	Pipe plug (Allen) **½** Briggs std.	40
0136	Adjustable yoke No. **10-32** S. A. E. std	45
0137	Escutcheon pin No. **12** (.109) x 2'' long	40
0138	Countersunk head rivet **⅛** x ¼	40
0139	Round head rivet **⅛** x 7/16	40
0140	Hex hd. cap screw **5/16-24** x 1½ S. A. E. med. thd.	41
0141	Pipe plug (Allen) **⅜** Briggs std.	40
0142	Jam nut **⅜-24** S. A. E. med. thd.	37
0143	Plain cut washer **13/32 ID 13/16 OD 1/16** th (⅜ S. A. E.)	44
0144	Castle nut **⅜-24** S. A. E. med. thd.	36
0145	Trunk rivet No. **12** x ⅝	41
0146	Ball **5/16** dia.	36
0147	Castle nut **⅜-24** S. A. E. med. thd.	36
0148	Castle nut **½-20** S. A. E. med. thd.	36
0149	Cotter pin **3/32** x 1	39
0150	Cotter pin **3/32** x ⅝	39
0151	Round head rivet **¼** x ¾	40
0152	Cotter pin **⅛** x ⅞	40
0153	Hex. hd. cap screw **5/16-24** x ¾ S. A. E. med. thd.	41
0154	Hex. hd. cap screw **⅜-24** x 1¼ S. A. E. med. thd.	41
0155	Cotter pin **⅛** x 1½	40
0156	Hex. hd. cap screw **5/16-24** x 1¼ S. A. E. med. thd.	41
0157	Plain cut washer **9/32 ID ⅝ OD 1'16** thick (¼ S. A. E.)	44
0158	Wire No. **18** (.049) B. W. G. bulk material	45
0159	Round head rivet **¼** x ⅝	40
0160	Hex hd. cap screw **5/16-24** x ½ S. A. E. med. thd.	41
0161	Hex hd. cap screw **5/16-24** x 1¾ S. A. E. med. thd.	41
0163	Hex. hd. cap screw **⅜-24** x 4¾ S. A. E. med. thd.	41
0164	Castle nut **½-20** S. A. E. med. thd.	36
0165	Hex. hd. cap screw **5/16-24** x ⅞ S. A. E. med. thd.	41
0167	Round head rivet **5/16** x 1	40
0168	Hex. hd. cap screw **⅜-24** x 1	41
0169	Castle nut **9/16-18** S. A. E. med. thd.	36
0170	Cotter pin **⅛** x 1¼	40

PART NO.	DESCRIPTION	PAGE
0171	Cotter pin 3/32 x 1⅛	40
0173	Plain hex nut 7/16-20 S. A. E. med. thd.	38
0174	Countersunk head rivet .187 x 7/16	40
0175	Countersunk head rivet 3/16 x ¼	40
0176	Button hd. rivet .187 x 7/16	40
0177	Hex. hd. cap screw 5/16-24 x ⅜ full thd.	41
0178	Hex. hd. cap screw ⅜-24 x ⅞ S. A. E. med. thd.	41
0179	Fillister hd. mach. screw 8-32 x ¾	43
0180	Cotter pin 1/16 x ¾	40
0181	Round head rivet 5/16 x ⅞	40
0182	Zerk lubricator fitting (straight) ⅛ P th.	36
0183	Fillister hd. mach. screw No. 10-24 x ¼ S. A. E. med. thd.	43
0185	Round gasket 57/64 ID 1⅛ OD 3/32 thick	36
0186	Castle nut 5/16-24	36
0187	Hex. hd. cap screw 7/16-20 x 1¼ S. A. E. med. thd.	42
0188	Hex. hd. cap screw ¼-28 x ¾ S. A. E.	42
0189	Flared tube union nut ⅜ tube S. A. E. long (1-5/16)	39
0190	Plain cut washer 7/32 ID ½ OD 1/16th (No. 10 S. A. E.)	45
0191	Hex. hd. cap screw ⅜-24 x 3 S. A. E. med. thd.	42
0192	Round hd. mach. screw No. 10-32 x ½ S. A. E. med. thd.	43
0194	Plain hex nut ¼-28 S. A. E. med. thd.	38
0195	Hex hd cap screw 5/16-18 x 1¾	42
0196	Fillister hd. mach screw No. 10-24 x 7/16	43
0197	Filister hd. mach. screw No. 12-24 x ⅝	43
0199	French hd. mach. screw 5/16-24 x ⅞	43
0200	Round head rivet 5/16 x 1¼	40
0201	Flat hd. mach. screw No. 10-32 x 1¼	43
0202	Flat hd. rivet ¼ x ⅜	40
0203	Round hd. wood screw No. 8 x ⅝	44
0204	Hex. hd. cap screw 5/16-24 x 1⅞ S. A. E. med. thd.	42
0205	French hd. mach. screw 5/16-24 x 1⅝ S. A. E. med. thd.	43
0206	French hd. mach. screw 5/16-24 x 1⅛ S. A. E. med. thd.	43
0207	French hd. mach. screw 5/16-24 x 1½ S. A. E. med. thd.	43
0208	Flat hd. mach. screw ¼-28 x ⅞ S. A. E. med. thd.	43
0209	Split rivet 9/64 x ½ flat head	40
0210	Hex. hd. cap screw ⅜-24 x 1⅜	42
0211	Hex. hd. cap screw 9/16-18 x 3½	42
0212	Hex. hd. cap screw 9/16-18 x 3¾	42
0213	Filister hd. mach. screw No. 10-24 x ¾	43
0214	Filister hd. mach. screw No. 10-24 x 1	43
0215	Filister hd. mach. screw No. 12-24 x 1½	43
0216	Round head rivet 3/16 dia. x ¼	41
0217	Round head rivet 3/16 dia. x 5/16	41
0218	Hex. hd. cap screw 5/16-24 x 2¾ S. A. E. med.	42
0219	Flare tube union ⅜ dia. tbe. x ¼ pipe thd. S. A. E. std.	36
0220	Flat hd. wood screw No. 8 x ⅝ long	44
0221	Flare tube elbow ¼ tbe. x ⅛ pipe thd. S. A. E. std.	36
0222	Jam nut ¼-28 U. S. F. 5/32 thick	37
0223	Square hd. set screw ¼-20 x ½	44
0224	Filister hd. mach. screw No. 8-32 x ¼	43
0225	Pipe plug Allen ¾ Briggs std.	40
0227	Hex. hd. cap screw 5/16-18 x ¾	42
0228	Lockwasher ¼ x 3/32 x 3/64 thick	44
0229	Filister hd. mach. screw No. 12-24 x ½	43
0230	Hex hd cap screw ⅜-16 x ⅞	42
0232	Lockwasher ⅜ x ⅛ x 3/32 thick	44
0233	Hex. hd. cap screw ⅜-16 x ¾	42
0234	Hex. hd. cap screw 5/16-18 x ⅞	42
0235	Hex hd. cap screw 5/16-18 x 3¼	42
0236	Hex hd cap screw 5/16-18 x 2⅜	42
0237	Lockwasher 5/16 x ⅛ x 3/32 thick	44
0238	Hex. hd. cap screw 7/16-20 x 1¼	42
0239	Jam nut 7/16-14	37
0240	Jam nut 5/16-24	37
0241	Hex. hd. cap screw ⅜-16 x 1⅛	42
0242	Hex. hd cap screw ⅜-24 x ⅝	42
0243	Lockwasher 7/16 x 5/32 x ⅛ thick	44
0244	Compression nut 5/16 dole 3 U roll ball	37
0245	Compression sleeve 5/16 dole 3 U roll ball	44

PART NO.	DESCRIPTION	PAGE
0246	Hex hd. cap screw 5/16-24 x 2¼ S. A. E. med. thd.	42
0247	Hex. hd. cap screw 5/16-24 x 2½ S. A. E. med. thd.	42
0248	Flat hd. mach. screw No. 14-24 x ⅝ A. S. M. E.	43
0249	Hex hd. cap screw ¼-28 x ⅜ S. A. E.	42
0250	Plain hex nut 14 x 24 A. S. M. E.	38
0251	Jam nut 9/16 x 5/16 thick	37
0252	Lamp bulb 3 C P G-6	36
0253	Flare tube union nut short ¼″ S. A. E.	39
0254	Flare tube straight union ¼ T x ⅛ P T	36
0255	Flared tube nut ⅜ dia. tube S. A. E.	39
0256	Flare tube union nut (short) 5/16 dia. tube S. A. E.	39
0257	Flare tube elbow 90 ⅜ dia. tube S. A. E.	36
0258	Flare tube connector S. A. E. ⅜ tube ¼ pipe thd.	36
0259	Flat head wood screw No. 6 x ¾	44
0260	Pipe nipple ⅛ I P 3″ long	36
0261	Pipe coupling ⅛ I. P.	36
0263	Rod end pin 5/16 S. A. E. std.	39
0264	Hex hd. cap screw ⅜-16 x ⅝ U. S.	42
0265	Plain hex nut 9/16-18 S. A. E.	38
0266	Plain hex nut No. 10-24 A. S. M. E.	38
0267	Plain hex nut No. 8-32 A. S. M. E.	38
0268	Escutcheon pin No. 15 (.072) x ½	40
0269	Flare tube union nut S. A. E. short 5/16	39
0270	Flare tube union nut S. A. E. short ¼	39
0271	Jam nut ½-20 x 5/16 thick	37
0272	Wire terminal sherman No. 4 x .032 thick	44
0273	Hex. hd. cap screw ¼-28 x ½	42
0274	Lock washer S. A. E. heave ⅜ x ⅛ x ⅛	44
0275	Clevis pin 3/16 x (7/16) S. A. E.	39
0276	French hd. mach. screw No. 8-32 x ¼	43
0277	Jam nut ⅝-18 S. A. E. x 5/16 thick	37
0278	Lock washer ⅝ x 13/64 x′ 3/32	44
0279	Adjustable yoke end No. 10-32 S. A. E.	45
0280	Plain hex nut No. 10-32 S. A. E. med. thd.	38
0281	Plain yoke end No. 19 (3/16) S. A. E.	36
0282	Knurled nut No. 8-32 thd. (7/16 dia. hd. 5/16 high)	37
0283	Square hd. mach. bolt 3/16-24 U. S. F. x ½ long	36
0284	Square nut 3/16-24 for mach. bolt 0283	38
0285	Jam nut 7/16-20	37
0287	Hex. hd. cap screw ¼-28 x 1¼	42
0288	Hex. hd. cap screw 5/16-24 x ⅝	42
0289	Hex. hd. cap screw ⅜-24 x 1½	42
0290	French hd. mach. screw 5/16-24 x ⅝	43
0291	French hd. mach. screw 5/16-24 x 1¼	43
0292	Hex. hd. cap screw 7/16-20 x 1½	42
0293	Round hd. mach. screw No. 8-32 x 1⅛	43
0294	Plain hex. nut 7/16-20 S. A. E.	38
0295	Plain cut washer 15/32 ID 15/16 th. S. A. E.	45
0296	Countersunk head rivet .250 dia. x ¾ long	40
0297	Countersunk head rivet dia. x ¾ long	40
0298	Hex. head cap screw 7/16-20 x 1¾ OS	42
0299	Plain cut washer 32 I. D. 16 O. D. 16 th.	45
0300	Hex. hd. cap screw 5/16-24 x 1″ S. A. E.	42
0301	Fill hd. cap screw 5/16-24 x 1″	41
0302	Lock washer 9/16 x 3/16 x ⅛	44
0303	Round head mach. screw No. 12-24 x ½	43
0304	Plain cut washer ¼ I. D. 9/16 OD 1/16 th.	45
0305	Clevis pin ¼ S. A. E.	39
0307	Flare tube straight connector ¼ tube and ⅛ pipe thd.	36
0308	Flare tube straight connector 5/16 tube x ⅛ pipe thd.	36
0309	Cotter pin 5/32 x ¾	40
0310	Taper pin No. 4 x 1	40
0311	Fill. hd. cap screw 5/16-24 x ¾	41
0312	Round hd. carriage bolt ¼-20 x 1¼ (9/16 head dia. less nut)	36
0313	Square nut (mach. bolt) ¼ 20 for carriage bolt 0312	38
0314	Hex. hd. cap screw 5/16-24 x 1¼ S. A. E.	43
0315	Lock washer ¼ x 3/32 x 1/16 S. A. E.	44
0316	Adjustable yoke end ⅜-24 S. A. E. std.	36
0317	Clevis pin ⅜-S.A. E. std.	39

PART NO.	DESCRIPTION	PAGE
0318	Hex. hd. cap screw 3⁄8-24 x 5 S. A. E.	43
0319	Hex. hd. cap screw 1⁄4-28 x 1⅜	43
0320	Flat hd. mach. screw 1⁄4-28 x 1 S. A. E. thd.	43
0321	Round hd. rivet 3⁄16 x 1⁄2	41
0322	Round hd. rivet 5⁄32 x 1⁄4	41
0323	French hd. mach. screw No. 10-32 x 1⁄2	42
0324	Lock washer No. 10 S. A. E. x 1⁄16 x 3⁄64	44
0325	Hex. hd. cap screw 3⁄8-16 x 1¾ U. S.	43
0326	Hex. hd. cap screw 1⁄2-20 x 1½ S. A. E.	43
0327	Plain hex. nut 1⁄2-20 S. A. E.	38
0328	Hex. hd. cap screw 5⁄16-18 x 1⅛ U. S.	43
0329	Taper pin No. 0 x 3⁄4	40
0330	Woodruff key No. 4 (5⁄8 x 3⁄32)	36
0331	Hex. hd. cap screw 1⁄4-28 x 1 S. A. E.	43
0332	Round hd. mach screw No. 10-32 x 1⁄2	44
0333	Hex. hd. cap screw 1⁄2-20 x 1⅛ S. A. E.	43
0334	Alemite fitting Z-36 AA 1⁄8 P. th. 67 1⁄2° elbow	36
0335	Plain hex. nut 1⁄4-20	38

Body Parts

It is impossible to supply a parts list of the various types of bodies installed on our chassis for this reason; when body parts are desired it will be necessary to make up a special order giving complete detailed information for each part as listed below:

1. Car number

2. Body number

3. Body make and type

4. Small sketch or sample of part desired

Upon reciept of order for body material we will endeavor to obtain these parts from the respective manufacturers and ship direct to you.

Prices quoted upon application at time of order.

Index

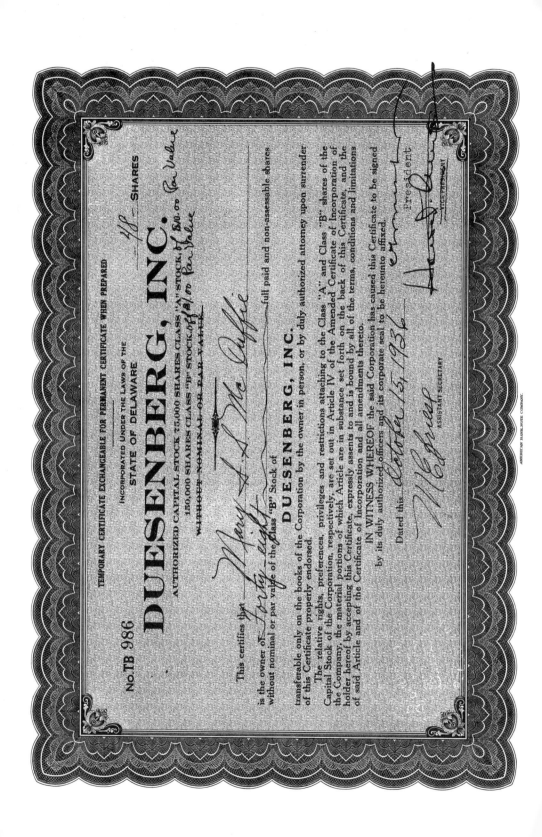

TEMPORARY CERTIFICATE EXCHANGEABLE FOR PERMANENT CERTIFICATE WHEN PREPARED

INCORPORATED UNDER THE LAWS OF THE
STATE OF DELAWARE

No. TB 986

DUESENBERG, INC.

AUTHORIZED CAPITAL STOCK 75,000 SHARES CLASS "A" STOCK, of $10.00 Par Value
150,000 SHARES CLASS "B" STOCK, of $3.00 Par Value
WITHOUT NOMINAL OR PAR VALUE

48 SHARES

This certifies that _Mary A. McCuffie_

is the owner of _forty eight_

without nominal or par value of the Class "B" Stock of

DUESENBERG, INC.

full paid and non-assessable shares

transferable only on the books of the Corporation by the owner in person, or by duly authorized attorney upon surrender of this Certificate properly endorsed.

The relative rights, preferences, privileges and restrictions attaching to the Class "A" and Class "B" shares of the Capital Stock of the Corporation, respectively, are set out in Article IV of the Amended Certificate of Incorporation of the Company, the material portions of which Article are in substance set forth on the back of this Certificate, and the holder hereof by accepting this Certificate, expressly assents to and is bound by all of the terms, conditions and limitations of said Article and of the Certificate of Incorporation and all amendments thereto.

IN WITNESS WHEREOF the said Corporation has caused this Certificate to be signed by its duly authorized officers and its corporate seal to be hereunto affixed.

Dated this _October 15, 1936_

President

VICE-PRESIDENT

ASSISTANT SECRETARY

AMERICAN BANK NOTE COMPANY

SUPERCHARGER
PARTS SUPPLEMENT

Duesenberg

MODEL J

Compiled by the

General Service Department

DUESENBERG, INC.

Indianapolis, Ind., U. S. A.

SUPERCHARGER

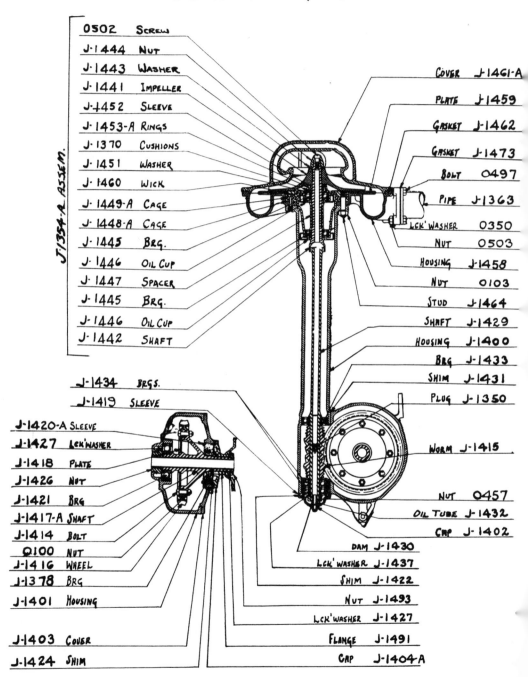

J·1354-A ASSEM.

0502	SCREW
J·1444	NUT
J·1443	WASHER
J·1441	IMPELLER
J·1452	SLEEVE
J·1453-A	RINGS
J·1370	CUSHIONS
J·1451	WASHER
J·1460	WICK
J·1449-A	CAGE
J·1448-A	CAGE
J·1445	BRG.
J·1446	OIL CUP
J·1447	SPACER
J·1445	BRG.
J·1446	OIL CUP
J·1442	SHAFT

J·1434	BRGS.
J·1419	SLEEVE
J·1420-A	SLEEVE
J·1427	LCK'WASHER
J·1418	PLATE
J·1426	NUT
J·1421	BRG
J·1417-A	SHAFT
J·1414	BOLT
Q100	NUT
J·1416	WHEEL
J·1378	BRG
J·1401	HOUSING
J·1403	COVER
J·1424	SHIM

COVER	J·1461-A
PLATE	J·1459
GASKET	J·1462
GASKET	J·1473
BOLT	0497
PIPE	J·1363
LCK'WASHER	0350
NUT	0503
HOUSING	J·1458
NUT	0103
STUD	J·1464
SHAFT	J·1429
HOUSING	J·1400
BRG	J·1433
SHIM	J·1431
PLUG	J·1350
WORM	J·1415
NUT	0457
OIL TUBE	J·1432
CAP	J·1402
DAM	J·1430
LCK'WASHER	J·1437
SHIM	J·1422
NUT	J·1493
LCK'WASHER	J·1427
FLANGE	J·1491
CAP	J·1404A

IMPELLER & DRIVE ASSEMBLY
J-1350-A

SUPERCHARGER   J-1410-A

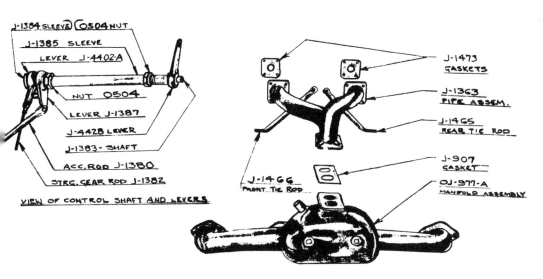

Parts on Intake Side

View of Control Shaft and Levers (left diagram):

J-1384 SLEEVE
0504 NUT
J-1385 SLEEVE
LEVER J-4402-A
NUT 0504
LEVER J-1387
J-4428 LEVER
J-1383 - SHAFT
ACC. ROD J-1380
STRG. GEAR ROD J-1382

VIEW OF CONTROL SHAFT AND LEVERS

Right diagram:

J-1473 GASKETS
J-1363 PIPE ASSEM.
J-1465 REAR TIE ROD
J-907 GASKET
OJ-977-A MANIFOLD ASSEMBLY
J-1466 FRONT TIE ROD

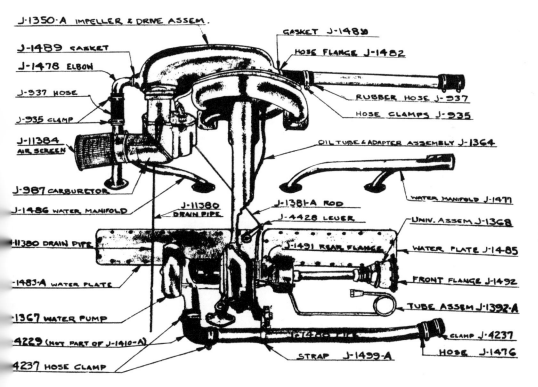

Parts on Exhaust Side labels:

J-1350-A IMPELLER & DRIVE ASSEM.
J-1489 GASKET
J-1478 ELBOW
J-937 HOSE
J-935 CLAMP
J-11384 AIR SCREEN
J-987 CARBURETOR
J-1486 WATER MANIFOLD
J-11380 DRAIN PIPE
J-1485-A WATER PLATE
J-1367 WATER PUMP
J-4229 (NOT PART OF J-1410-A)
J-4237 HOSE CLAMP

GASKET J-1489
HOSE FLANGE J-1482
RUBBER HOSE J-937
HOSE CLAMPS J-935
OIL TUBE & ADAPTER ASSEMBLY J-1364
WATER MANIFOLD J-1477
J-11380 DRAIN PIPE
J-1381-A ROD
J-4428 LEVER
J-1491 REAR FLANGE
UNIV. ASSEM. J-1368
WATER PLATE J-1485
FRONT FLANGE J-1492
TUBE ASSEM. J-1392-A
CLAMP J-4237
HOSE J-1476
STRAP J-1499-A

Parts on Exhaust Side

SUPERCHARGER

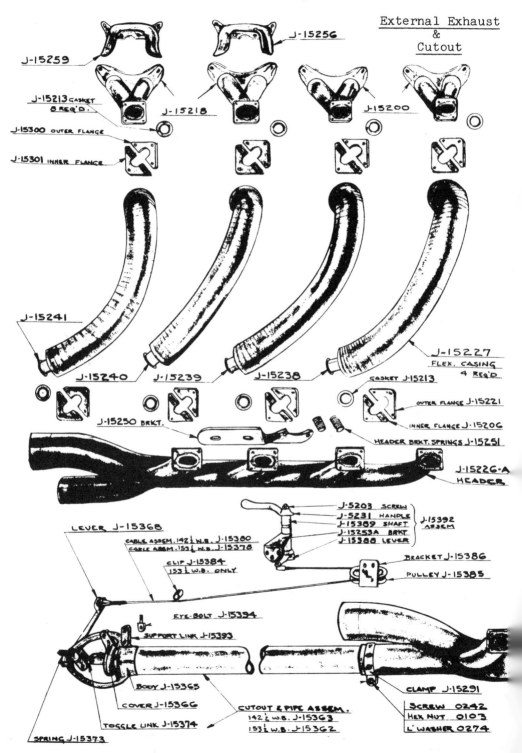

J-15259

J-15256

J-15213 GASKET 8 REQ'D.

J-15218

J-15200

J-15300 OUTER FLANGE

J-15301 INNER FLANGE

J-15241

J-15240

J-15239

J-15238

J-15227 FLEX. CASING 4 REQ'D

GASKET J-15213

OUTER FLANGE J-15221

INNER FLANGE J-15206

J-15230 BRKT.

HEADER BRKT. SPRINGS J-15251

J-15226-A HEADER

J-5203 SCREW
J-5231 HANDLE
J-15389 SHAFT
J-15253A BRKT.
J-15388 LEVER
J-15392 ASSEM.

LEVER J-15368

CABLE ASSEM. 142½ W.B. J-15380
CABLE ASSEM. 153½ W.B. J-15378

CLIP J-15384
153½ W.B. ONLY

BRACKET J-15386
PULLEY J-15385

EYE-BOLT J-15394

SUPPORT LINK J-15393

BODY J-15365

COVER J-15366

TOGGLE LINK J-15374

CUTOUT & PIPE ASSEM.
142½ W.B. J-15363
153½ W.B. J-15362

CLAMP J-15291

SCREW 0242
HEX NUT 0103
L' WASHER 0274

SPRING J-15373

MODEL J - SJ

DUESENBERG SUPERCHARGER PARTS SUPPLEMENT

No. Used Per Car	Description	Part Number	Price Each
1	SUPERCHARGER and EXHAUST MANIFOLD INST. 142½W.B. -	J-11394	2250.00
	Consists of		
1	SUPERCHARGER ASSEMBLY- - - - - - - - - - - - - -	J-1410-A	1585.85
	For Detail see under J-11395		
1	EXHAUST MANIFOLD INSTALLATION 142½ W.B.- - - - -	J-15354	927.75
	For Detail see this part number.		
1	SUPERCHARGER and EXHAUST MANIFOLD INST. 153½W.B. -	J-11395	2250.00
	Consists of		
1	SUPERCHARGER ASSEMBLY- - - - - - - - - - - - - -	J-1410-A	1585.85
	Consists of		
10	Nuts--Cylinder Head- - - - - - - - - - - - -	J-148	.35
1	Stud--Super, Carburetor- - - - - - - - - - -	J-215	.15
8	Assembly--Connecting Rod - - - - - - - - - -	-OJ-375	28.20
3	Screw--Super Purolator Bracket Short - - - -	J-778	.90
2	Gasket--Super Pipe Manifold- - - - - - - - -	J-907	.35
6	Clamp--Super Water Hose- - - - - - - - - - -	J-935	.40
3	Hose--Super Water- - - - - - - - - - - - - -	J-937	.30
1	Assembly--Carburetor - - - - - - - - - - - -	-OJ-987	90.00
4	Gasket--Water Manifold - - - - - - - - - - -	J-995-AA	.10
4	Gasket--Oil Filter - - - - - - - - - - - - -	J-998	.05
4	Ring--Oil Filter Seal- - - - - - - - - - - -	J-1001	.10
4	Screw--Acorn Head Cap (5/16-24 x 5/8)- - - -	J-1011	.35
2	Cover--Super Impeller Hsg. Cover Water H.- -	J-1050	.40
1	SUPER IMPELLER and DRIVE ASSEMBLY- - - - - -	J-1350-A	695.75
	Consists of		
24	Screw--Fil. Hd. Cap (1/4-24 x 5/8) - - - - -	J-124	.15
1	SUPER DRIVE WORM WHEEL and HOUSING ASSEMBLY- -	J-1351-A	224.75
	Consists of		
1	SUPER DRIVE WORM WHEEL and HOUSING ASSEMBLY- -	J-1358-A	46.50
	Consists of		
1	Sleeve--Super Drive Housing Drain- - - - -	J-1395	.50
1	Housing--Super Drive Worm Wheel- - - - - -	J-1401	44.75
2	Dowel--Super Drive Housing - - - - - - - -	J-1440	.25
1	Plug--Heat Indicator Manifold- - - - - - -	J-5546	.90
1	Gasket--Heat Indicator Manifold Plug - - -	J-5548	.05
1	SUPER DRIVE WORM WHEEL and SHAFT ASSEMBLY- - -	J-1359-A	174.25
	Consists of		
1	SUPER DRIVE WORM WHEEL SHAFT ASSEMBLY- - - -	J-1361-A	46.25
1	Shaft--Super Drive Worm Wheel- - - - - - -	J-1417-A	42.90
1	Plate--Super Drive Worm Wheel Shaft- - - -	J-1418	3.25

PLEASE GIVE CAR NUMBER AND MOTOR NUMBER WHEN ORDERING PARTS

Printed in U.S.A.

March 1, 1934

MODEL J - SJ

DUESENBERG SUPERCHARGER PARTS SUPPLEMENT

No. Used Per Car	Description	Part Number	Price Each
	SUPER DRIVE WORM WHEEL and SHAFT ASSEMBLY (CONTINUED)		
1	Bearing--Super Drive Worm Wheel Frt.- - - -	J-1378	6.00
1	SUPER DRIVE HOUSING OIL FEED NOZZLE ASSEMBLY-	J-1397	2.85
	Consists of		
1	Fitting--Super Drive Housing Oil Feed Tube-	J-1379	.50
1	Nozzle--Super Drive Housing Oil Feed- - - -	J-1396	2.50
1	Cover--Super Drive Worm Wheel Housing - - -	J-1403	17.10
1	Cap--Super Drive Worm Wheel Housing Bearing	J-1404-A	10.75
8	Bolt--Super Drive Worm Wheel- - - - - - - -	J-1414	.15
1	Wheel--Super Drive Worm - - - - - - - - - -	J-1416	42.50
1	Sleeve--Super Drive Worm Wheel Frt. Bearing	J-1420-A	18.25
1	Bearing--Super Drive Worm Wheel - - - - - -	J-1421	5.20
1	Shim--Super Drive Worm Wheel Frt. Bearing Sl.	J-1424	1.70
1	Nut--Super Drive Worm Wheel Rear Bearing- -	J-1426	5.90
2	Washer--Super Drive Worm Wheel Brg.Nt.Lock-	J-1427	1.25
1	Flange--Super Universal Joint Rear- - - - -	J-1491	10.35
1	Nut--Super Universal Joint Rear Flange- - -	J-1493	3.60
8	Nut--Plain Hex 5/16-24- - - - - - - - - - -	0100	.02
6	Screw--Hex Head Cap 5/16-24 x 7/8 - - - - -	0505	.15
1	Gasket--Super Drive Housing Cover - - - - -	J-1409	2.65
14	Screw--Hex Head Cap 5/16-24 x 3/4 - - - - -	0520	.15
1	SUPER DRIVE WORM and HOUSING ASSEMBLY - - - - -	J-1352-A	144.25
	Consists of		
1	SUPER DRIVE WORM HOUSING ASSEMBLY - - - - - -	J-1356	33.25
	Consists of		
1	Housing--Super Drive Worm - - - - - - - - -	J-1400	32.75
1	Adapter--Super Impeller Bearing Oil Tube- -	J-11365	.50
1	SUPER DRIVE WORM and SHAFT ASSEMBLY - - - - - -	J-1357	107.25
	Consists of		
1	SUPER DRIVE WORM SHAFT ASSEMBLY - - - - - - -	J-1360	52.75
	Consists of		
1	Shaft--Super Drive Worm - - - - - - - - - -	J-1429	51.25
1	Dam--Super Drive Worm Shaft - - - - - - - -	J-1430	1.10
1	Plug--Super Drive Worm Shaft- - - - - - - -	J-11350	.75
1	Worm--Super Drive - - - - - - - - - - - - -	J-1415	35.50
1	Sleeve--Super Drive Worm Lower Bearing- - -	J-1419	10.75
1	Shim--Super Drive Worm Lower Bearing Sleeve	J-1422	1.45
1	Key--Super Drive Worm - - - - - - - - - - -	J-1428	.60
1	Bearing--Super Drive Worm Upper Rad.- - - -	J-1433	3.50
1	Bearing--Super Drive Worm Lower Double Row-	J-1434	2.90
1	Washer--Super Drive Worm Thrust Bearing Oil	J-1435	2.95

PLEASE GIVE CAR NUMBER AND MOTOR NUMBER WHEN ORDERING PARTS

Printed in U.S.A.   March 1, 1934

MODEL J - SJ

DUESENBERG SUPERCHARGER PARTS SUPPLEMENT

No. Used Per Car	Description	Part Number	Price Each
	SUPER DRIVE WORM and SHAFT ASSEMBLY (CONTINUED)		
1	Washer--Super Drive Worm Th. Bearing Lock -	J-1437	1.50
1	Washer--Super Drive Worm Th. Bearing Ret. -	J-2232	.05
1	Nut--Check 5/8 - 18 x 3/8 Th. - - - - - - -	0457	.05
1	SUPER DRIVE WORM HOUSING CAP ASSEMBLY - - - -	J-11366	3.85
	Consists of		
1	Cap--Super Drive Worm Housing - - - - - - -	J-1402	3.10
1	Tube--Super Drive Worm Housing Cap Oil- - -	J-1432	1.10
4	Screw--Hex Head Cap 5/16-24 x 7/8 - - - - -	0505	.15
1	SUPER IMPELLER HOUSING and PLATE ASSEMBLY - -	J-1353	52.75
	Consists of		
1	Housing--Super Impeller - - -. - - - - - - -	J-1458	39.50
1	Plate--Super Impeller Housing - - - - - - -	J-1459	13.50
9	Screw--Flat Head Machine #12-24 x 1/2 - - -	0499	.02
1	SUPER IMPELLER and BEARING ASSEMBLY - - - - -	J-1354-A	187.25
	Consists of		
2	Cushion--Super Impeller Upper Brg. Sl. Ring	J-1370	.05
1	Impeller--Supercharger- - - - - - - - - - -	J-1441	70.75
1	Shaft--Supercharger Impeller- - - - - - - -	J-1442	29.75
1	Washer--Supercharger Impeller - - - - - - -	J-1443	1.35
1	Nut--Supercharger Impeller- - - - - - - - -	J-1444	2.15
2	Bearing--Super Impeller - - - - - - - - - -	J-1445	2.50
2	Cup--Super Impeller Bearing Oil - - - - - -	J-1446	4.75
1	Spacer--Super Impeller Bearing- - - - - - -	J-1447	3.85
1	Cage--Super Impeller Lower Bearing- - - - -	J-1448-A	17.75
1	Cage--Super Impeller Upper Bearing- - - - -	J-1449-A	14.50
1	Cover--Super Impeller Upper Bearing - - - -	J-1450-A	22.25
1	Washer--Super Impeller Upper Bearing Seal -	J-1451	2.25
1	Sleeve--Super Impeller Upper Bearing Seal -	J-1452	3.80
2	Ring--Super Impeller Upper Bearing Seal - -	J-1453-A	1.10
1	Dowel--Super Impeller Bearing Cage- - - - -	J-1454	.30
1	Wick--Super Impeller Upper Bearing Oil- - -	J-1460	.35
1	Gasket--Super Impeller Outer Bearing Cover-	J-11351	1.30
1	Gasket--Super Impeller Upper Bearing Cage -	J-11352	1.45
2	Screw--Flat Head Machine #12 - 24 x 3/4 - -	0492	.05
2	Screw--Flat Head Machine #12 - 24 x 1/2 - -	0499	.02
1	Screw--Fil. Head Machine #14 - 24 x 3/4 - -	0502	.05
1	Pin--Super Impeller Upper Seal Ring - - - -	J-11392	.45
1	SUPER IMPELLER HOUSING COVER ASSEMBLY - - - -	J-1355	77.75
	Consists of		
1	Cover--Super Impeller Housing - - - - - - -	J-1461-A	77.50
1	Plug--Pipe 1/8 Allen- - - - - - - - - - - -	0133	.12
2	Plug--Headless Pipe 3/4 (sq. hole)- - - - -	0225	.15

PLEASE GIVE CAR NUMBER AND MOTOR NUMBER WHEN ORDERING PARTS

Printed in U. S. A.   March 1, 1934

MODEL J - SJ

DUESENBERG SUPERCHARGER PARTS SUPPLEMENT

No. Used Per Car	Description	Part Number	Price Each
	SUPER IMPELLER and DRIVE ASSEMBLY (CONTINUED)		
1	Gasket--Super Drive Worm Housing- - - - - -	J-1431	2.95
1	Gasket--Super Impeller Housing Cover- - - -	J-1462	.45
6	Stud--Super Impeller Housing- - - - - - - -	J-1464	.25
1	Gasket--Super Impeller Bearing Cover Cage -	J-11351	1.30
6	Nut-- Plain Hex 3/8-24- - - - - - - - - - -	0103	.03
5	Screw--Hex Head Cap 5/16-24 x 2-1/2 - - - -	0247	.30
2	Screw--Flat Head Cap #12 - 24 x 1/2 - - - -	0499	.02
1	SUPER PUROLATOR BRACKET ASSEMBLY- - - - - -	J-1362	16.25
	Consists of		
1	Bracket--Super Purolator- - - - - - - - - -	J-1479	15.85
2	Plug--Pipe 1/4 Allen- - - - - - - - - - - -	0134	.12
1	Connector--Flare Tube Straight 3/8 T x 1/4	0258	.30
1	SUPER MANIFOLD PIPE ASSEMBLY- - - - - - - -	J-1363	54.85
	Consists of		
1	Pipe--Super Front Manifold- - - - - - - - -	J-1470	N.S.S.
1	Pipe--Super Rear Manifold - - - - - - - - -	J-1471	N.S.S.
2	Flange--Super Manifold Upper- - - - - - - -	J-1472	N.S.S.
1	Flange--Super Manifold Lower- - - - - - - -	J-1474	N.S.S.
1	SUPER IMPELLER BEARING OIL TUBE ASSEMBLY- - -	J-1364	1.50
	Consists of		
1	Tube--Super Impeller Bearing Oil- - - - - -	J-1457	N.S.S.
2	Bushing--Junction 5/32 (Not Plated) - - - -	J-6039	.05
2	Sleeve--Compression 5/32 (not Plated) - - -	J-6040	.05
1	INTAKE D. D. MANIFOLD ASSEMBLY- - - - - - -	OJ-977-A	114.75
	Consists of		
1	Manifold--Down Draft Intake - - - - - - - -	J-977-A	107.50
4	Plugs--Intake Manifold Core Hole- - - - - -	J-983	1.35
4	Gasket--Intake Manifold Core Hole Plug- - -	J-989	.10
1	Plug--Square Head Pipe 1/8" - - - - - - - -	0445	.15
1	Fitting--Intake Manifold Water Jacket In. -	J-931	1.35
1	Fitting--Intake Manifold Water Jacket out.-	J-930	.65
1	Pin--Down Draft Control Pivot - - - - - - -	J-4414-A	.35
1	SUPER WATER PUMP ASSEMBLY - - - - - - - - -	J-9367	75.50
1	SUPER UNIVERSAL JOINT ASSEMBLY - - - - - -	J-1368	78.50
1	SUPER CYL. HEAD OIL TUBE & ADAPTER ASSEMBLY -	J-1369	1.10
	Consists of		
1	Tube--Super Cyl. Head Oil - - - - - - - - -	J-1455	.35
1	Adapter--Super Cyl. Head Oil Tube - - - - -	J-1456	.85
1	SUPER ACCELERATOR ROD ASSEMBLY- - - - - - -	J-1380	5.25
	Consists of		
1	Rod--Supercharger Acc - - - - - - - - - - -	J-11376	N.S.S
1	End--Adjustable Rod (Not Plated)- - - - - -	J-5504	.35
1	Nut--Jam (Not Plated) - - - - - - - - - - -	0222	.05

PLEASE GIVE CAR NUMBER AND MOTOR NUMBER WHEN ORDERING PARTS

March 1, 1934

MODEL J - SJ

DUESENBERG SUPERCHARGER PARTS SUPPLEMENT

No. Used Per Car	Description	Part Number	Price Each
	SUPER ASSEMBLY (CONTINUED)		
1	SUPER CARBURETOR CONTROL ASSEMBLY- - - - - -	J-1381-A	3.75
	Consists of		
1	Rod--Supercharger Carb. Control- - - - - -	J-11368	N.S.S.
1	Yoke--Adjustable - - - - - - - - - - - -	0279	.30
1	Nut--Plain Hex - - - - - - - - - - - - -	0280	.15
1	Yoke--Plain (Not Plated) - - - - - - - -	0281	.20
1	SUPER CARB. STRG. GEAR ROD ASSEMBLY- - - - -	J-1382	2.55
	Consists of		
1	Rod--Super Carb. Strg. Gear- - - - - - - -	J-11367	N.S.S.
1	Yoke--Adjustable - - - - - - - - - - - -	0279	.30
1	Nut--Plain Hex - - - - - - - - - - - - -	0280	.15
1	Sleeve--Super Carb. Control Shaft Brg. - -	J-1385	2.65
1	SUPER CARB. CONTROL SHAFT ASSEMBLY - - - - -	J-1388	8.15
	Consists of		
1	Shaft--Super Carb. Control - - - - - - - -	J-1383	2.25
1	Sleeve--Super Carb. Control Shaft Lever- -	J-1384	1.75
1	Lever--Super Carb. Control Shaft Accel.- -	J-1387	2.45
1	Lever--Super Carb. Control Stop- - - - - -	J-4402-A	1.45
1	Pin--Super Carb. Control Shaft Lever - - -	J-5260	.05
1	SUPER GEAR OIL NOZZLE TUBE ASSEMBLY- - - - -	J-1392-A	4.50
	Consists of		
1	Tube--Super Drive Worm Oil Feed- - - - - -	J-1393	N.S.S.
2	Nut--Flare Tube- - - - - - - - - - - - -	0513	.35
1	Packing--Super Drive Housing Drain - - - -	J-1394	.30
1	Bracket--Super Drive Housing Cover - - - -	J-1408	.90
1	Plate--Super Crankcase Reinforcing Front -	J-1411	.85
1	Plate--Super Crankcase Reinforcing Rear- -	J-1412-A	1.25
4	Stud--Super Drive Housing Cylinder - - - -	J-1413	.05
1	Nut--Super Universal Joint Rear Flange Lock	J-1427	1.25
2	Spacer--Super Drive Housing Drain- - - - -	J-1463	.35
1	Rod--Super Rear Tie - - - - - - - - - - -	J-1465	5.50
1	Rod--Super Front Tie - - - - - - - - - - -	J-1466	5.25
2	Gasket--Super Manifold Pipe- - - - - - - -	J-1473	.40
1	Hose--Super Water Pump - - - - - - - - - -	J-1476	.55
1	Manifold--Front Water- - - - - - - - - - -	J-1477	20.50
1	Elbow--Super Water Inlet Hose- - - - - - -	J-1478	2.25
1	Plate--Super Water Pump Drive- - - - - - -	J-1480	15.25
1	Shaft--Super Water Pump Drive- - - - - - -	J-1481	8.50
1	Flange--Super Water Outlet Hose- - - - - -	J-1482	2.60
1	Plate--Super Cyl. Water Inlet- - - - - - -	J-1483-A	6.60
1	Deflector--Super Cyl. Water Inlet- - - - -	J-1484	1.25
1	Plate--Super Cyl Water Shaft - - - - - - -	J-1485	4.75
1	Manifold--Super Rear Water - - - - - - - -	J-1486	23.75
1	Manifold--Super Rear Outlet- - - - - - - -	J-1487	2.75

PLEASE GIVE CAR NUMBER AND MOTOR NUMBER WHEN ORDERING PARTS

Printed in U.S.A.   March 1, 1934

MODEL J - SJ

DUESENBERG SUPERCHARGER PARTS SUPPLEMENT

No. Used Per Car	Description	Part Number	Price Each
	SUPER ASSEMBLY (CONTINUED)		
1	Pipe--Super Rear Pump Inlet - - - - - - - -	J-1488	7.75
2	Gasket--Super Rear Hose Flange- - - - - - -	J-1489	.35
4	Bolt--Super Universal Joint Rear- - - - - -	J-1490	.10
1	Flange--Super Universal Joint Rear- - - - -	J-1491	10.35
1	Flange--Super Universal Joint Front - - - -	J-1492	4.75
1	Nut--Super Universal Joint Rear Flange- - -	J-1493	3.60
1	Nut--Super Universal Joint Front Flange - -	J-1494	2.35
1	Shaft--Super Water Pump Sprocket- - - - - -	J-1495	19.75
1	Seal--Super & Water Pump Sprocket Shaft Oil	J-1496	5.85
1	Washer--Super Water Pump Sprocket Shaft Thrust	J-1497	3.75
6	Bolt--Super Universal Joint Front - - - - -	J-1498	.10
1	Strap--Super Water Pump Inlet Pipe- - - - -	J-1499-A	2.60
1	Grommet - - - - - - - - - - - - - - - - - -	JA-3126	.05
1	Lever--Super Carb. Control Shaft Clamp- - -	J-4428	1.95
1	Screw--Super Purolator Bracket Long - - - -	J-11353	.75
4	Bolt--Super Purolator Attaching - - - - - -	J-11362	.90
1	Pipe--Super Carb. Drain - - - - - - - - - -	J-11380	1.35
1	SUPER AIR SCREEN ASSEMBLY - - - - - - - - - -	J-11384	13.25
	Consists of		
1	Band--Super Carb. Air Screen Front- - - - -	J-11385	N.S.S.
1	Band--Super Carb. Air Screen Rear - - - - -	J-11386	N.S.S.
1	Sleeve--Super Carb. Air Screen Slotted- - -	J-11387	N.S.S.
1	End--Super Carb. Air Screen - - - - - - - -	J-11388	N.S.S.
1	Cylinder--Super Carb. Air Screen- - - - - -	J-11389	N.S.S.
4	Screw--Hex Head Cap 5/16-18 x 7/8 - - - - -	J-11391	.55
4	Nut--Plain Hex 5/16-24- - - - - - - - - - -	0101	.03
4	Nut--Plain Hex 3/8-24 - - - - - - - - - - -	0102	.02
1	Nut--Plain Hex 10-32- - - - - - - - - - - -	0105	.03
1	Pin--Cotter 1/8 x 1-14- - - - - - - - - - -	0122	.01
4	Pin--Cotter 1/16 x 3/8- - - - - - - - - - -	0123	.01
4	Pin--Clevis 3/16 S.A.E. - - - - - - - - - -	0127	.20
2	Plug--Pipe (1/8)- - - - - - - - - - - - - -	0133	.12
4	Rivet--Round Head 1/4 x 3/4 - - - - - - - -	0151	.02
1	Nut--Plain Hex 7/16 - 20- - - - - - - - - -	0173	.03
2	Screw--Hex Head Cap 3/8 - 24 x 7/8- - - - -	0178	.05
8	Nut--Plain Hex 1/4 - 28 - - - - - - - - - -	0193	.03
2	Screw--Hex Head Cap 3/8-24 x 1-3/8- - - - -	0210	.05
4	Washer--Lock 3/8 x 1/8 x 3/32 - - - - - - -	0232	.02
1	Washer--Lock 7/16 x 5/32 x 1/8- - - - - - -	0243	.02
1	Screw--Hex Head Cap 7/16-20 x 1-3/4 - - - -	0298	.05
4	Screw--Hex Head Cap 5/16 - 24 x 1-1/4 - - -	0314	.30
6	Washer--Lock 1/4 x 3/32 x 1/16- - - - - - -	0315	.02

PLEASE GIVE CAR NUMBER AND MOTOR NUMBER WHEN ORDERING PARTS

MODEL J - SJ

DUESENBERG SUPERCHARGER PARTS SUPPLEMENT

No. Used Per Car	Description	Part Number	Price Each
	SUPER ASSEMBLY (CONTINUED)		
1	Screw--Round Head Mach. 10-32 x 1/2 - - - -	0332	.05
1	Nut--Plain Hex- - - - - - - - - - - - - - -	0335	.06
12	Washer--Lock 5/16 x 1/8 x 1/16- - - - - - -	0350	.01
11	Screw--Round Head Machine - - - - - - - - -	0428	.03
8	Screw--Hex Head Cap 5/16-24 x 1 - - - - - -	0497	.30
17	Nut--Plain Hex 5/16 - 24- - - - - - - - - -	0503	.10
2	Nut--Plain Hex 1/2 - 20 - - - - - - - - - -	0504	.15
2	Screw--Hex Head Cap 3/8 - 16 x 7/8- - - - -	0507	.30
4	Screw--Hex Head Cap 5/16 - 24 x 1-1/2 - - -	0519	.15
1	Union--Compression Half 1/4 T x 1/8 P - - -	0524	.20
1	Nut--Compression 1/4" - - - - - - - - - - -	0525	.20
1	Sleeve--Compression 1/4" - - - - - - - - -	0526	.05
1	**EXTERNAL EXHAUST 153½" W. B. INSTALLATION** - -	J-15355	929.75
	Consists of		
1	**EXTERNAL EXHAUST INSTALLATION ASSEMBLY**- - - -	J-5380-C	432.50
	Consists of		
4	Gasket--Exhaust Manifold- - - - - - - - - -	J-969-**AA**	.40
8	Nuts--Acorn 3/8 - 24- - - - - - - - - - - -	J-1000	.60
8	Nuts--Exhaust Manifold Small- - - - - - - -	J-1003	.45
4	Nuts--Exhaust Manifold Large- - - - - - - -	J-1004	.65
1	Pan--Ext. Exh. Right Rear Center Side - - -	JR-7179	2.75
8	Nut--Engine Side Pan - - - - - - - - - - -	J-7280	.25
2	Branch--External Exhaust Front Y- - - - - -	J-15200	11.75
4	Flange--External Exhaust Pipe Split Inner -	J-15206	2.70
8	Gasket--External Exhaust Pipe Roung - - - -	J-15213	.10
2	Branch--External Exhaust Rear Y - - - - - -	J-15218	12.25
4	Flange--External Exhaust Pipe Split Outer -	J-15221	2.50
1	Header--External Exhaust- - - - - - - - - -	J-15226-**A**	70.75
4	Casing--External Exhaust Pipe Flex - - - -	J-15227	20.50
1	External Exhaust #1 Pipe Assembly - - - - -	J-15238	32.50
1	External Exhaust #2 Pipe Assembly - - - - -	J-15239	32.50
1	External Exhaust #3 Pipe Assembly - - - - -	J-15240	32.50
1	External Exhaust #4 Pipe Assembly - - - - -	J-15241	32.50
1	Bracket--External Exhaust Header- - - - - -	J-15250	3.15
2	Spring--External Exhaust Header Bracket - -	J-15251	.75
2	Cover--External Exhaust Rear Y Branch - - -	J-15256	16.50
4	Stud--External Exhaust Rear Y Branch & Cover	J-15257	.35
4	Stud--External Exhaust Front Y Branch - - -	J-15258	.30
4	Flange--Ext. Exh. Pipe Split Outer - Enameled	J-15300	3.10
4	Flange--Ext. Exhaust Pipe Split Inner " -	J-15301	3.10

PLEASE GIVE CAR NUMBER AND MOTOR NUMBER WHEN ORDERING PARTS

Printed in U.S.A.   March 1, 1934

MODEL J - SJ

DUESENBERG SUPERCHARGER PARTS SUPPLEMENT

No. Used Per Car	Description	Part Number	Price Each
	EXTERNAL EXHAUST INSTALLATION ASSEMBLY (CONT'D)		
1	Pan--Ext. Exh. Right Front Center Side- - -	J-17150	2.85
34	Nut--Plain Hex - - - - - - - - - - - - - -	0103	.03
2	Screw--Hex Head Cap - - - - - - - - - - -	0289	.05
2	Washer--Plain Cut 7/16 x 1 x 5/64 - - - - -	0374	.02
26	Screw--Hex Head Cap - - - - - - - - - - - -	0523	.05
6	Screw--Hex Head Cap (At Covers & Brkt.) - -	0528	.10
6	Clip--External Exh. Pipe Flex. Casing - - -	J-15237	.60
1	EXTERNAL EXHAUST FENDER & COLLARS INST. - - -	J-7351	125.50
	Consists of		
1	Assembly--Front Fender R. H.- - - - - - - -	J-7350	87.50
1	Collar--External Exhaust Fender #1- - - - -	J-15246	9.75
1	Collar--External Exhaust Fender #2- - - - -	J-15247	9.75
1	Collar--External Exhaust Fender #3- - - - -	J-15248	9.75
1	Collar--External Exhaust Fender #4- - - - -	J-15249	9.75
18	Washer--Lock- - - - - - - - - - - - - - - -	0459	.02
18	Screw--French Head Machine- - - - - - - - -	0521	.03
18	Nut--Plain Hex- - - - - - - - - - - - - - -	0522	.03
1	REAR CUTOUT 153½"W.B. INSTALLATION- - - - -	J-15360	51.90
	Consists of		
1	CUTOUT & PIPE 153½" W.B.- - - - - - - - - - -	J-15362	35.50
	Consists of		
1	CUTOUT ASSEMBLY - - - - - - - - - - - - - - -	J-15364	27.50
	Consists of		
1	CUTOUT BODY & LEVER ASSEMBLY- - - - - - - - -	J-15367	18.75
	Consists of		
1	Body--Cutout- - - - - - - - - - - - - - - -	J-15365	12.50
1	Lever--Cutout - - - - - - - - - - - - - - -	J-15368	5.75
1	Shaft--Cutout Lever - - - - - - - - - - - -	J-15369	.45
1	Pin--Cutout Lever Shaft - - - - - - - - - -	J-15370	.25
1	Spring--Cutout- - - - - - - - - - - - - - -	J-15373	.30
1	Cover--Cutout - - - - - - - - - - - - - - -	J-15366	4.85
1	Link--Brake Toggle- - - - - - - - - - - - -	J-15374	27.50
2	Pin--Cutout Cover Toggle- - - - - - - - - -	J-15371	.35
1	Pin--Cutout Lever Toggle- - - - - - - - - -	J-15372	.60
6	Pin--Cotter 1/8 x 7/8 - - - - - - - - - - -	0152	.01
1	Pipe--Cutout 153½" W. B.- - - - - - - - - -	J-15375	7.15
1	Bolt--Cutout Support Eye- - - - - - - - - -	J-15394	1.30
2	Link--Cutout Support- - - - - - - - - - - -	J-15393	.55
2	Screw--Hex Head Cap 3/8 - 24 x 1-1/4 Drl. -	J-5255	.05
2	Nut--Castle 3/8 - 24- - - - - - - - - - - -	0147	.03
2	Pin--Cotter- - - - - - - - - - - - - - - -	0180	.02

PLEASE GIVE CAR NUMBER AND MOTOR NUMBER WHEN ORDERING PARTS

Printed in U.S.A.   March 1, 1934

MODEL J - SJ

DUESENBERG SUPERCHARGER PARTS SUPPLEMENT

No. Used Per Car	Description	Part Number	Price Each
	REAR CUTOUT 153½" W.B. INST. (CONTINUED)		
2	Nut--Plain Hex 3/8 - 24 - - - - - - - - - -	0103	.03
2	Washer--Lock 3/8- - - - - - - - - - - - - -	0274	.02
1	Clamp--Cutout Pipe- - - - - - - - - - - - -	J-15291	1.85
1	Screw--Hex Head Cap 3/8 - 24 x 3/4- - - - -	0242	.05
1	CUTOUT CONT. HANDLE & BRACKET ASSEMBLY- - - -	J-15392	5.25
	Consists of		
1	Bracket--Cutout Control Handle- - - - - - -	J-15253-A	2.30
1	Shaft--Cutout Control - - - - - - - - - - -	J-15389	.55
1	Lever--Cutout Control Bottom- - - - - - - -	J-15388	.65
1	Screw--Hex Head Cap 5/16 - 24 x 7/8 - - - -	0165	.05
1	Pin--Muffler Cutout Control Shaft - - - - -	J-5260	.05
1	Handle--Muffler Cutout Control- - - - - - -	J-5231	1.45
1	Screw--Muffler Cutout Control Handle- - - -	J-5203	.25
5	Screw--Hex Head Cap 5/16 - 24 x 1 - - - - -	0300	.05
5	Nut--Plain Hex 5/16 - 24- - - - - - - - - -	0101	.03
5	Washer--Lock 5/16 - - - - - - - - - - - - -	0237	.02
1	CUTOUT CONTROL CABLE & PULLEY ASSEMBLY- - - -	J-15390	8.15
	Consists of		
1	Assembly--Cutout Control Cable 153½" W. B.-	J-15378	2.65
1	Pulley--Cutout Control Cable- - - - - - - -	J-15385	1.85
1	Bracket--Cutout Control Cable Pulley- - - -	J-15386	3.10
1	Bushing--Cutout Control Cable Pulley- - - -	J-15387	.30
1	Screw--Hex Head Cap 5/16 - 24 x 1-1/8 - - -	0509	.03
1	Nut--Plain Hex 5/16 - 24 - - - - - - - - - -	0101	.03
1	Washer--Lock 5/16 - - - - - - - - - - - - -	0237	.02
2	Washer--Plain Cut 5/16- - - - - - - - - - -	0299	.03
1	Joint--Ball 1/4 - 28 x 1/4 - 28 - - - - - -	J-5392	.30
1	Nut--Plain Hex 1/4 - 28 - - - - - - - - - -	0194	.03
1	Pin--Clevis 1/4" S.A.E. - - - - - - - - - -	0305	.05
1	Pin--Cotter 1/16 x 1/2- - - - - - - - - - -	0368	.01
1	Nut--Plain Hex 1/4 - 28 - - - - - - - - - -	0194	.03
1	Guard--Cutout Control Cable - - - - - - - -	J-15384	.50
	For Service in Field to replace front mounted cutout include		
1	Adapter--Rear Mounted Cutout Exh. Header	J-15284-S	2.25

PLEASE GIVE CAR NUMBER AND MOTOR NUMBER WHEN ORDERING **PARTS**

Printed in U.S.A.   March 1, 1934

MODEL J - SJ

DUESENBERG SUPERCHARGER PARTS SUPPLEMENT

No. Used Per Car	Description	Part Number	Price Each
	EXT. EXH. 153½" W. B. INST. (CONTINUED)		
1	HOOD COMPLETE ASSEMBLY- - - - - - - - - - - -	J-17100	338.60
	Consists of		
4	Button--Hood Rest - - - - - - - - - - - - -	JA-3858	.25
1	Top--Hood Right - - - - - - - - - - - - - -	J-7163-A	27.25
1	Top--Hood Left- - - - - - - - - - - - - - -	J-7164-A	27.25
1	Pin--Hood Center Hinge- - - - - - - - - - -	J-7254-A	1.25
2	Pin--Hood Side Hinge- - - - - - - - - - - -	J-7298-A	1.25
1	HOOD RIGHT SIDE UPPER PANEL ASSEMBLY- - - - -	J-17101	74.50
	Consists of		
1	Angle--Hood Right Side Upper Reinf. - - - -	J-7376	3.55
2	Half--Hood Panel Toggle Lock Upper- - - - -	J-7382	1.20
1	Panel--Hood Right Side Upper- - - - - - - -	J-17104	12.25
1	HOOD RIGHT SIDE UPPER SCREEN ASSEMBLY - - - -	J-17105	31.25
	Consists of		
1	Screen--Hood Right Side Upper - - - - - - -	J-17110	19.25
	(Does not include Plating)		
1	Frame--Hood Right Side Upper Screen - - - -	J-17111	2.80
	(Does not include Plating)		
6	Nut--Plain Hex 8-32 - - - - - - - - - - - -	0267	.03
17	Nut--Plain Hex 6-32 - - - - - - - - - - - -	0450	.03
23	Washer--Lock#8 x 5/64 x 3/64- - - - - - - -	0459	.02
6	Screw--French Head Mach. 8-32 x 3/4 - - - -	0508	.06
17	Washer--Plain 9/64 ID 7/16 OD 1/32 Th.- - -	0510	.02
6	Washer--Plain 11/64 x 7/16 x 1/32 - - - - -	0511	.02
17	Screw--French Head Mach. #6 - 32 x 1/2- - -	0521	.03
1	HOOD RIGHT SIDE LOWER PANEL ASSEMBLY- - - - -	J-17102	85.25
	Consists of		
1	Washer--Hood Lock Lever Spring- - - - - - -	JA-1601-A	.10
2	Button--Hood Pest- - - - - - - - - - - - -	JA-3858	.25
1	Lock--Hood- - - - - - - - - - - - - - - - -	J-7214	2.50
2	Stud--Hood Hook Pivot - - - - - - - - - - -	J-7217	.15
2	Bracket--Hood Hook- - - - - - - - - - - - -	J-7218	.95
1	Screw--Hood Lock Cylinder Spring- - - - - -	J-7219	.70
1	Bumper--Hood Center Bracket Rubber- - - - -	J-7226	.10
1	Handle--Hood Operating- - - - - - - - - - -	J-7229	1.60
1	Spring--Hood Lock Cylinder Ejector- - - - -	J-7231	.05
1	Plate--Hood Lock Cyl. Retaining - - - - - -	J-7232	.05
1	Bracket--Hood Lock Center - - - - - - - - -	J-7233	1.75

PLEASE GIVE CAR NUMBER AND MOTOR NUMBER WHEN ORDERING PARTS

MODEL J - SJ

DUESENBERG SUPERCHARGER PARTS SUPPLEMENT

No. Used Per Car	Description	Part Number	Price Each
1	Lever--Hood Lock Operating- - - - - - - - -	J-7234	1.50
1	Hook--Hood R. H.- - - - - - - - - - - - - - -	J-7240	1.40
1	Hook--Hood L. H.- - - - - - - - - - - - - - -	J-7241	1.40
2	Bushing--Hood Hook Pivot- - - - - - - — - - -	J-7244	.10
2	Washer--Hood Hook Retainer- - - - - - - - - -	J-7245	.10
1	Angle--Hood Right Side Lower Reinforc.- - - -	J-7377	3.50
2	Half--Hood Panel Toggle Lock Lower- - - - -	J-7383	1.20
2	Key--Hood Panel Toggle Lock - - - - - - - -	J-7384	.50
1	Panel--Hood Right Side Lower- - - - - - - -	J-17106	5.40
1	HOOD RIGHT SIDE LOWER SCREEN ASSEMBLY - - - -	J-17107	22.15
	Consists of		
1	Screen--Hood Right Side Lower - - - - - - -	J-17112	19.15
1	Frame--Hood Right Side Lower Screen - - - -	J-17113	2.80
3	Pin-Cotter- - - - - - - - - - - - - - - - -	0120	.05
3	Nut--Castle - - - - - - - - - - - - - - - -	0147	.03
2	Rivet--Round Head - - - - - - - - - - - - -	0176	.03
2	Nut--Plain Hex- - - - - - - - - - - - - - -	0194	.03
6	Nut--Plain Hex 8-32 - - - - - - - - - - - -	0267	.03
20	Rivet--Round Head - - - - - - - - - - - - -	0390	.02
1	Screw--Round Head Machine - --- - - - - - --	0418	.04
17	Nut--Plain Hex 6-32 - - - - - - - - - - - -	0450	.03
23	Washer--Lock #8 x 5/64 x 3/64 - - - - - -	0459	.02
6	Screw--French Head Mach. 8-32 x 3/4 - - - -	0508	.06
17	Washer--Plain 9/64 ID 7/16 OD 1/32 Th.- - -	0510	.02
6	Washer--Plain 11/64 x 7/16 x 1/32 - - - - -	0511	.02
17	Screw--French Hd. Mach. #6 - 32 x 1/2 - - -	0521	.03
1	HOOD LEFT SIDE PANEL ASSEMBLY - - - - - - - -	J-17103	102.25
	Consists of		
1	Washer--Hood Lock Lever Spring- - - - - - -	JA-1601-A	.10
2	Button--Hood Rest- - - - - - - - - - - - -	JA-3858	.25
1	Lock--Hood- - - - - - - - - - - - - - - - -	J-7214	2.50
2	Stud--Hood Hook Pivot - - - - - - - - - - -	J-7217	.15
2	Bracket--Hood Hook- - - - - - - - - - - - -	J-7218	.95
1	Screw--Hood Lock Cyl. Spring- - - - - - - -	J-7219	.10
1	Bumper--Hood Center Bracket Rubber- - - - -	J-7226	.10
1	Handle--Hood Operating- - - - - - - - - - -	J-7229	1.60
1	Spring--Hood Lock Cyl. Ejector- - - - - - -	J-7231	.05
1	Plate--Hood Lock Cyl. Retaining - - - - - -	J-7232	.05
1	Bracket--Hood Lock Center - - - - - - - - -	J-7233	1.75
1	Lever--Hood Lock Operating- - - - - - - - -	J-7234	1.50

PLEASE GIVE CAR NUMBER AND MOTOR NUMBER **WHEN** ORDERING PARTS

Printed in U.S.A.

March 1, 1934

MODEL J - SJ

DUESENBERG SUPERCHARGER PARTS SUPPLEMENT

No. Used Per Car	Description	Part Number	Price Each
	HOOD LEFT SIDE PANEL ASSEMBLY (CONTINUED)		
1	Hook--R.H.- - - - - - - - - - - - - - - - - -	J-7240	1.40
1	Hook--L.H.- - - - - - - - - - - - - - - - - -	J-7241	1.40
2	Bushing--Hood Hook Pivot- - - - - - - - -	J-7244	.10
2	Washer--Hood Hook Retaining - - - - - - -	J-7245	.10
1	HOOD LEFT SIDE SCREEN ASSEMBLY- - - - - - -	J-7373	44.25
	Consists of		
1	Screen-Hood Left Side (Not Plated)- - - -	J-7374	38.25
1	Frame--Hood Left Side Screen (Not Plated-	J-7375	5.60
1	Panel--Hood Left Side - - - - - - - - - -	J-17108	9.75
3	Pin--Cotter - - - - - - - - - - - - - - -	0120	.05
3	Nut--Castle - - - - - - - - - - - - - - -	0147	.03
2	Rivet--Round Head - - - - - - - - - - - -	0176	.03
2	Nut--Plain Hex- - - - - - - - - - - - - -	0194	.03
20	Rivet--Round Head - - - - - - - - - - - -	0390	.02
1	Screw--Round Head Machine - - - - - - - -	0418	.04
35	Nut--Plain Hex 6-32 - - - - - - - - - - -	0450	.03
35	Washer--Lock #8 x 5/64 x 3/64 - - - - - -	0459	.02
35	Washer--Plain 9/64 ID 7/16 OD 1/32 Th.- -	0510	.02
35	Screw--French Head Mach. #6 - 32 x 1/2- -	0521	.03
4	Nut--Plain Hex- - - - - - - - - - - - - -	0194	.03
1	EXTERNAL EXHAUST 142½" W.B. INSTALLATION- - -	J-15354	927.75
	Consists of		
1	EXTERNAL EXHAUST PIPE & HEADER INST.- - - - -	J-538p-C	432.50
	See List Above		
1	FENDERS & COLLARS INSTALLATION- - - - - - -	J-7351	125.50
	See List Above		
1	CUTOUT 142½" W.B. INSTALLATION- - - - - - -	J-15361	50.90
	Consists of		
1	CUTOUT & PIPE 142½" W.B. ASSEMBLY - - - - -	J-15363	34.25
	Consists of		
1	CUTOUT ASSEMBLY - - - - - - - - - - - - - - -	J-15364	27.50
	Consists of		
1	CUTOUT BODY & LEVER ASSEMBLY- - - - - - - -	J-15367	18.75
	Consists of		
1	Body-Cutout - - - - - - - - - - - - - - -	J-15365	12.50
1	Lever--Cutout - - - - - - - - - - - - - -	J-15368	5.75
1	Shaft--Cutout Lever - - - - - - - - - - -	J-15369	.45
1	Pin--Cutout Lever Shaft - - - - - - - - -	J-15370	.25

PLEASE GIVE CAR NUMBER AND MOTOR NUMBER WHEN ORDERING PARTS

Printed in U.S.A.   March 1, 1934

MODEL J - SJ

DUESENBERG SUPER CHARGER PARTS SUPPLEMENT

No. Used Per Car	Description	Part Number	Price Each
	CUTOUT ASSEMBLY (CONTINUED)		
1	Spring--Cutout- - - - - - - - - - - - - - -	J-15373	.30
1	Cover--Cutout - - - - - - - - - - - - - - -	J-15366	5.75
1	Link--Brake Toggle- - - - - - - - - - - - -	J-15374	1.10
2	Pin--Cutout Cover Toggle- - - - - - - - - -	J-15371	.35
1	Pin--Cutout Lever Toggle- - - - - - - - - -	J-15372	.60
6	Pin--Cotter 1/8 x 7/8 - - - - - - - - - - -	0152	.01
1	Pipe--Cutout 142½" W.B. - - - - - - - - - -	J-15376	5.75
1	Bolt--Cutout Support Eye- - - - - - - - - -	J-15394	1.30
2	Link--Cutout Support- - - - - - - - - - - -	J-15393	.55
2	Screw--Hex Head Cap 3/8 - 24 x 1-1/4 Drld.-	J-5355	.05
2	Nut--Castle 3/8 -24 - - - - - - - - - - - -	0147	.03
2	Pin--Cotter - - - - - - - - - - - - - - - -	0180	.02
2	Nut--Plain Hex 3/8 - 24 - - - - - - - - - -	0103	.03
2	Washer--Lock 3/8- - - - - - - - - - - - - -	0274	.02
1	Clamp--Cutout Pipe - - - - - - - - - - - - -	J-15291	1.85
1	Screw--Hex Head Cap 3/8 - 24 x 3/4- - - - -	0242	.05
1	CUTOUT CONT. HANDLE & BRACKET ASSEMBLY- - -	J-15392	5.25
	Consists of		
1	Bracket--Cutout Control Handle- - - - - -	J-15253-A	2.30
1	Shaft--Cutout Control - - - - - - - - - -	J-15389	.55
1	Lever--Cutout Control Bottom- - - - - - -	J-15388	.65
1	Screw--Hex Head Cap 5/16 - 24 x 7/8 - - -	0165	.05
1	Pin--Muffler Cutout Control Shaft - - - -	J-5260	.05
1	Handle--Muffler Cutout Control- - - - - -	J-5231	1.45
1	Screw--Muffler Cutout Control Handle- - -	J-5203	.25
5	Screw--Hex Head Cap 5/16 - 24 x 1 - - - -	0300	.05
5	Nut--Plain Hex 5/16 - 24- - - - - - - - -	0101	.03
5	Washer--Lock 5/16- - - - - - - - - - - - -	0237	.02
1	CUTOUT CONTROL CABLE & PULLEY ASSEMBLY - - -	J-15391	8.10
	Consists of		
1	CUTOUT CONTROL CABLE 142½" W.B. ASSEMBLY- -	J-15380	2.55
	Pulley--Cutout Control Cable- - - - - - -	J-15385	1.85
1	Bracket--Cutout Control Cable Pulley- - -	J-15386	3.10
1	Bushing--Cutout Control Cable Pulley- - -	J-15387	.30
1	Screw--Hex Head Cap 5/16 - 24 x 1-1/8 - -	0509	.03
1	Nut--Plain Hex 5/16 - 24- - - - - - - - -	0101	.03
1	Washer--Lock 5/16- - - - - - - - - - - - -	0237	.02
2	Washer--Plain Cut 5/16- - - - - - - - - -	0299	.03
1	Joint--Ball 1/4 - 28 x 1/4 - 28 - - - - -	J-5392	.30
1	Nut--Plain Hex 1/4 - 28 - - - - - - - - -	0194	.03

PLEASE GIVE CAR NUMBER AND MOTOR NUMBER WHEN ORDERING PARTS

MODEL J - SJ

DUESENBERG SUPERCHARGER PARTS SUPPLEMENT

No. Used Per Car	Description	Part Number	Price Each
	CUTOUT 142½" W.B. INST. (CONTINUED)		
1	Pin--Clevis 1/4" S.A.E. - - - - - - - - - -	0305	.05
1	Pin--Cotter 1/16 x 1/2- - - - - - - - - - -	0368	.01
1	Nut--Plain Hex 1/4-28 - - - - - - - - - - -	0194	.03
	For Service in field to replace front mounted cutout include		
1	Adapter--Rear Mounted Cutout Exh. Header- -	J-15284-S	2.25
1	HOOD COMPLETE ASSEMBLY - - - - - - - - - - -	J-17100	338.60
	See List Above		

NOTE: N. S. S. - Not Serviced Separately.

SUPERCHARGER PART NUMBER INDEX GIVING PAGE LOCATION

PLEASE GIVE CAR NUMBER AND MOTOR NUMBER WHEN ORDERING PARTS

MODEL J - SJ

SUPERCHARGER PART NUMBER INDEX GIVING PAGE LOCATION

Part No.	Page No.	Part No.	Page No.
J-995-**AA**	1	J-1400	2
J-998	1	J-1401	1
J-1000	7	J-1402	3
J-1001	1	J-1403	2
J-1003	7	J-1404-**A**	2
J-1004	7	J-1408	5
J-1011	1	J-1409	2
J-1050	1	J-1410-**A**	1
J-1350-**A**	1	J-1411	5
J-1351-**A**	1	J-1412-**A**	5
J-1352-**A**	2	J-1413	5
J-1353	3	J-1414	2
J-1354-**A**	3	J-1415	2
J-1355	3	J-1416	2
J-1356	2	J-1417-**A**	1
J-1357	2	J-1418	1
J-1358-**A**	1	J-1419	2
J-1359-**A**	1	J-1420-**A**	2
J-1360	2	J-1421	2
J-1361-**A**	1	J-1422	2
J-1362	4	J-1424	2
J-1363	4	J-1426	2
J-1364	4	J-1427	2 & 5
J-1367	4	J-1428	2
J-1368	4	J-1429	2
J-1369	4	J-1430	2
J-1370	3	J-1431	4
J-1432	3	J-1481	5
J-1433	2	J-1482	5
J-1434	2	J-1483-**A**	5
J-1435	2	J-1484	5
J-1437	3	J-1485	5
J-1440	1	J-1486	5
J-1441	3	J-1487	5
J-1442	3	J-1488	6
J-1443	3	J-1489	6
J-1444	3	J-1490	6
J-1445	3	J-1491	2 & 6
J-1446	3	J-1492	6
J-1447	3	J-1493	2 & 6
J-1448-**A**	3	J-1494	6
J-1449-**A**	3	J-1495	6
J-1450-**A**	3	J-1496	6

PLEASE GIVE CAR NUMBER AND MOTOR NUMBER **WHEN** ORDERING PARTS

Printed in U.S.A.   March 1, 1934

MODEL J - SJ

SUPERCHARGER PART NUMBER INDEX GIVING PAGE LOCATION

PLEASE GIVE CAR NUMBER AND MOTOR NUMBER WHEN ORDERING PARTS

Printed in U.S.A.   March 1, 1934

MODEL J - SJ

SUPERCHARGER PART NUMBER INDEX GIVING PAGE LOCATION

Part No.	Page No.	Part No.	Page No.
J-7351	8 & 12	J-15246	8
J-7373	12	J-15247	8
J-7374	12	J-15248	8
J-7375	12	J-15249	8
J-7376	10	J-15250	7
J-7377	11	J-15251	7
J-7382	10	J-15253-**A**	9 & 13
J-7383	11	J-15256	7
J-7384	11	J-15257	7
J-11350	2	J-15258	7
J-11351	3 & 4	J-15284-S	9 & 14
J-11352	3	J-15291	9 & 13
J-11353	6	J-15300	7
J-11362	6	J-15301	7
J-11365	2	J-15354	1 & 12
J-11366	3	J-15355	7
J-11367	5	J-15360	8
J-11368	5	J-15361	12
J-11376	4	J-15362	8
J-11380	6	J-15363	12
J-11384	6	J-15364	8 & 12
J-11385	6	J-15365	8 & 12
J-11386	6	J-15366	8 & 13
J-11387	6	J-15367	8 & 12
J-11388	6	J-15368	8 & 12
J-11389	6	J-15369	8 & 12
J-15370	8 & 12	0127	6
J-15371	8 & 13	0133	3 & 6
J-15372	8 & 13	0134	4
J-15373	8 & 13	0147	8, 11, 12 & 13
J-15374	8 & 13	0151	6
J-15375	8	0152	8 & 13
J-15376	13	0165	9 & 13
J-15378	9	0173	6
J-15380	13	0176	11 & 12
J-15384	9	0180	8 & 13
J-15385	9 & 13	0193	6
J-15386	9 & 13	0194	9, 11, 12 & 14
J-15387	9 & 13	0210	6
J-15388	9 & 13	0222	4
J-15389	9 & 13	0225	3
J-15390	9	0232	6

PLEASE GIVE CAR NUMBER AND MOTOR NUMBER WHEN ORDERING PARTS

Printed in U.S.A.   March 1, 1934

MODEL J - SJ

SUPERCHARGER PART NUMBER INDEX GIVING PAGE LOCATION

Part No.	Page No.	Part No.	Page No.
J-15391	13	0237	9 & 13
J-15392	9 & 13	0242	9
J-15393	8 & 13	0243	6
J-15394	8 & 13	0247	4 & 13
J-17100	10 & 14	0258	4
J-17101	10	0267	10 & 11
J-17102	10	0274	9 & 13
J-17103	11	0279	5
J-17104	10	0280	5
J-17105	10	0281	5
J-17106	11	0289	8
J-17107	11	0298	6
J-17108	12	0299	9 & 13
J-17110	10	0300	9 & 13
J-17111	10	0305	9 & 14
J-17112	11	0314	6
J-17113	11	0315	6
J-17150	8	0332	7
		0335	7
0100	2	0350	7
0101	6, 9, 13	0368	9 & 14
0102	6	0374	8
0103	4, 8, 9, 13	0390	11 & 12
0105	6	0418	11 & 12
0120	11 & 12	0428	7
0122	6	0445	4
0123	6	0450	10, 11 & 12
0457	3	0511	10 & 11
0459	8, 10, 11 & 12	0513	5
0492	3	0519	7
0497	7	0520	2
0499	3 & 4	0521	8, 10, 11 & 12
0502	3	0522	8
0503	7	0523	8
0504	7	0524	7
0505	2 & 3	0525	7
0507	7	0526	7
0508	10 & 11	0528	8
0509	9 & 13		
0510	10, 11 & 12		

PLEASE GIVE CAR NUMBER AND MOTOR NUMBER WHEN ORDERING PARTS

Printed in U.S.A.   March 1, 1934

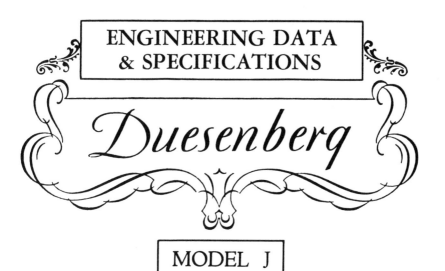

ENGINEERING DATA
& SPECIFICATIONS

Duesenberg

MODEL J

Compiled by the

General Service Department

DUESENBERG, INC.

Indianapolis, Ind., U. S. A.

ENGINEERING DATA

DUESENBERG MODEL J SPECIFICATIONS

GENERAL ENGINE

```
Number of cylinders - - - - - - - - - - - - - - - - - - - - - - - - 8
Valve Arrangement  - - - - - - - - - - - - - - - 4-valve. Overhead
Bore and Stroke - - - - - - - - - - - - - - - - - - 3-3/4 x 4-3/4
Engine Mounting - - - - - Bolts through rubber pads & springs.
                                            (Front & Rear)
Number of points suspension - - - - - - - - - - - - - - - - - - - 4
Engine Make - - - - - - - - - - - - - - - - - - - - - - - Duesenberg
Model Designation - - - - - - - - - - - - - - - - - - - - - - - "J"
Cylinder Arrangement - - - - - - - - - - - - - - - - - Straight 8
Cylinder Bore Finish - - - - - - - - - - - - - - - - - - - Ground
Number of Cylinders cast en bloc - - - - - - - - - - - - - - 8
Crankcase Material, upper half - - - - - - Gray Cast Iron
Crankcase Material, lower half - - - - - - - - Aluminum
Piston Displacement - - - - - - - - - - - - - - - 420 cu. in.
Taxable Horsepower - - - - - - - - - - - - - - - - - - - - - 45
Maximum Developed Horsepower at 4200 R.P.M. - - - - - - - 265
Compression ratio - - - - - - - - - - - - - - - - - - - 5.2 to 1
Engine serial numbers begin with - - - - - - - - - - - J-099
Intake side - - - - - - - - - - - - - - - - - - - - - - - - - Left
Exhaust side - - - - - - - - - - - - - - - - - - - - - - - - Right
Engine Oil Filler side - - - - - - - - - - - - - - - - - Left
Flywheel Diameter - - - - - - - - - - - - - - - - - - - 14 15/16
Engine weight approx. - - - - - - - - - - - - - - - - - 1150#
```

PISTON AND RINGS

```
Piston Make - - - - - - - - - - - - - - - - - - - - - - - Ray-Day
Piston Material - - - - - - - - - - - - - - - - - Aluminum Alloy
Piston, Distance between bosses - - - - - - - - - - - 1-9/16
Piston Type - - - - - - - - - - - - - - - - - - Split Full Skt.
Piston Weight in ounces - - - - - - - - - - - - - - - - - 20
Piston Length - - - - - - - - - - - - - - - - - - - - - 4-3/8
Piston Clearance, top - - - - - - - - - - - - - - - - - .022"
Piston Clearance, bottom - - - - - - - - - - - - - - - .0035"
Piston Diameter - - - - - - - - - - - - - - - - - - - - 3.747"
Piston Ring Groove Depth, Oil - - - - - - - - - - - - .166"
Piston Ring Groove Depth, Compression - - - - - - - - .161"
Lower Oil Groove Drilled Radially - - - - - - - - - - Yes
Piston Clearance, second land - - - - - - - - - - - - .018"
Piston Clearance, third land - - - - - - - - - - - - - .018"
Piston Clearance, fourth land - - - - - - - - - - - - .018"
Number of Oil Rings used per piston - - - - - - - - - - - 1
Width of Oil Ring - - - - - - - - - - - - - - - - - - - 3/16"
Number of Compression Rings used per piston - - - - - - - 3
Width of Compression Ring - - - - - - - - - - - - - - - 1/8"
Maximum wall thickness of rings - - - - - - - - .140" to .150"
Piston Ring Make - - - - - - - - - - - - - - - Perfect Circle
Number of rings above pin - - - - - - - - - - - - - - - - 4
Piston length, top to pin center - - - - - - - - - - 2-5/8"
Pin Hole Diameter - - Finish ream 1.06225 - 1.060175 Room tem.
Total Number Piston Rings used - - - - - - - - - - - - - 4
```

DUESENBERG MODEL J SPECIFICATIONS

PISTON AND RINGS

```
Width of Compression Ring - - - - - - - - - - - - - - 1/8"
Maximum wall thickness of rings - - - - - - - .140" to .150"
Piston Ring Make - - - - - - - - - - - - - - Perfect Circle
Number of rings above pin - - - - - - - - - - - - - - - 4
Piston length, top to pin center - - - - - - - - - - 2-5/8"
Pin Hole Diameter - - Finish ream 1.06225 - 1.06175 Room tem.
Total Number Piston Rings used - - - - - - - - - - - - - 4
```

RODS AND PINS

```
Wristpin length - - - - - - - - - - - - - - - - - - 3-17/64"
Wristpin diameter - - - - - - - - - - - - - - - - - 1-1/16"
Is Wristpin locked in rod or floating - - - - - - Floating
Wristpin Locking method - - - - - - - - - - - - - Lockrings
Wristpin Bushing length - - - - - - - - - - - - - -1-15/32"
Wristpin Bushing outside diameter - - - - - - - - - 1.254"
Wristpin Bushing inside diameter - - - - - - Rough 1.046"
Wristpin Hole finish after assem. - - - 1.0625 Diamond Bored
Connecting Rod Length, center to center - - - - - 9-13/16"
Connecting Rod Material - - - - - - - - Duralumin Forging
Connecting Rod Cap Material - - - - - - - - - Steel   "
Connecting Rod Weight in ounces Less cap bolts & bushing - 18
Connecting Rod Bearing Material - - - - - - - - Mogul Alloy
Connecting Rod Bearing Make - - - - - - - - - - Duesenberg
Connecting Rod Bearing Finish - - - - - - - - - - Reamed
Crankpin diameter and length - - - - - - - 2.4375  x  1.753
                                            2.4365  x  1.747
Connecting Rod Bearing Clearance - - - - - - - - - - .002"
Connecting Rod Bearing poured or separate - - - - - Poured
```

CRANKSHAFT, COUNTERWEIGHTS, & VIBRATION DAMPER

```
Vibration Damper Used - - - - - - - - - - - - - - - - Yes
Vibration Damper Type - - - - - - - - - Duesenberg Mercury
Front Flywheel Used - - - - - - - - - - - - - - - - - No
Crankshaft Completely machined - - - - - - - - - - - Yes
Crankshaft Counterweights, number used - - - - - - - - 8
Amount of Crankshaft offset - - - - - - - - - - - - 1/4"
Which Main bearing takes Thrust - - - - - - - - - Front
Crankshaft end play - - - - - - - - - - - - - - - .003"
Main Bearing Material - - - - - - - - - - - - Mogul Alloy
Main Bearings, number of - - - - - - - - - - - - - - 5
Main Bearings interchangeable? - - - - - - - - - - - No
No. 1 Main Brg.Journal dia. x length - - - 2-3/4 x 3-5/16"
```

CRANKSHAFT, COUNTERWEIGHTS, & VIBRATION DAMPER

```
No. 2 Main Brg. Journal dia. x length - - - 2-3/4 x 1-7/8"
No. 3 Main Brg. Journal dia. x length - - - 2-3/4 x 2-3/8"
No. 4 Main Brg. Journal dia. x length - - - 2-3/4 x 1-7/8"
No. 5 Main Brg. Journal dia. x length - - - 2-3/4 x 2-7/8"
Crankshaft Sprocket Make - - - - - - - - - - - Link Belt
```

DUESENBERG MODEL J SPECIFICATIONS

CAMSHAFT AND CHAIN DRIVE

```
Camshaft Drive - - - - - - - - - - - - - - - - - - - - - - Chain
Timing Chain Make - - - - - - - - - - - - - - - - - - Link Belt
Upper Timing Chain Length - - - - - - - - - - - - - - 51-3/4"
Upper Timing Chain Width - - - - - - - - - - - - - - 1-11/16"
Lower Timing Chain Length - - - - - - - - - - - - - - 47-1/4"
Lower Timing Chain Width - - - - - - - - - - - - - - - 2"
Timing Chain Pitch - - - - - - - - - - - - - - - - - - 3/8"
Timing Chain Adjustment - - Automatic takeup eccentric & Spring
```

VALVES

```
Intake Valve Make - - - - - - - - - - - Thompson Products, Inc.
Exhaust Valve Make - - - - - - - - - - - Thompson Products, Inc.
Intake Valve Head Material - - - - - - - Chrome-nickel steel
Exhaust Valve Head Material - - -- - - - Silchrome Steel #1
Intake Valve Head Actual overall dia. - - - - - - - - 1-1/2"
Exhaust Valve Head Actual overall dia. - - - - - - - 1-7/16"
Angle of Intake Valve Seat - - - - - - - - - - - - - 30 degrees
Angle of Exhaust Valve Seat - - - - - - - - - - - - 30 degrees
Intake Valve Stem Material - - - - - - - - - Chrome-nickel Steel
Exhaust Valve Stem Material - - - - - - Silchrome Steel #1
Intake Valve Stem length - - - - - - - - - - - - - - 5.002
Exhaust Valve Stem Length - - - - - - - - - - - - - 4.992
Intake Valve Stem dia. - - - - - - - - - - - - - - - 11/32"
Exhaust Valve Stem dia. - - - - - - - - - - - - - - 11/32"
Intake Valve Stem end style - - - - - - - - - - - - 3 grooves
Exhaust Valve Stem end style - - - - - - - - - - - - 3 grooves
Intake Valve lift - - - - - - - - - - - - - - - - - - .360"
Exhaust Valve lift - - - - - - - - - - - - - - - - - .360"
Are Valves with oversized stems made for replacement? - No
Are Valve Guides removable - - - - - - - - - - - - - - Yes
Distance from top of seat to end of stem inlet - - - 5-5/64"
Distance from top of seat to end of stem exhaust - - 5-5/64"
Inner Valve Spring Pressure and length with valve
                    closed - - - - - - 26 lb.@1-15/16
Inner Valve Spring Pressure & length with valve
                    open - - - - - 36-40 lb. @ 1-19/32
Outer Valve Spring Pressure & length with valve
                    closed - - - - 35-40 lb. @ 1 29/32
Outer Valve Spring Pressure & length with valve
                    open - - - - 65-70 lb. @ 1 1/4
Tappet Clearance for valve timing, intake - - - - - - - .025"
Tappet clearance for valve timing, exhaust - - - - - - - .025"
Valve Timing, intake opens - - - - - - - - - - - 6° B.T.C.
Valve Timing, intake closes - - - - - - - - - - - 40° P.B.C.
Valve Timing, exhaust opens - - - - - - - - - - - 40° B.B.C.
Valve Timing, exhaust closes - - - - - - - - - - 14° P.T.C.
```

STARTING MOTOR

```
Starting Motor Make - - - - - - - - - - - - - - - - Delco-Remy
Starting Motor Type of Drive - - - - - - - - - - - - Bendix
```

DUESENBERG MODEL J SPECIFICATIONS

STARTING MOTOR

```
Starting Motor pinion Meshes with front or rear of
                         flywheel - - - - - - - - - - - Front
Number of teeth in flywheel - - - - - - - - - - - - - - - - 119
Face width of flywheel Teeth - - - - - - - - - - - - - 11/16"
Flywheel teeth integral or steel ring? - - - - - - Stl. Ring
Gear Ratio between starter armature & flywheel? - 10 to 119
Location of starting motor - - - Left side in front of flywheel
Starting switch location - - - - - - - - - On Starting Motor
Starting switch control - - - - - - - - - - - - Pull wire
```

GENERATOR

```
Generator Make - - - - - - - - - - - - - - - - Delco-Remy
Generator Drive - - - Flexible Coupling Accessory Shaft
Generator Voltage Regulation, type of - - - - - - - - 3 Brush
Cutout Relay Make - - - - - - - - - - - - - - - - - Delco-Remy
Generator Field Fuse Capacity - - - - - - - - - - None Used
Generator Armature speed at cutout closing - - - - - - - 500
Generator Armature speed at cutout opening - - - - - - - 200
Voltage at cutout closing - - - - - - - - - - - - - 7 to 7.5
Amperes to open cutout - - - - - - - - - - - - - - Reverse 2.5
Ammeter Make - - - - - - - - - - - - - - - - - - - - National
Generator to Engine Speed Ratio - - - - - - - - - - - 1 to 1
```

IGNITION

```
Ignition Unit Make - - - - - - - - Duesenberg Spe. Delco-Remy
Ignition Unit Current Source - - - - - - - - - - - Battery
Ignition Unit Manual Advance, degrees - - - Crankshaft 20°
Ignition Unit Automatic Advance, degrees -      "      18°
Ignition Unit Breaker Gap - - - - - - - - - - - - .018 - .024"
Timing in degrees with spark advanced manually - - - - - -
                      1 1/2" on 14 15/16" dia. flywheel
Firing order - - - - - - - - - - - - - - - 1-6-2-5-8-3-7-4
Ignition Coil Make - - - - - - - - - - - - - - - Delco-Remy
Ignition switch make - - - - - - - - - - - - - Delco -Remy
Spark Plug Thread - - - - - - - - - - - - Metric 18 x 1-1/2 mm.
Spark Plug Make - - - - - - - - - - - - - - Champion
Spark Plug Gap - - - - - - - - - - - - - - - - - .025
Ignition Cable Make - - - - - - - - - - - - - Packard
Location of Coil - - - - - - - - - - - - - Back of Inst. Bd.
```

LAMPS & HORN

```
Lighting Switch Make - - - - - - - - - - - - - - Delco-Remy
Location of Switch - - - - - - - - At lower end of Strg. Gear
Candle Power of Headlights - - - - - - - - - - - - - 21 c. p.
Method by which lights are dimmed - - - - - - - Depressed Beam
Candle Power of Cowl Lamps - - - - - - - - - - - - - 3 c. p.
Candle Power of Tail Light - - - - - - - - - - - - - 3 c. p.
Candle Power of Stop Light - - - - - - - - - - - - - 21 c. p.
Candle Power of Backup Light - - - - - - - - - - - 21 C. p.
   (i.e  Tail, Stop & Backup lights integral in one housing)
```

DUESENBERG MODEL J SPECIFICATIONS

LAMPS & HORN

```
Are Tail and Dash Lights in Series - - - - - - - - - No
Headlight Make - - - - - - - - - - - - - Special for Duesen-
                                          berg (I.L.)
Headlight Reflector Type - - - - - - - Special for Duesen-
                                          berg (I.L.)
Headlight Lens Make - - - - - - - - - - Monogram
Headlight Lens Diameter - - - - - - - - - - - - - - 11-1/2"
Cowl Light Make - - - - - - - - - - - - Special for Duesen-
                                          berg (I.L.)
Tail Light Make - - - - - - - - - - - - Special for Duesen-
                                          berg (I.L.)
Instrument Board Lights - - - - - - - - Duesenberg
Instrument Board Light Candlepower - - - - - - - - - 3 c. p.
Signal Lights on Instrument Board - - - - - - - - Duesenberg
Candlepower of Signal Lights - - - - - - - - - - 1-1/2 c. p.
Horn - - - - - - - - - - - - - - - - - - - - - Delco-Remy Trumpet
                                                            Type
Location - - - - - - - - - - - - - - - - - - Under Headlamps
Horn type, vibrator or motor - - - - - - - - Vibrator
Amperage Draw of Horn - - - - - - - - - - - - Single 8-11
                                          Matched Pair 14-16
```

BATTERY

```
Battery Make ---------------------------Exide
Battery Model --------------------------3-XCRV-21-2-G
Battery Length -------------------------20-7/16"
Battery Width --------------------------5-1/2"
Battery Height -------------------------8-11/16"
Battery Cell Arrangement ---------------Longitudinal
Battery Shipped Wet or Dry -------------As Specified
Battery Capacity, Ampere Hours ----------160
Battery Voltage ------------------------6 - 8
Which Battery Terminal is grounded ------Negative
Engine Connection ----------------------Ground Strap to Frame
Battery Location -----------------------Right Running Bd.
```

SIGNAL BOX

```
Make -----------------------------------Duesenberg
Purpose ------------------1. To operate signal lights on
                            inst. board showing how chassis
                            lubrication is functioning, when
                            battery needs water, & when
                            motor needs lub.
                         2. To compel chassis Lubricator
                            Pump to operate once every 60
                            to 80 miles.
Location -----------On Left Side of Engine in rear of Oil
                    Filler, in front of Fuel Pump
Type of Mechanism-----------------Planetary Gear Reduction
Method of Drive -------------------Special Drive Shaft
```

DUESENBERG MODEL J SPECIFICATIONS

SIGNAL BOX

Material of Housing ---------------Die Cast Alloy
Material of Housing Cover --------Die Cast Alloy
Bearings ------------------------One for Drive Shaft (Die
                                                    Cast Alloy)

LUBRICATION METHODS

Overhead Cams & Valve Tappets -----------Oil Bath
Lubricating System --------------------Pressure
Oil Pressure to Main Bearings? ----------Yes
Oil Pressure to Conn Rods? --------------Yes
Oil Pressure to Wristpins? --------------Yes
Oil Pressure to Camshaft Bearings? ------Yes
Timing Gear Lubrication -----------------Positive
Oil Pump Type --------------------------Gear Duesenberg
Normal Oil Pressure -------------------50 lbs. at 50 MPH
Pressure at which relief valve opens --25#
Capacity of Oil Reservoir, quarts -----12 qts.
Oil Pressure Gauge Make --------------National
Drain Oil, Miles ---------------------700
Type of Oil Drain --------------------Hand Valve
Oil Reservoir Gauge Type -------------Float Duesenberg
External Oil Filter Make -------------Motor Improvements
                                    Purolator Duesenberg Spec.
Chassis Lubrication Type -------------Duesenberg Spec. Bijur.
Chassis Lubrication Make -------------Duesenberg and Bijur
Crankcase Ventilating System ----------Breathers
Cylinder Wall ------------------------Side Hole in Rods

LUBRICATION RECOMMENDATIONS
For 1929-30-31

REAR AXLE
    Capacity - 2 quarts
    Use Standard Oil Co. Lubricant "Number 4848"
    Winter and Summer

TRANSMISSION
    Capacity - 5 pints.
    Use Standard Oil Co. Lubricant "Stanolind - 200"
    Winter and Summer

STEERING GEAR

    Use Standard Oil Co. Lubricant "Number 20"
    Winter and Summer

MOTOR
    Capacity - 12 quarts
    An "extra heavy grade of oil should be used for the warm
    seasons, with specifications as follows:
                        Viscosity at 100°F---1421 Saybolt

DUESENBERG MODEL J SPECIFICATIONS

LUBRICATION RECOMMENDATIONS

Viscosity at 210°F---105 Saybolt
Flash----------------455°F
Cold Test ----------16°F

This grade of oil may be obtained in many nationally
advertised brands and is classified in most cases as "extra
heavy" or SAE Specification 0.60. Use only the very best oil
obtainable. For the winter months the next lightest grade
should be used, which is SAE No. 50, or where the cold
weather is extremely severe, SAE No. 40 oil may be desirable.

KNUCKLE PINS--TIE ROD BALL SOCKETS--FRONT WHEEL BEARINGS
Use soft cup grease similar to Alemite

CHASSIS LUBRICATOR
Use only Bijur special oil "Heavy" for mild climates
Use only Bijur special oil moderately "Heavy" for
cold climates

FUEL SYSTEM

Gasoline Tank Make - - - - - - - - - - - - - - - - - Duesenberg
Gasoline Tank Capacity - - - - - - - - - - - - - - - 26 Gal.
Fuel Feed Type - - - - - - - - - - - - - - - - - - - Pump
No. of Pumps - 2
Main Pump - Duesenberg
Location - - - - - - - - - - - - - - - - On left side of engine
Capacity - - - - - - - - - - - - - - - - - - 30 Gal. per hour
Auxiliary Pusher Pump Make - - - - - - - - - Stewart-Warner
Location - Gas Tank
Capacity -
Type of Main Pump - - - - - - - - - - - - - Mechanical Bellows
Type of Auxiliary Pump - - - - - - - - - - - - - - Electric
Auxiliary Pump Control - - - - - - - - - - - - - - Automatic
Type of Pressure Control - - - - - - - - - - - - Elec. Switch
Location of Switch - - - - - - - - - - - - - Between Carburetor
                                             and Mechanical Pump
Pressure Setting of Switch - - - - - - - - - - - - 2 lbs.
Pressure Control Switch Make - - - - - - - - - Stewart-Warner
Gasoline Filter Make - - - - - - - - - - - - - - - Duesenberg
Carburetor Make - - - - - - - - - - - - - - - Wheeler-Schebler
Downdraft or Updraft - - - - - - - - - - - - - - - Updraft
Carburetor Size - - - - - - - - - - - - - - - - - $1\frac{1}{2}$"
Carburetor Type - - - - - - - - - - - - - - - - Duplex-Air mtrg.
Method of heating intake mixture - - - - - By pass from Exhaust
Heat Adjustment - - - - - - - - - - - - Water Temp. Automatic
Heat Control - - - - - - - - - - - - - - - - Manual Shutoff
Air Cleaner - No
Muffler Make - - - - - - - - - - - - - - - - - Special for
                                             Duesenberg (Hamilton)
Exhaust Pipe - - - - - - - - - 2-3/8" for both branches at front
                               3-1/2" for rear end

DUESENBERG MODEL J SPECIFICATIONS

GENERAL CHASSIS

Chassis serial numbers begin with #2125

```
No. of wheelbases in production - - - - - - - - - - - - - 2
Long wheelbase in inches - - - - - - - - - - - - - - - - 153-1/2"
Short wheelbase in inches - - - - - - - - - - - - - - - -142-1/2"
Tread, front - - - - - - - - - - - - - - - - - - - - - - 57-1/2"
Tread, rear - - - - - - - - - - - - - - - - - - - - - - - 58"
Wheels, Make - - - - - - - - - - - - - - - - - - -Kelsey-Hayes
Wheels, Size - - - - - - - - - - - - - - - - - - - - - -19.00 x 5
Type - - - - - - - - - - - - - - - - - - - - - - - - - - Wire
Standard Finish - - - - - - - - - - - - - - - - - - - - Chromium
Tire size standard equip. - - - - - - - - - - - - - - - -7.00 x 19
Tire inflation - - - - - - - - - - - 40 lbs. front, 38 lbs. rear
Overall Length of Car with Bumpers--142½"  WB - - - - - - 211½"
Overall Length of Car with Bumpers--153½"  WB - - - - - - 222½"
Weight of Standard 5 Pass. 4-door Sedan--142½"  WB - - 5450 lbs.
Overall Length less Bumpers 142½"  WB - - - - - - - - 197-3/16"
Overall Length less Bumpers 153½"  WB - - - - - - - - 208-3/16"
Width of Car - - - - - - - - - - - - - - - - - - - - - - -72"
Spare Wheels - - - - - - - - - - - - - - - - - - - One each side
Tool Box - - - - - - - - - - - - - - - - - - - - - Left running board
```

FRAME

```
Frame Make - - - - - - - - - - - - - - - - - - - - - - - Parish
Frame Material - - - - - - - - - - - - - - - - - - - Alloy Steel
Frame Depth - - - - - - - - - - - - - - - - - - - - - 8-1/2"
Frame Thickness - - - - - - - - - - - - - - - - - - - 7/32"
Frame Flange Width - - - - - - - - - - - - - - - - - 2-3/4"
Type - - - - - - - - - - - - - - - - - - - - - - - - Double Drop
No. of Cross Members - - - - - - - - - - - - - - - - - 6
Type - - - - - - - - - - - - - - - - - Round and Square Tubular
```

SPRINGS

```
Front Spring Type - - - - - - - - - - - - - - - - Semi-Elliptic
Front Spring Make - - - - - - - - - - - - - - - - Detroit Stl.
Front Spring Material - - - - - - - - - - - - - - Spring Steel
Front Spring Length - - - - - - - - - - - - - - - - - - 41"
Front Spring Width - - - - - - - - - - - - - - - - - - 2-1/2"
Front Spring Number of Leaves - - - - - - - - - - - - - 12
Front Spring Shackled Front or Rear - - - - - - - - - - Rear

Rear Spring Type - - - - - - - - - - - - - - - - - Semi-Elliptic
Rear Spring Make - - - - - - - - - - - - - - - - - Detroit Stl.
Rear Spring Material - - - - - - - - - - - - - - - Spring Steel
Rear Spring Length - - - - - - - - - - - - - - - - - - 62½"
Rear Spring Width - - - - - - - - - - - - - - - - - - 2½"
Rear Spring Number of Leaves--5 pass. Sedan - - - - - - - 12
Rear Spring Number of Leaves--7 pass. Sedan - - - - - - - 13
Rear Spring Number of Leaves--Coupe or Roadster - - - - - 11
Spring Shackles Type and Make - - - - Bronze Bush. Duesenberg
Lubrication - - - - - - - - - - - - - Automatic Chassis Lub.
```

DUESENBERG MODEL J SPECIFICATIONS

SHOCK ABSORBERS

```
Front Shock Absorbers Type - - - - - - - - - - - - - -Rubber Flow
Front Shock Absorbers Make - - - - - - - - - - - - - - - Watson
Rear Shock Absorbers Type - - - - - - - - - - - - - - Hydraulic
Rear Shock Absorbers Make - - - - - - - - - - - - - Delco-Lovejoy
Lubrication of Arm Joints - - - - - - - - Automatic Chassis Lub.
```

COOLING SYSTEM

```
Cooling Circulation, type of - - - - - - - - - Pump
Water Pump Type - - - - - - - - - - - - - - - - - -Impeller
Water Pump Make  - - - - - - - - - - - - - - - - - - Duesenberg
Water Pump Drive - - - - - - - - - - - - - - - Accessory Shaft
Thermostat Make - - - - - - - - - - - - - - - - - Pines
Radiator Shutter Make - - - - - - - - - - - - - Pines
Radiator Shutter Control - - - - - - - - - - - - Automatic
Radiator Core Type - - - - - - - - - - - - - - - Honeycomb
Radiator Core Make - - - - - - - - - - - - - - - Winchester
Radiator Shell - - - - - - - - - - - - - - - - - Steel
Cooling System Capacity - - - - - - - - - - - - 8 gals.
Lower Radiator Hose, inside diameter - - - - - - 1-3/4"
Lower Radiator Hose, Length - - - - - - - - - 5½" Elb.
Upper Radiator Hose, Inside diameter - - - - - - 1-3/4"
Upper Radiator Hose, Length - - - - - - - - - 9-3/8" Elb.
Fan Belt Type - - - - - - - - - - - - - - - - - V
Fan Belt, Coupling or Endless Type - - - - - - - Endless
Fan Belt Make - - - - - - - - - - - - - - - - - Goodrich
Fan Belt Length - - - - - - - - - - - - - - - 36.521 ins. cir.
Fan Belt Width - - - - - - - - - - - - - - - - - 3/4"
Fan Make - - - - - - - - - - - - - - - - - Schwitzer-Cummins
Location of Drain - - - - - - - - - - - - - Radiator left side
Cyl. Block Drain - - - - - - - - - - - - - - Rear Right Side
Fan Ratio - - - - - - - - - - - - - - - - - - - 1.4 Eng.
Fan Diameter and Width -- 4 Blade - - - - - - - 17 x 1-7/8"
```

CLUTCH

```
Clutch Make - - - - - - - - - - - - - - - - Long
Clutch Model - - - - - - - - - - - - - - Special for Duesenberg
Clutch Type - - - - - - - - - - - - - - - Dual Plate, Dry Disc.
Method of Vibration Insulation - - - - - - Springs
Number of Clutch Driving Discs - - - - - - 3
Number of Clutch Driven Discs - - - - - - - 2
Clutch Operation (In oil or dry) - - - - - Dry
Clutch Facing Material - - - - - - - - Special Moulded Composition
Clutch Facing inside diameter - - - - - - - 6½"
Clutch Facing outside diameter - - - - - - 11"
Clutch Facing thickness - - - - - - - - - - .137"
Number of Clutch Facings required - - - - - 4
Is Clutch Adjustable? - - - - - - - - - - - Yes
Is Clutch Brake Used? - - - - - - - - - - - Special
Is Clutch Brake Standard or Optional? - - - Optional
Location of Clutch Brake - - - - - - On bottom of Transmission
Clutch Brake Make - - - - - - - - - - - - - Duesenberg
```

DUESENBERG MODEL J SPECIFICATIONS

FREEWHEEL UNIT

```
Standard or Optional Equipment - - - - - - Optional
Make - - - - - - - - - - - - - - - - - - - Duesenberg
Type - - - - - - - - - - - - - - L. G. S. Expanding Spring
Outside diameter of Spring - - - - - - - - 4"
Overall Length of Spring - - - - - - - - - 2-31/32"
Pilot Bearing - - - - - - - - - - Hoffman   RXLS 2-3/8" Special
Tail Shaft Bearing - - - - - - - - - - - - #1308-M
Part of Transmission or separate unit - - - Separate
Location - - - - - - - - - - - - - - - - - Rear of Transmission
Control - - - - - - - - - - - - - - - - - - Lockout Lever
Reverse Lock Control - - - - - - - - - - - Automatic
Reverse Lock Release - - - - - - - - - - - Automatic
```

TRANSMISSION AND DRIVE SHAFT

```
Transmission - - - - - - - - Warner T-72 Special for Duesenberg
Location - - - - - - - - - - - - - - - - - Rear of Motor
Forward Speeds - - - - - - - - - - - - - - 3
Transmission Ratio in second - - - - - - - 1.397 - 1.000
Transmission Ratio in low - - - - - - - - - 2.485 - 1.000
Transmission Ratio in reverse - - - - - - - 2.917 - 1.000
Transmission Oil Capacity - - - - - - - - - - - - - 5 pints
Transmission to Axle Torque Tube Drive - - 2 Universal Joints
                                              and Shaft
Universal Joint Make - - - - - - Spicer Special for Duesenberg
Front Universal Type - - - - - - - - - Rubber Cushion Inserts
Rear Universal Type - - - - - - - - - - - - - - - Mechanical
```

REAR AXLE AND DIFFERENTIAL

```
Rear Axle Make - - - - - - - - - - - - - - - - - Duesenberg
Rear Axle Type - - - - - - - - - - - - Torque Tube-Hypoid Gear
                                          Semi-Floating Shaft
Minimum Road Clearance under Rear Axle, Tires inflated - - - 9"
Rear Axle Oil Capacity - - - - - - - - - - - - - - - 2 qts.
Gear Ratios used - - - - - - - - - - 53-14, 53-13, 56-13, 55-12
```

```
                    53-14 - 3.78-1
                    53-13 - 4.08-1
                    55-12 - 4.58-1
                    56-13 - 4.30-1
```

```
Method in which Pinion is adjusted - - - - - - - - - - - Shims
```

FRONT AXLE AND STEERING

```
Front Axle Make - - - - - - - - - - - - - - - - - - Duesenberg
Front Axle Section - - - - - - - - - - - - - - - I-Beam Forged
I-Beam Material - - - - - - - - - - - Chrome Molybdenum Alloy
Type of Ends - - - - - - - - - - - - - - - - - - Reverse Elliot
Steering Gear Type - - - - - - - - - - - - - - - -Cam and Lever
```

DUESENBERG MODEL J SPECIFICATIONS

FRONT AXLE & STEERING

```
Steering Gear Make - - - - - - - - - - - - - - - - - - - Ross 660
Steering Gear Ratio - - - - - - - - - - - - - - - - - - Variable
No. of turns of strg. wheel for full left to right turn - - - 3
Castor Angle - - - - - - - - - - - - - - - - - - - - - - 1° to 3°
Camber Angle (each side) - - - - - - - - - - - - - - - - 1°
Toe-in ( 2" below wheel center ) - - - - - - - - - - - 1/8" to 1/4"
Toe-in adjustment - - - - Right and Left Hand Thread on Tie Rod
```

BRAKES

```
Foot Brakes, Make - - - - - - - - - - - - - - - - - - - Duesenberg
Number of Complete Brakes, including Hand Brake - - 5
Foot Brake, Type of Mechanism - - - - - - - - - - - Hydraulic
Location of Service Brakes - - - - - - - - - - - - Each Wheel
Vacuum Brake Booster Make - - - - - - - - - - - - - Bragg-Kliesrath
Master Cylinder Make - - - - - - - - - - - - - - - Wagner-Duesenber
Brake Lining Make - - - - - - - - - - - - - - - - - Molded Gatke
Rear Brake Drum Diameter - - - - - - - - - - - - - 15"
Operation of Brakes - - - - - - - - - - - - - - - - Internal Expand
Service Brake Lining Length - - - - - - - - - - - - 14-3/8"
No. Shoes per Wheel - - - - - - - - - - - - - - - - 2
Material Brake Shoe - - - - - - - - - - - - - - - - Aluminum
Foot Brake (Service) Lining Width - - - - - - - - - 2¼"
Foot Service Brake Lining Thickness - - - - - - - - 17/64"
Rear Brake Clearance - - - - - - - - - - - - - - - - .010
Front Brake Clearance - - - - - - - - - - - - - - - .010
Front Brake Drum Diameter - - - - - - - - - - - - - 15"
Total Foot Brake Area - - - - - - - - - - - - - - - 1.8 Sq. Ft.
     (4 wheels)
Hand Brake Location - - - - - - - - - - - - - - Trans.-Driveshaft
Operation of Hand Brake - - - - - - - - - - - Extern. Contr.
Hand Brake Drum Diameter - - - - - - - - - - - - 7-3/4"
Hand Brake Lining per Shoe - - - - - - - - - - - 8-1/4"
No. of Shoes - - - - - - - - - - - - - - - - - - 2
Hand Brake Lining Width - - - - - - - - - - - - - 3"
Hand Brake Lining Thickness - - - - - - - - - - - ¼"
Hand Brake Clearance - - - - - - - - - - - - - - .025
```

BEARING LIST

BALL BEARINGS

Item	Make	Brg. No.	Name	No. Reqd.	Duesenberg Number
1		#16 Mag.Type	Fan Pulley Front Ball Bearing	1	J-785-9
2		#20 Mag.Type	Fan Pulley Rear Ball Bearing	1	J-785-12
3	Gurney	#211-CT	Clutch Release Ball Bearing	1	J-1505

DUESENBERG MODEL J SPECIFICATIONS

BALL BEARINGS

Item	Make	Brg. No.	Name	No. Reqd.	Duesenberg Number
4	Schubert	#405	Front Whl. Hub Outer Ball Bearing	2	JA-1654
5	Schubert	#311	Rear Axle Wheel Ball Bearing	2	JX-1901
6	(JA-1654)	.002 oversize)	Front Whl Hub Outer Ball Bearing	2	JA-1654-A
7	Schubert	#212	Differential Loft Ball Bearing	1	JX-2042
8	Federal	#1308-M	Transmission sht.rr. Ball Bearing	1	J-2043
9	Schubert	#9310	Drive Pinion Front Ball Bearing	1	JX-2064
10	Schubert	#309	Front Wheel Inner and Prop. Shaft Bearing	3	J-2505
11	Federal	#211-M	Trans. main Drive Shaft Ball Bearing	1	J-2040
12	Schubert	#5206-W	Strg. Knuckle Radial Ball Bearing	2	J-2534

ROLLER BEARINGS

Item	Make	Brg. No.	Name	No. Reqd.	Duesenberg Number
13	Hyatt	#RA-147	Clutch Pilot Roller Bearing	1	J-1507
14	Hyatt	#RA-00527	Trans. Cntrshaft Gear Roller Bearing	2	J-1977
15	Hyatt	#NC-212	Trans. Eccentric Gear Roller Bearing	1	J-2027
16	Hyatt	#211	Trans. Main Shaft Front Roller Bearing	1	J-2047
17	Nrm.Hffmn.	#R-355-LL	Diff. Inner Pinion Roller Bearing	1	J-3071

SPECIAL BEARINGS

Item	Make	Brg. No.	Name	No. Reqd.	Duesenberg Number
18	Schubert	#7205-5	Strg. Pivot Pin Thrust Ball Bearing	2	J-2528-A
19	Schubert	#9212-5	Diff. Right Side Ball Bearing	1	J-3034

He drives a Duesenberg

DOMESTIC DISPLAY ADVERTISING

Duesenberg

MODEL J

DUESENBERG, INC.

Indianapolis, Ind., U. S. A.

E. L. CORD *Announces Plans for*

Duesenberg

THIS interesting announcement has been awaited for more than two years. Even now it would be delayed, if Mr. Cord and his engineers could conceive of any possible way in which to improve upon the new Duesenberg, in either kind or degree.

This presentation will cause surprise, because it is totally different from any ever made by any other automobile manufacturer.

We will not give specifications, nor attempt a description. Suffice it to say Mr. Cord's aim is for America unquestionably to lead Europe in producing the world's finest automobile. Of course, exclusive body styles.

We will not announce prices. In this connection, however, Duesenberg will not charge for snobbery. The Duesenberg price will be based entirely upon innate value. Of course, this new Duesenberg is a different kind of automobile both in its design and construction. It is built to win, through sheer merit, world wide recognition for absolute superiority in every way over every other automobile on earth.

Such a motor car cannot be measured by ordinary standards.

The introduction of this new Duesenberg is the fulfillment of another step in Mr. Cord's long-planned program to give the world the benefits of what leading engineers can do when not handicapped by time, expense nor in any way.

Fred S. Duesenberg needs no introduction. His name is a synonym for authority. He built America's first Straight Eight, the first small cubic inch piston displacement race car, America's first hydraulic brakes, and the only American car to win the Grand Prix. In the crucible of racing, in which Duesenberg cars have been dominant winners, have been born innumerable fundamentals that have advanced the entire automotive industry.

For years he has created high priced custom cars upon special orders.

But, basic manufacturing changes were necessary before his genius could be made available to the public in the present Duesenberg automobile.

This too is a tremendous step forward.

Now, the fruition of these years of concentration represent an achievement in which every American may justly take pride.

DUESENBERG, INC., INDIANAPOLIS, INDIANA

"The World's Finest Motor Car"

Duesenberg

To be the world's finest automobile, the New Duesenberg must excel every other motor car in every way with finality. It does!

Ready now for your inspection

265 horsepower
chassis $8,500.00

DUESENBERG, INC., Indianapolis, Indiana

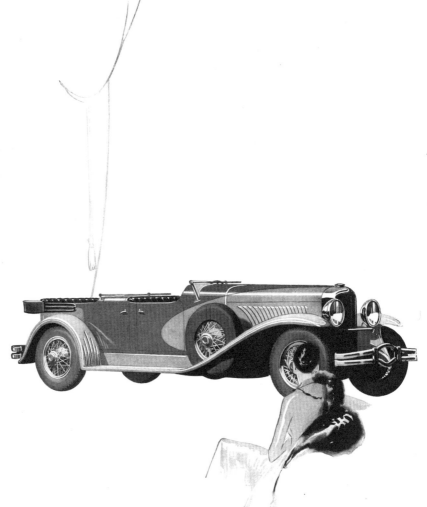

"The World's Finest Motor Car"

Duesenberg

The world's finest automobile, the new
Duesenberg, has 265 horsepower. Its entire construction is proportionately strong, thereby insur-
ing greatest safety, endurance and absolute
dominion. It excels equally in every other respect.

Chassis $8,500

DUESENBERG, INC., INDIANAPOLIS, INDIANA

"*The World's Finest Motor Car*"

With double the horsepower of any other motor
car, it equally outclasses all others in smoothness, ease of handling, road steadiness, riding
quality, comfort, stamina, longevity and luxury.

Chassis $8,500

DUESENBERG INC., INDIANAPOLIS, INDIANA

"The World's Finest Motor Car"

Duesenberg

265 h. p.

The Duesenberg Catalogue Just Published Says:

THE OBJECT of this book is to be informative; to give you a partial insight into the design, the structural strength, the metallurgy and the numerous exclusive ways in which Duesenberg provides for your utmost safety, comfort and enjoyment. . . . . The same motives which actuate the creation of any masterpiece prompt the building of this, the world's finest motor car. In every realm of human endeavor there is innate in certain men the driving desire to produce something that excels with finality. Always there is devotion to an ideal with only one thought in mind: to produce the best, forgetful of cost or expediency or any other consideration. When this is finally accomplished the work is acclaimed a masterpiece by those who are in a position to know; it is recognized as a standard by which all other things of its kind are judged . . . . This is true, whether the creation be a Taj Mahal, a Grecian vase, Cellini's metal craft, a Rembrandt painting, or—a Duesenberg car.

We say this without egotism. The superlatively fine has no need to be boastful. So confident is Duesenberg of the unquestioned supreme position its product occupies, that a nameplate is considered superfluous. Nowhere on the car do you find the name Duesenberg. But everywhere throughout the car you discover those master strokes of engineering and design and construction obtainable nowhere else than in a Duesenberg . . . . Yet the Duesenberg is marketed on the same basis as the most popular-priced car: dollar-for-dollar value. The Duesenberg price is set by the car's inherent worth.

Necessarily, its appeal is to only a very few. Any masterpiece can only be appreciated by those who understand the principles upon which its greatness is based. Therefore the ownership of a Duesenberg reflects discernment far above the ordinary. . . . . We are not the first to have had the ambition to build the world's finest motor car. But in our case this achievement was made possible by the experience and the creative genius of the man who designed it. . . . . For many years the world has recognized his name as a synonym for scientific pioneering, for high precision standards, and for performance attainments outdistancing all others. The climax of Fred S. Duesenberg's lifetime of effort and study is summed up in this new car . . . We submit the new Duesenberg, after more than two years of untiring zeal to excel every other car in the world, in every way.

Chassis $8,500

DUESENBERG, INC., INDIANAPOLIS, IND.

Convertible Coupe

Sport Phaeton

All Weather Cabriolet

5 Passenger Sedan

"The World's Finest Motor Car"

Duesenberg

265 *Horsepower*

THERE are decided advantages in having at your command, twice the horsepower possessed by any other car. The greatest benefit is that of tremendous reserve power. No motor car gives the best performance when operated at its maximum of power or speed. With the average automobile, 65 miles an hour is such a strain on the motor that engine noise and vibration become excessive and result in discomfort and nervous fatigue to driver and passengers. . . . To a Duesenberg, 65 miles an hour is little more than idling along. Noise and vibration are hardly perceptible. The throttle is not even half open. Only 60 horsepower is required, leaving a vast reserve of power for acceleration and hill-climbing. . . . Nor is it in engine power alone that a Duesenberg surpasses all other motor cars. In the preponderance of aluminum parts that make for lighter weight, in the far greater strength of frame, in the unique automatic lubrication system, in superlative driving ease and riding comfort, and in all those refinements of mechanism that make for automotive perfection, a Duesenberg definitely earns its title of The World's Finest Motor Car.

Chassis $8,500

DUESENBERG, INC., INDIANAPOLIS, IND.

"The World's Finest Motor Car"

Duesenberg

265 H. P.

One Reason for Unvarying Steadiness

DUESENBERG superiority starts with its foundation, the frame. Duesenberg strength and rigidity, its steady performance, exceptional endurance and hitherto unprocurable safety are largely the result of its expert design and abnormally strong frame. These great factors of safety and durability, are characteristic of the car's construction, throughout.... It is because Duesenberg DOES excel all other cars mechanically, that for the first time, a car of this character is marketed on a Dollar-for-Dollar value basis.

Chassis, $8,500
DUESENBERG, INC., INDIANAPOLIS, IND.

"The World's Finest Motor Car"

Duesenberg

265 h. p.

The Duesenberg is sold on exactly the same basis as the world's cheapest automobile, that is, on dollar for dollar value. The price of the Duesenberg is not based on the intangible but on its structural superiority.

THE DUESENBERG is simpler and easier to operate even than small cars of short wheelbase. It is more readily and safely controlled. In driving, it places the very minimum of effort upon the man or woman at the wheel. Gear shifting is easy, due to special Duesenberg "light shaft" construction. Gearshift and brake levers stand high, so that they are easily reached. The steering wheel is placed at a more nearly vertical angle for better handling of the car, and its height is adjustable. Only a moderate pressure of the foot upon the pedal is required, to bring the car to a smooth, quick stop, as the specially designed four-wheel brakes are unusually powerful.

In care as well, the Duesenberg is as nearly automatic as a motor-propelled vehicle can be. A pair of signal lights on the dash glows at every eighty miles to indicate that the automatic system of complete chassis lubrication is functioning; a light glows to remind the driver that oil should be changed and another warns that the battery may need water. Among the other valuable aids to easier driving found on the most complete instrument board ever supplied to an automobile are a tachometer, a split-second stop clock, a 150 mile speedometer and an altimeter barometer, suggesting that Duesenberg's striving toward motor car perfection extends to even the minutest details.

Chassis, $8,500

DUESENBERG, INC., INDIANAPOLIS, IND.

LIMOUSINE—*with top up, partition and side glasses up.*
TOWN CAR—*front of top rolled back and partition up.*
OPEN PHAETON—*with top and partition down.*

All-Weather Cabriolet

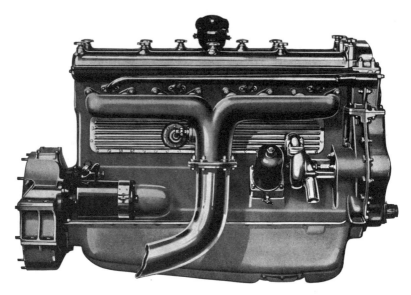

The Power Plant That Spells Safety

WHY should a man want a car whose engine develops 265 horsepower? Not to be able to drive 100 miles an hour, or more . . . although that is possible without any special effort in a Duesenberg; not so that he can go 90 miles an hour in second gear . . . although there are times when this advantage proves priceless; but rather that when a man purchases a motor car he wants to fortify himself and his family with every protection obtainable. The safety of a Duesenberg owner starts with his sense of security, with his mental attitude when he gets in to his car to fare forth into traffic, with the knowledge that this is the world's strongest, most powerfully built motor car, in every respect. He has as a result, complete mastery, which spells protection; mastery of road conditions, mastery of traffic emergencies, mastery of every situation. Strains which would wreck another car, leave a Duesenberg unharmed. Its superb strength in every part, the perfection of its balance, the ease with which this mighty giant is subservient to your every wish, the steadiness with which it holds the road at all speeds, its tremendously powerful and efficient brakes, all combine to produce what Duesenberg after all stands for: The Utmost in Safe Transportation.

Chassis $8,500

DUESENBERG, INC., INDIANAPOLIS, IND.

"The World's Finest Motor Car"

Duesenberg

265 h.p.

"The World's Finest Motor Car"

Duesenberg

265 h.p.

The Duesenberg is sold on exactly the same basis as the world's lowest priced automobile, that is, on dollar for dollar value. The price of the Duesenberg is not based on the intangible but on its structural superiority.

A Power Giant's Backbone

Engineering skill was never put to more severe test than in designing the crankshaft for a motor car engine developing 265 Horsepower. The demands made upon any crankshaft are most trying, but particularly so in a motor as powerful as Duesenberg's. It must be extremely rigid to withstand the terrific strain placed upon it by tremendous centrifugal forces; at the same time, this huge mass of metal must be as finely balanced as the most delicate scales. This rare combination is successfully achieved in the Duesenberg's crankshaft, by employing the finest double-heat-treated alloy steel of extraordinary diameter, $2\frac{3}{4}$ inches, and by smoothing out any periodic vibrations, through the use of a specially designed mercury vibration dampener. This is typical of the painstaking care exercised with each one of a Duesenberg's more than 7000 parts, to make certain that it will definitely and outstandingly excel the same part on any other car built.

Chassis, $8,500
DUESENBERG, INC., INDIANAPOLIS, IND.

Convertible Five-Passenger Sedan-Limousine; body by Willoughby; combination owner or chauffeur-driven automobile.

"The World's Finest Motor Car"

Duesenberg

265 h.p.

Reproductions from actual photographs of Duesenberg Town Cabriolet

DUESENBERG, INC., INDIANAPOLIS, IND.

Duesenberg Winner of Elegance Rallye

At Cannes and again at Pau, in competition with
150 of the world's costliest

"The World's Finest Motor Car"

Duesenberg

THOUGH it is a matter for just pride that an American car should receive first place at two of the most important fine car exhibitions in France, this victory for Duesenberg is only logical. The Duesenberg is definitely planned and designed and engineered to be The World's Finest Motor Car.

IN ORDER TO merit this distinction, a Duesenberg must not merely excel all other cars in every respect, but must do it so definitely and by so great a margin as to establish a motor realm all its own. This Duesenberg does, with finality.

ITS DOMINATING SUPERIORITY begins with the engine, a Straight Eight developing 265 Horsepower—nearly twice that of any automobile motor in the world. While having so much power enables the car to attain extremely high speed, that is not the primary purpose. The greatest benefits from this abundance of power are revealed under continuous ordinary requirements. In day after day driving, the car's resources are never taxed; its capacities are never even approached; there is an absence of effort and strain, due to having at all times a vast protective reserve. Thus, because it is the most powerful, a Duesenberg becomes the most safe. Because a Duesenberg does its work with so little effort, the car does not wear itself out. It will go on giving the same high degree of service, year after year, almost indefinitely. The driver and passengers in a Duesenberg ride shielded in absolute security from all driving annoyances, to a degree never before accomplished in any motor vehicle.

THE DUESENBERG ENGINE'S unprecedented power and high mechanical efficiency are due to skillful designing, rather than mere size. Here, as in all other parts of the car, Fred Duesenberg, one of the world's greatest automotive engineers, displays his remarkable genius in adapting the lessons learned on the race track, to meet the requirements of the very finest passenger car that man has yet devised. While other automobile engines have two valves to each cylinder, a Duesenberg has four, which greatly facilitates the intake and exhaust. Instead of a single purifying, all oil entering the Duesenberg motor is triple filtered. The crankshaft is abnormally rigid and provided with a mercury balancer, designed exclusively for this car and smoothing out the slightest power vibration. To obtain lightness and strength, more aluminum parts are used than by any other motor car manufacturer.

ALL THROUGH THE car, from the super-strong frame down to the minutest details of construction, a Duesenberg excels in the same outstanding way. Bodies are custom designed, the work of the world's leading coach builders, who have spared no effort to produce designs of marked originality, and of quality in keeping with the car's mechanical excellence.

IT WILL INTEREST those who would take pride in owning so fine a car, to know that the Duesenberg is sold on exactly the same basis as the world's lowest priced automobile, dollar for dollar value. The price of the Duesenberg is not based on the intangible, but on its structural superiority.

Intake side of Duesenberg 265 H. P. Engine. The cylinder block and upper half of crank case are a single rigid casting

DUESENBERG, INC., INDIANAPOLIS, IND.

A Duesenberg Takes Perfection As Its Goal

Transcends All Present Day Standards
of Motor Car Construction

ANY great masterpiece can be appreciated only by those who understand the principles upon which its greatness is based. This is true whether the creation be a painting by Goya, a piece of furniture by Phyfe, a composition by Debussy — or a car by Duesenberg.

To THE "man on the street" a Duesenberg may mean—a high priced, large car; high powered; capable of great speed. But in every community there are those discerning enough to realize that these are only the most obvious aspects of the car's greatness, and that its true significance goes much deeper.

THE DUESENBERG cannot be considered in the same terms as other cars. In designing it, Fred S. Duesenberg plunged fearlessly into the future and established an automotive domain all his own, far beyond the outposts that others had set. He was eminently equipped to do this by experience which began with that testing place of theory, the race track, and which extended through long years of experimenting and designing and building fine motor cars. Three years ago he set out deliberately to create a motor car that would excel any automobile built, and excel to so marked a degree that it would become with absolute finality The World's Finest Motor Car. This position the Duesenberg occupies today.

THE DUESENBERG establishes a new conception of motoring that cannot be obtained from any other car. When a man of wealth buys a Duesenberg he assures himself and his family that background of

luxury, that extensive equipment of service, that completeness of comfort and freedom from all outside annoyances, that security to which he is accustomed in his home.

DRIVER AND PASSENGERS in a Duesenberg ride at all times in perfect serenity, knowing that the engine's 265 horsepower provides a protective reserve equal to every emergency; that the brakes are tremendously powerful, that the car's frame is the strongest ever built under an automobile; in short, that this is the world's safest motor car.

AT THE SAME TIME, the Duesenberg is simpler and easier to operate than smaller, less powerful cars. It requires far less attention. Care of this car makes no demands upon the driver; chassis lubrication is entirely automatic; a unique system of signal lights warns when servicing will be required.

EQUALLY TYPICAL of Duesenberg's anticipation of the driver's slightest need is the instrument board, which includes many important gauges not generally found except on aircraft; yet adding greatly to the fullest enjoyment of fine car driving.

THE FINAL PROOF of a man's discernment in choosing the Duesenberg is in the price he pays, which is not based on something intangible, but is set by the car's inherent worth, its intrinsic value alone. The Duesenberg is marketed on the same basis as the world's lowest priced automobile, Dollar for Dollar Value.

DUESENBERG, INC., INDIANAPOLIS, IND.

"The World's Finest Motor Car"

Duesenberg

Why This Is The World's Finest Motor Car

The Duesenberg a Result of Man's Inherent Desire to Produce That Which Excels —

BACK of every great creative work is a history of never-failing devotion to an ideal, with only one thought in mind: to produce the best, without regard to precedent, or time, or cost or any other consideration. It is this spirit which actuates everyone connected with the designing and engineering and building of a Duesenberg. This car must markedly excel all others, in every respect, and with finality.... When Fred S. Duesenberg's pioneering mind conceived the idea that oil should be triple-filtered before entering the engine, it made no difference that other builders were satisfied to use a single filter, or that the new method was more costly. The only fact of any importance to Duesenberg was, that by this means alone could be assured the complete purity of every drop of engine oil, and that this absolute freedom from impurity was essential to the most efficient performance. That is why this important advancement was adopted, and for similar reasons, many others that place the Duesenberg years in the forefront. . . . It is by the sum total of all these mechanical superiorities, that a Duesenberg's price is set — by the inherent worth of the car. DUESENBERG, INC., INDIANAPOLIS, INDIANA.

Perfect Engine Lubrication

is assured on the Duesenberg, by the use of two wire mesh screens and a special Purolator; in addition, small pockets in the crank pins imprison any slight particles which the filters may not catch.

"The World's Finest Motor Car"

Duesenberg

All Weather Town Brougham

Duesenberg

265 *H.P.*

" T H E   W O R L D ' S   F I N E S T   M O T O R   C A R "

THE BEVERLY

Duesenberg

"THE WORLD'S FINEST MOTOR CAR"

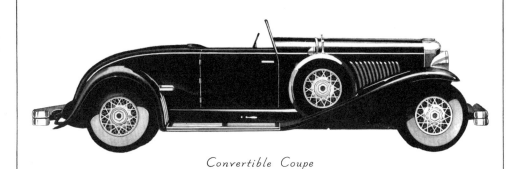

Convertible Coupe

Duesenberg

With Top Up

*With Top Down
and door windows up*

265 H.P.

"THE WORLD'S FINEST MOTOR CAR"

WORKS: INDIANAPOLIS, IND.

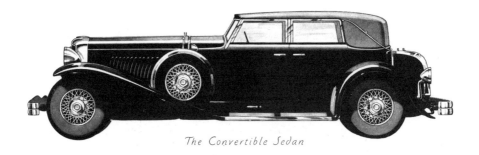

The Convertible Sedan

Duesenberg

265 Horsepower

With Top Down

"THE WORLD'S FINEST MOTOR CAR"
WORKS: INDIANAPOLIS, IND.

THE PHAETON

265 HORSEPOWER

"THE WORLD'S FINEST MOTOR CAR"
WORKS: INDIANAPOLIS, IND.

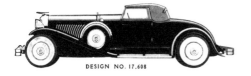

DESIGN NO. 17,608

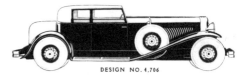

DESIGN NO. 4,706

DESIGN NO. 9,762

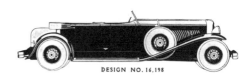

DESIGN NO. 16,198

DESIGN NO. 13,543

DESIGN NO. 4,369

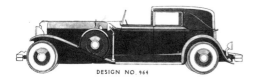

DESIGN NO. 964

DESIGN NO. 8,001

Duesenberg

265
HORSEPOWER

Typical of Duesenberg's unique creative service are these designs prepared recently for persons desiring strictly custom motor cars. Our artists would deem it a pleasure to sketch for you an automobile embodying your own thoughts regarding details of comfort and appearance.

"THE WORLD'S FINEST MOTOR CAR"
WORKS, INDIANAPOLIS, IND.

She drives a
Duesenberg

He drives a Duesenberg

She drives a Duesenberg

He drives a Duesenberg

She drives a
Duesenberg

He drives a Duesenberg